UNWRAPPED

UNWRAPPED
My Autobiography

Freddie Starr
with Alan Wightman

This edition first published in Great Britain in 2002 by
Virgin Books Ltd
Thames Wharf Studios
Rainville Road
London W6 9HA

First published in Great Britain in 2001 by Virgin Books Ltd

A catalogue record for this book is available from the British Library.

ISBN 0 7535 0694 7

Typeset by TW Typesetting, Plymouth, Devon
Printed and bound by Mackays of Chatham PLC

ACKNOWLEDGEMENTS

Alan Wightman, co-writer. I'd like to thank Alan for all of his input: for coming to Spain and spending many a long hour sitting by the pool, eating me out of house and home, drinking endless cups of coffee, and – oh yes – helping me write this book.

I consider you as a true friend, a very talented writer, and an all round great bloke. Look forward to working together on part two. Cheers.

Brian Shaw, for getting this book off the ground, and for all of your help with touring up and down the country for the past twenty years. And maybe you'll drop your commission for the next book.

To all my friends and family, wherever you are, thanks for believing in me. There are too many to mention, but you know who you are.

And finally to my wife, Donna, who provided us with a bottomless teapot and a steady stream of sandwiches. I love you with all of my heart, and wouldn't swap you for a herd of elephants – sheep maybe – but not elephants.

CHAPTER ONE

Freddie Starr. When you hear that name, what images does it conjure up in your mind? A madman running around a stage, wearing a Hitler moustache, ridiculous shorts and a pair of Wellington boots, reducing an audience to helpless laughter? Perhaps you immediately recall tabloid headlines concerning my alleged consumption of a small furry rodent? How about those sensational newspaper reports concerning court cases, ex-wives, gardeners and several hundred dancers who alleged I tried to seduce them – in one very busy weekend! You might even recall how I became an 'overnight success' after my appearance on the 1970 *Royal Variety Show*? Or you may well flinch at the memory of the night I tied up TV critic Garry Bushell in front of an audience of celebrities and covered him in thousands of 'maggots'? Well, I can't blame you for thinking about me in those terms. Because that's the public's perception of me. A crazy guy who lives a crazy life, in and out of the spotlight.

Until now I've put up with all that nonsense. If you work in showbusiness, then you have to accept that people are going to want to read and hear about what you do. Or sometimes, what you haven't done or *wish* you could have done, if only you had the time and the equipment. So when I read about myself in the papers, or friends tell me something they'd heard on the radio, I usually smile and shrug. I know it's going to happen. Sometimes it does get to me – who wouldn't get upset if you read something that you know is the opposite of what actually happened, or is completely made up – but what can I do about it? Well, actually quite a lot. For a start I can write this book and let you know directly, without the press getting in the way, exactly what happened in my life. I can write what I think about the people I've worked with, some of the really great performers that I've been lucky enough to work with and even call my friends. And I can say it the way I choose, which is more than I've had the chance to do before. It'll make a nice change to read my own words on my life.

Having said all that, all performers, and I include myself here without any apology, occasionally need the help of the papers to publicise their new TV series or film or stage play or book.

I've been big enough to admit that performers need the help of newspapers from time to time. But what *no* journalist would ever admit to is this – they need us more than we need them . . . *every day of the week*. Newspapers have relied on showbusiness stories and scandals to make money for themselves since the first words were carved into the first stone. Going back to the Dark Ages, I expect there were headlines in the *Camelot Gazette* along the lines of 'Crazy Freddo The Court Jester Ate My Ferret!' It's probably because showbiz stories and their accompanying pictures provide a little light-hearted nonsense between reports and interviews dealing with the harsh reality and tragedy of real life. There has always been an uneasy truce between the press and showbusiness. One uses the other. I scratch your back, you can rub some sun-tan cream into mine. I'm aware that the game has changed a lot in the past few years, and what was Fleet Street doesn't get all its own way anymore as stars employ people (usually ex-journalists themselves) to get their stories told their way.

Once I decided to write this book, I hid myself away and spent many months scribbling and burning the midnight oil. I really *had* to burn the midnight oil because my local electricity company cut me off due to a silly dispute over an alleged unpaid bill. They said I hadn't paid it. I said I had paid it. This went on for weeks until one morning this fellah in a uniform and cap knocked on my front door and said, 'Mr Starr, I've come to turn you off!' I said. 'Well, you certainly don't turn me *on*!'

So I wrote page after page, as I recalled incidents that had happened in my life going back to the 1940s. I'll give you all the small details as we go along. Dates, names, places. I know that's what you expect. But what might surprise you is how honest I am about the ups and downs of my life. Truthfully,

I've always had a healthy cynicism about the business I'm in and have not once been taken in by the 'Darling you were marvellous' brigade who inhabit it.

This book doesn't look at the world of showbusiness through rose-tinted spectacles. Have you *seen* the cost of rose-tinted spectacles at SpecSavers? They charge a bloody fortune and they take far more than an hour to make. I've been a performer for over forty years and a star since 1970. You may say I've been lucky. I would point out that the harder I've worked, the luckier I've become. OK, there's no doubt that a little bit of luck does make a helluva difference in my business, as it does in any profession, but it's definitely possible to 'make your own luck'. By that I mean, whatever you do for a living, if you work hard, learn your trade, keep your wits about you and whenever you see an opening that you think might suit you, be the first to jump at it, you *might* have made the right career decision. In which case you'd consider that your luck had changed for the better.

Look, if you promise to keep this to yourself, I'll share with you what I think is the best definition of 'luck' I've ever heard. I can't remember who said it, but whoever he or she was, they knew what they were talking about. Ready?

'Luck occurs when opportunity meets experience.'

That's bloody brilliant, isn't it? Because if, for example, you're a young comedian and you're given an opportunity – say a guest spot on a big TV show – and you're not experienced or confident enough, you could end up looking a right prat in front of millions of viewers. But . . . if you've gained enough experience in the clubs and holiday camps and small summer shows and you know what you're doing and what you're going to say and how to work an audience, that opportunity could change your life. As a nine-minute routine on the 1970 *Royal Variety Show* totally changed mine.

Mind you, Lady Luck can be a right awkward cow when she wants to be. Sometimes when she's bored or frustrated because she hasn't had a good seeing-to for months, she likes to point her finger at a struggling performer, to give him a break, only to decide a couple of months later, 'I've changed my mind. I think I'll let the bugger go back to struggling again.' Now that's cruel. Giving someone a taste of the big time then snatching it away just as they were enjoying it. That's how heartless the world of showbusiness is. It's bloody tough to make it to the top and it's even tougher to *stay* on top.

Since the early 1970s I've worked on hundreds of TV shows, from *Who Do You Do* to *Freddie Starr's Madhouse* and my two *Audience With* . . . specials, and although I've stayed on the top of my profession, I've seen other big-name performers rise and fall. Some of them do manage to rise again and I'm always the first in line to congratulate them. I've known some brilliantly talented performers who deserved to become major stars never get the chance to put their foot on the ladder and today they just about make a living in the clubs. I've watched people whose egos were bigger than their talents become household names.

Dredging up memories and names and incidents from my past as I wrote this book was, for the most part, great therapy. I did touch on one or two old wounds and the occasional wistful regret, naturally. There's no one walking around on this planet today who doesn't regret that they hadn't said something to a friend or relative who's no longer around, or made the effort to make that phone call or write that letter that may have helped to patch up a long-simmering argument or put right a silly misunderstanding. It's human nature.

And as hard as some people find this to believe, comedians are as human as most people. Sometimes, and I don't want to get too deep here, comedians are a little more human than most people because we believe we have an insight into 'the human condition'. We make jokes about things that concern everybody. Universal subjects like sex, marriage, money, doctors, crime, crap foreign holidays, pain-in-the-arse relatives, supermarket shopping, public transport, chronic flatulence etc. Well maybe the last subject concerns *me* more than *you*. We'll leave it there. I said we'll leave it. Right? Comedians aren't afraid of talking about things that might affect us or our families and friends no matter what our station in life is.

My station in life happens to be St Pancras. But that may not necessarily be true of everybody reading this book. In fact I'm glad it isn't or they'd be no bloody room left on Platform Three. The bottom line is, comedians are just like most people. We just get *paid* more than most people!

By the way, if you bought this book yourself or if someone bought it for you, I genuinely hope you enjoy it and find the contents a fascinating and sometimes amusing insight into my roller-coaster of a life. If however, you're just standing in a bookshop, idly browsing through this until the rain stops outside, I've got two suggestions. Either get your wallet out, walk over to the counter and buy this book. Or you can quietly put it back on the shelf, walk over to the front door and piss off out of the shop so the people who *really* want to know about the life of Freddie Starr can get on with reading it. Thank you so very much.

'There's no business like show business', wrote Irving Berlin. He should also have said, 'Because it breeds more rogues, crooks, swindlers, villains, pilferers, thieves, spivs and smooth-talking sharks-in-suits than any other walk of life.'

I'll let you in on a secret. If you're considering a change of career at the moment and you have any sort of criminal record, absolutely no morals and hold your fellow man in complete disdain, let me help you make the right decision. You should become a showbusiness accountant, showbusiness lawyer or a comedian's personal manager. You'll clean up, you really will!

Set yourself up as a personal manager to the stars and there will always be hundred of naive performers lining up outside your office, waiting to hand over their hard-earned cash to you. Because performers can't cope with bureaucracy. They're not built for it. The performer's sole function is to *perform*. That's what they have to be focused on. They don't want to be bothered with accounts and VAT and bills and invoices, so if you can convince them you're a shit-hot showbiz account-ant who they can trust with their lives, wives, girlfriends and every penny they earn, they'll leave it all to you to sort out. But there's no need for you to work hard for your clients. Just place all their paperwork in a drawer and ignore the tax demands that will inevitably drop through your letterbox. Go out and have a three-hour lunch break and close up the office around four o'clock.

If a performer starts to worry about pressure being applied by the tax man, just string him along for a while, pretending everything's sorted and feed him a juicy piece of showbiz gossip to send him away with a smile on his face. With practice you could keep this up for two or three years before they smell a rat. Then when the heat starts being turned up, you can bugger off somewhere warm with half a million quid in readies. I'm sure there are people who've tried this.

Of course showbusiness isn't *all* about slogging away night after night, dealing with career disappointments, and having to watch your back all the time in case you're well and truly shafted by managers and accountants. No, just 90 per cent of it is. So, what attracts people to this business? When I ask people this they always give me the same answer. 'The glamour.' Excuse me? Glamour? Tell me what's glamorous about a fifty-date tour of Great Britain, travelling from one town to another?

Ideally, a well-planned tour would mean just a couple of hours driving between venues. But that's not how it works out. Sometimes it involves driving from Southampton to Newcastle, then the following day driving back down to Cornwall. So you arrive at the venue completely knackered at three in the afternoon, hanging your stage gear on some dusty old clothes rail, then going out into the draughty theatre to take a sound check with the band. You then find out the drummer's missing because he's still a hundred miles away, sitting on the side of the motorway because his engine blew up. While he's waiting for the RAC man to get him back on the road, you finish your sound check and go back to your tiny dressing room to grab forty winks on a battered old couch that looks like it came straight from Steptoe's yard. You wake up feeling worse than ever, sip cold tea and nibble on a cheese sandwich with edges shaped by curling tongs, before showering and getting into your stage suit, while feeling sick as a pig with nerves, before stepping out on to the stage, knowing that straight after the show you face a two-hundred-mile car journey home before you can crash into bed. If that's glamorous, Jo Brand is Weightwatcher of the Year.

Alright. I didn't mean to paint quite so bleak a picture of the touring life. I'm a comedian for goodness sakes! I'm supposed to bring laughter and joy into people's lives and I've got you reaching for the aspirin bottle! So I'll lighten up a little. Of course I know that compared to most people, performers do have a very enjoyable lifestyle most of the time. We don't work set hours. Our souls aren't destroyed by a lifetime of clocking-on at the factory gates at six in the morning, or battling twenty-foot waves in the North Sea hoping to catch a netful of cod, or sitting at a supermarket check-out eight hours a day. But the business does have its own ways of chipping away at the soul of anyone who has ever tried to make a living as an entertainer, especially a comedian. It can be tough when you start out and audiences don't laugh at you, or insult you or even throw things at you and you slink out of the back door of the club, having been paid off. But when you've made a bit of a name for yourself and you get some respect from your peers and club owners and theatre managers and TV executives, being a performer can be an extraordinarily pleasant way to make a living. The longer you stay a 'star' you can earn fabulous money, afford to stay at luxury hotels, drive amazing limousines, learn to fly planes and helicopters and even afford to pay the coalman once a month.

But all that isn't just given to you on a plate because you're a nice person with a sense of humour. No, you only get it after you sign 'The Devil's Comedy Contract'! Have I mentioned that before? No? Well, it's really quite simple and I guarantee there's not one successful comedian past or present who hasn't signed the document in blood, sweat and tears. 'The Devil's Comedy Contract' declares that 'A comedian will be given wealth, possessions, jewellery, mansions, swimming pools, exotic holidays, beautiful women – and the occasional ugly one – in return for agreeing to do one thing. *Every time he walks on stage or in front of a television camera, whether he feels like it or not . . . **he has to be funny**. That's **every single time**. No argument. If he fails to be funny on just **one single*** *occasion,* he agrees that his glittering prizes will be taken away from him, one . . . by . . . one!' Please sign here!

It's entirely different for singers, actors, jugglers, concert pianists and every other job in the business. If they have a bad night or they're not quite on form, no one thinks they're on the slide. But comedy performers are always expected to be side-splittingly funny 24 hours a day. When a star comedian walks out in front of 2,000 people, he *knows* he's got them in the palm of his hand before he's opened his mouth. He knows that this hall-full of expectant, smiling, strangers love him. He can *feel* their laughter and applause and his years of experience help him cope with this explosion of admiration. It's a fantastic feeling. An audience going crazy for *you*? You can't beat it, my friend. You never want it to end. You're King Of Comedy for a night.

But eventually the crowd does let you go and the stage is bare and the lights are switched off and after you sign a few autographs, you carry your suit to the car and drive home. That's it. In case any of you were wondering, that's by and large exactly what a comedian does after making 2,000 people rock with laughter. He goes home. Some performers might retire to a nearby bar or club and down a few bevvies. Me, I don't drink, never have. So I go straight home. Just like a factory worker or an insurance clerk or a shop assistant goes home when their working day is over, to eat, watch a bit of telly and sleep, a comedian does the same after he finishes work. The only difference being, he gets back to a darkened house at half-past three in the morning, makes a cup of tea, switches on the TV and falls asleep in front of *Job Finder*.

But before any comedian can reach the stage of his career where he's a 'hot' name and television contracts are dangled in front of him and people recognise him in the street and want his autograph and he can pack out theatres twice a night, life can be a struggle. Work might be irregular so money will be tight. If he's married, he will have constant rows with his wife about the hours he works. She may put pressure on him to get a 'proper job'. She may even be jealous of his going out to work in the clubs at night, suspicious that he might have a bit on the side. All this doesn't help to spread sweetness and harmony around the house. Then, when he eventually does 'make it', their relationship faces an even bigger challenge, because he has to be so focused on his career that his wife, children, family and friends and any 'social life' will always come a poor second.

As the money starts rolling in, he'll be able to afford the house of his dreams in several acres of land, surrounded by celebrity neighbours. But he, the performer, hardly ever gets a chance to sleep there because he's always touring or in a long summer season or stuck in a TV studio for weeks on end. As the years go by, and believe me when you're working at this pace they *fly* by, he sees less and less of his family until eventually they stop relating to him as a husband or father. The harder he works for them, bitterness and resentment build up, not on his part, theirs.

All he becomes to them is the man who bought them the big house and pays all their bills. Like all fathers and husbands, there are times when he wants to hug his family and tell them all how much he loves them, but that's not always possible when they're living in Berkshire and he's performing twice-nightly, six days a week in Blackpool from June to November, with additional concerts every Sunday in Skegness or Scarborough. Watertight, cast-iron contracts created between his management and the shows' producers make it impossible for him to get home even for a day.

Trying to keep in touch with regular, long-distance phone calls doesn't really help, because after the opening 'Hellos' and 'How are you's' they're often filled with long, awkward silences. When his three-month tour or long summer season finishes and he does return home, some of those long awkward silences are often hidden away in the luggage he brings in through the front door. Ready to relax and chat and spend some real time with his family, he finds himself in the house of his dreams, the one he's been working his bollocks off all summer to pay for, surrounded by the people he loves most in all the world . . . *and they've got absolutely nothing to say to him.*

I'm telling you all this, not as some sort of 'this might happen to you if you're not careful' warning to would-be comedians.

I'm telling you because it happened to me a few years ago.

And you may not be surprised to learn that it was around this time that I started to wonder why I ever bothered to become a performer.

So why and how *did* I become a performer? I wasn't born in a trunk. And unlike the Elephant Man, I wasn't born *with* a trunk. Yes, yes. I know the Elephant Man didn't actually have a trunk. I've seen the film. I was just having a little joke. There'll be a few more throughout this book. There'll be a prize for anyone who spots them all.

I didn't have showbiz blood running through my veins. No one else in my family showed signs of possessing any sort of talent, apart from knowing how to use their fists. All I can say is, when I was a young boy I used get a strange feeling in my stomach that there was something special waiting for me 'out there'. And it wasn't the khazi at the end of the garden.

It's difficult to describe the feeling all these years later. It was as if I *knew* that I wasn't going to spend all my life working on the docks or in a Liverpool factory. I didn't know how this was going to happen and I didn't daydream about being a big star one day. I just had this feeling that my destiny involved more than working five days a week on an assembly-line, living for the weekends and spending every night down the pub getting rat-arsed. It was around the same time, and I realise this is going to sound weird as I put it down in print, that I used to see spirits in my bedroom. Not the traditional spooks dressed in white sheets like they have in 'The Haunted Bedroom' scene in pantomimes. These spirits weren't scary at all. In fact they were comforting in a way. One in particular was a tiny little girl who would stand silently at the bottom of my bed before running around in circles. Yes, you could argue that I might well have been dreaming. But is it possible to have the same dream over and over, in which exactly the same things happen every time? Besides . . . I was wide awake every time I saw them. Scouts honour!

This chapter may give you a better insight into how the person you know as 'Freddie Starr' was formed. Let me be totally honest with you. I've never been great at remembering *specific* dates, names and places.

I was born Frederick Fowell at Number 10, Ulster Road, Liverpool in 1943. Yes, I was a war baby. My mother surrendered. Apparently, as soon as he got the news that I'd been born, Adolf Hitler ordered the Luftwaffe to bomb my home town because, as he wrote in his famous book of German humour, *Mein Kampf*, one of his psychic advisers had looked into the future and told him that one day little Freddie Fowell would grow up into a comedian who would earn a living by mercilessly taking the piss out of him. Which got right up inside his helmet.

While we're on the subject of Mein Führer, I'm told that some people, who must be one strawberry short of a punnet, actually think I dress up as wellie-wearing Adolf Hitler on stage, complete with swastikas on my shorts, because I'm a *fan* of that evil bastard. So let me take this opportunity to make myself absolutely, perfectly, never-again-to-be-misunderstood clear.

I do it because I think Hitler was a sub-human monster who allowed unforgivable atrocities to take place that were beyond the understanding of any rational-thinking person. And every time an audience laughs at the way I ridicule him, I'd like to think it ensures that Adolf's murderous arse, dick and bollock (I think it was him who only had one?) get another good singeing as he's rotated slowly on his very own private spit, over the red-hot burning coals of Hell, for all Eternity.

Now, class, are they any more questions?

We were a working-class family. My father, who held what today might be considered as Victorian principles, earned a living as a bricklayer during the day and made a few quid as a bare-knuckle fighter whenever the opportunity came along. My mother, who passed away five years ago, God bless her, brought up five of us – my three sisters Brenda, Hilda and Joan, my elder brother Richard and me. You'll be familiar with the expression 'we were poor but happy' and that could almost describe us. Except we were poor and bloody miserable. Well, only *most* of the time.

When I was four we moved from Ulster Road to Huyton. It was a brand new estate which had been built on the outskirts of Liverpool. We were one of the first families to move on to the estate and our new house was in Brookwood Road. For a while, the estate seemed half empty, but eventually more and more families moved out of the inner-city and moved in around us. But they didn't turn up in removal lorries or rented vans or even cars. At that time hardly anyone on the estate owned a car. In fact I'm sure some of our neighbours hadn't *seen* a car except in films. They'd arrive at their new homes with their few personal possessions and bits of furniture piled up on hand carts which they'd pushed all the way from the city. Some people were able to afford a horse and cart to do all the donkey work – if it's possible for a horse to do donkey work.

Looking back, life must have been tough for a kid growing up in the 1950s. But we just accepted everything as normal. If you only had one pair of school trousers and you ripped them, then you had to wear ripped trousers to school. If someone tried to take the piss out of you, you hit 'em. Hard. I've known kids come to school in the middle of winter just wearing a school shirt and short trousers, with holes in their shoes because their parents were skint and couldn't afford to buy them a coat and new shoes. Today, ripped jeans are considered 'cool'. We weren't cool in the 50s. We were bloody freezing.

So some days it was a real pleasure to go to school! At least they had those great big grey metal radiators that looked like they were made out of old battleships there. The junior school, which was brand new just like the estate, was five miles from my house.

Every day I'd walk there and back with my pals Peter, Charlie, Tony, Lawrie and the very first kid I got to know on the estate, Jimmy Haimer. Can you imagine the sort of things five little scallies like us got up to on that ten-mile round trip? Here's just one example . . .

Our marathon trek to school every day took us through a cowfield. If I was feeling poetic I could call it a 'meadow'. But there's nothing poetic about a field full of cowshit. Me and my mates were always laughing and joking about, and it may be true that I was the one with more mischief in him than the others. Which explains what happened one particular morning.

We were walking through this field and I noticed a huge cowpat in the grass that seemed to say to me 'Freddieeeee! Freddieeeee! Pick me up and throw me at one of your friends! It'll be fun! And you won't get into any trouble . . .!'

Now, it wasn't that I hadn't noticed cowpats before, because the field was covered in them every day. But this enormous pile was 'fresh out of the pan', so to speak and both caught my eye and my twisted sense of humour. I don't know what made me do it, but I picked up the steaming cow shit with both hands, threw it at one of my mates and it landed right on top of his head. For about ten seconds he looked like he was trying on a big flat cap ten sizes too big for him – except this particular big flat cap was made out of ripe, brown dung. I can't remember which mate it was who I christened in manure first, but I probably couldn't have recognised him anyway with all that khaki-coloured crap dripping down his face.

When they saw what I had done, my other mates all searched for fresh ammunition – they didn't have to look far – and before I knew it, the shit hit the fan (well, the side of my head) and a dung fight started, with giant cowpats flying through the air like noxious frisbees! (Noxious Frisbee? Wasn't he a famous West End actor of the 1930s?)

The fight only went on for five minutes, but I can assure you that was more than enough time to play with cowshit for *anyone*. We were all falling about laughing at the sight of ourselves, because none of the five of us had escaped. We were all plastered in the brown stuff. Our eyes, ears, noses, hair . . . even our pockets. We knew we couldn't go home in that state, because our parents would have murdered us. So what did us five bright sparks decide to do? We'd carry on our journey to school as if nothing had happened and just hope that no one noticed. Were we stupid or just completely dull?

I mean, how could no one notice five lads who were completely plastered from head to toe in recently evacuated manure? They must have picked up the stink on the Isle of

Man! Words can't adequately describe just how deadly this mixture of fresh cow shit and five sweaty, naughty, school-boys reeked. Every time I drive through the country and the fields are fresh with silage, it brings it back to me in a diluted form. But we didn't care what people thought, because we were *the lads!* We knew it all! Despite the fact that each of us was covered from head to toe in cow shit, we were *absolutely sure* we could brazen it out for an entire school day!

So what happened when we strolled into morning assem-bly? One by one all the other kids noticed the overpowering smell of the countryside right there in the middle of the school hall and it didn't take them long to work out where it was coming from. By the time the third kid had told us, in a very uncouth manner I must say, that we all stank, we'd had enough and started answering them back. So that got *their* backs up and within seconds, while the teachers kept on singing 'All Things Bright and Beautiful, All Creatures Great and Small', the five of us were, ironically, having a fight with dozens of other kids over the merits, or otherwise, of cow shit.

Luckily the bigger kids didn't get in too close, because they very quickly realised that every time they landed a punch anywhere on us, their fists would be covered in small, brown, wet, smelly lumps. So they'd wave their fists about an inch from us and 'pretend' to make contact with us. Out of the three hundred lads who joined in, some were shit at fighting and some were fighting at shit!

Ten minutes later all five of us were facing the Headmaster in his study. He looked at us and said, 'Now boys. I want you to tell me precisely how you all got in this disgusting mess!' No. That's not true, because he was firmly holding his nose between his thumb and forefinger at the time, so what it sounded to us like he was saying was 'Dow boyth. I bont you to dell be becithely dow you all got in diss dithguthting meth!' So naturally when we heard him talking like that we all pissed ourselves. Not literally, thank God, or the smell would have been even worse.

He tapped his desk impatiently with a small brown ruler. I think it was King Hussein of Jordan. Sorry. I slipped another joke in there. It won't happen again. The Headmaster was waiting for an explanation and as none of my mates could think of anything to say, guess who stepped forward one pace and offered to clarify the events that had put us in this dithguthting meth? Right first time. I said, 'Sir, I do apologise for our dreadful appearance. You see, my friends and I absolutely *adore* the countryside and on the way here this morning we stopped to rest for five minutes in a beautiful meadow and picked buttercups and daisies to bring in for our nature table. As we sat there, merrily selecting flowers and singing hymns, a beautiful Jersey cow we christened Daisy wandered over to see what we were doing and after a few minutes, satisfied we weren't up to any mischief, Daisy turned to walk away, lifted up her pretty little tail, gave out a gentle moo . . . and then shat all over us.'

The Headmaster just shook his head in despair and told us to get down to the showers straight away. We dived under the hot water fully dressed and washed as much of the shit off ourselves as we could.

When we came out of the showers, our clothes still dripping wet, we were told to go straight home, but the five of us knew we couldn't do that with our clothes soaking because our parents would have given us just as big a hiding as if we'd gone home covered in manure. So we walked out of the school gates in the direction of home and after a mile or so we got the ball out and played footie all day. By the time we got home the sun had dried us off, so I escaped getting a smacked arse. That time!

CHAPTER TWO

When it gets down to the nitty-gritty, showbusiness is no different from any other sort of business. Just like banking, estate agencies, scrap metal or the very latest dot.com mega-bucks winner, if there's money to be made out of it, it'll always attract the good, the bad and the downright pug-ugly. I'm not talking about looks here. I'm talking about people's behaviour. Their greed. Their plain *dishonesty*.

Agents, personal managers, accountants, club managers, impresarios, television executives – some of them are genuinely caring people and really want a performer to do well and rise to the top simply because they have faith in the performer and would like him or her to be a big star because they think that person is talented and deserves all the breaks.

But as soon as your TV ratings start dropping and people stop coming to see you when you're touring, you find all your 'best friends' disappearing into the woodwork. I'm not saying it's right or wrong. I'm just telling that's how the business works.

Of course there are always a few exceptions. The odd friend or two who will stick by you through thick and thin. But they're not usually people who rely on you to earn their living. You'll find about as much genuine loyalty in showbusiness as there are hairs on Paul Daniels's head. Basically bugger all.

Whereas the loyalty that exists among *criminals* is 150 per cent rock-solid. I'm not talking about those arsehole kids who go round nicking cars, belonging to hard-working people who might be struggling to keep up the monthly payments, and then deliberately crash them 'for a laugh'. And I'm not talking about the young toe-rags who kick open back doors so they can steal old ladies' purses from kitchen tables. They're not real criminals. They're just little shits who need a good hiding.

I'm talking about the real hard men of crime. The ones whose names and faces never get in the papers because they're too clever. They let their underlings do most of the street work. The hard men are tough as nails and you wouldn't want to cross them, but they don't get their hands dirty if they can help it. They plan. Organise. Arrange. *They get things sorted.* And their word is their bond. Because they're businessmen. Crime is their business and only a complete fool would mess around with. You see, the real hard men of crime have a certain look about them. They don't go around like the villains you see on TV *trying* to look hard. No, they don't have to *try*. They *are* hard. They have no fear. Remember that. These men fear *nothing!* I'm prepared to bet serious money that very few people reading this book can honestly say they fear *nothing!* Most of us fear something. Illness. Poverty. Redundancy. Death. Being mugged or burgled. Not these guys. Something about their demeanour tells you straight away, 'You don't fuck with me!'

How do I know? Listen, I've mixed with hardened criminals since I was a snotty nosed kid with his arse hanging out of his trousers in Liverpool. I've known violence, seen violence and been the victim of violence.

One of the first real fist-fights I ever witnessed (which I soon discovered was in a different league to the pathetic scraps that happened every day in the school playground) didn't involve criminals or teenage gangs or even the police. One morning, it must have been during the school holidays, my Dad got me out of bed around half-past six in the morning and said, 'Come on Fred. You're coming to work with me today!' I was about eleven or twelve I suppose and was excited at the prospect of working on a building site. I imagined I'd be carrying bricks in a hod up and down ladders or even doing a bit of plastering.

As it turned out, Dad, who was a foreman, had me making tea, running down the local cafe for bacon sandwiches and doing all the shitty little jobs the brickies wouldn't do. But I didn't really care. I wasn't in school, I was out on the fresh air and I knew my Dad might slip me a couple of bob for my endeavours at the end of the week. I felt really grown up. Especially hearing my Dad swear at his men if they were slacking, because I'd never heard Dad swear in the house. Mum would have clipped him one if he had. During the morning he must have said, 'Get a fucking move on with those fucking bricks you lazy bastards!' a hundred times and I pissed myself laughing every time. *My Dad* using the f-word! I couldn't wait to tell me mates!

One of the most popular Western series on television at that time was *Rawhide* which starred a young Clint Eastwood. He played a character called Rowdy Yates and there was a fellah who worked on the building site with my father, who looked a bit like Clint, so naturally, everybody called him Rowdy Yates.

Now unlike the screen version, *this* Rowdy was a big-headed, big-mouthed bully who constantly liked to taunt and insult everyone he worked with, including my Dad. It only took me a couple of hours that day to work out he was a nasty piece of work. What I didn't know was, he'd been really getting up my Dad's nose for weeks, but Dad, being the foreman, kept his temper under control and instead of giving him a right-hander, had limited himself to the odd verbal assault to keep this bastard in his place. Remember, my Dad was a bare-knuckle fighter who trained every day in our back garden. He was big and fit and well known in our area for being able to put a man down . . . fast! So either Rowdy must have, foolishly, thought he was tougher than Dad or he was completely off his trolley. Because even when the fellahs stopped for lunch, he still kept needling Dad. And Dad could only keep his temper under control for so long.

I remember what happened next as if it were yesterday. It's one of those moments in my life that I can run through my head any time I like, in glorious Technicolor and Cinemascope! It had started to rain, so instead of sitting around on the site, we were all huddled inside a builder's hut, eating our sandwiches and reading the papers. I'd say there were about twelve of us all together. Rowdy Yates finished eating and straightaway started insulting my Dad again. Dad ignored him at first and kept on reading his newspaper. But as Rowdy's insults became harder and cruder and nastier and more personal, Dad slowly put his paper down, took off his reading glasses and reached into his pocket. He pulled out a coin and flicked it towards Rowdy.

Rowdy caught the coin and said to my Dad, 'What the fuck is this for?'

My dad stood up, putting his glasses in his shirt pocket, and said, 'It's for you, son. So you can call an ambulance. Because in two minutes, you're going to need one, you nasty, loud-mouthed, bullying bastard! Now stand up or I'll hammer you where you sit!'

This was the moment Rowdy was waiting for and he jumped up, eyes ablaze, his fists clenched. His plan was to needle my Dad so much he would lose his rag and lash out at Rowdy in an undisciplined manner. Rowdy thought if he kept his cool, he could let Dad tire himself out and then move in to finish him off. That's what he thought. But he was an idiot. Rowdy must have been as thick as cowshit. He'd totally underestimated my Dad's strength, capabilities and intelligence. Oh dear!

My father, taking his bare-knuckle fighter stance, waited for Rowdy to throw the first punch. Rowdy, expecting Dad to run at him with his arms flailing in the heat of temper, was taken aback for a second. Just one second. Not a very long time in the history of the universe I admit. But long enough for Rowdy's IQ, which couldn't have been very high to start with, to fall 150 per cent. In that one second he lost all his logic and common sense . . . and the prat tried to throw a punch at my Dad. *My Dad!* The man who had used the f-word two thousand fucking times that day!

My father ducked and Rowdy's punch whistled past his head. Sitting there watching this I wanted to jump up and do something to this nasty piece of work who was trying to belt my Dad. But even as I thought about doing something, even as Rowdy's punch missed Dad's head, my father brought his right fist up and knocked the bugger out flat on the ground with one rock-solid punch! 'Wallop!' Rowdy's lip was bleeding badly and from the gormless expression on his face he looked as though he'd narrowly missed being hit by an express train. His eyes were still in their sockets but they weren't seeing very much.

My Dad stood over him and said, 'Get up you bullying bastard. I haven't finished with you yet!' Rowdy just sat there, wiping the blood off his mouth and shook his head to signify he'd had enough. But Dad wasn't satisfied with that. He knew his authority as a foreman and more importantly his reputation as a man and a local bare-knuckle fighter had been insulted. If he let Rowdy off with a single punch, once his lip had healed and the bruises had gone down, the odds were that one night he'd be sat in a pub getting pissed out of his head with his mates and one of them would say, "Ere. You ought to give that foreman a bleeding good hiding after what he done to you.' And the seed would be planted again and he'd want to have another go at him sometime, maybe with the help of his piss-artist mates. So he had to make sure Rowdy would never, ever pick a fight with him again.

He pulled Rowdy up by his hair and dragged him outside, where he proceeded to give him the hammering of his life. Rowdy was on his feet, just, but there was no fight left in him. Like all bullies, once you stand up to them, they're just hollow men with no guts. My father hit him hard in the ribs, gave him a double left hook and finished him off with a right hook. 'Boof!' Down he went like a sack of cold porridge. Everyone on the building site knew Rowdy Yates would never pick on anyone else again. Even if he were capable of it. One of the brickies tapped me on the shoulder and said, 'Freddie, your Dad is one of the best bare-knuckle fighters I've ever seen.'

What did he mean 'one of the best'? As far as I was concerned, after seeing how he'd put that arrogant bully down, my father was the best fighter in the entire world! I then realised why he trained so regularly and so hard.

Anyway, with the excitement over, the rest of us went back to work, though not before someone called for an ambulance. Rowdy 'Big-Mouthed Bastard' Yates spent a couple of weeks recovering in hospital. The site's accident book recorded that he'd fallen thirty-feet off scaffolding on to a pile of bricks. Yates's IQ must have been improved by the pounding he got from my father because he didn't once try to contradict the official version of events.

That was my first real sight of real violence and how it could be used to stop further violence. My Dad beat the shit out of Rowdy Yates, which was tough on the big-mouthed twat, but the chances were, after taking such a hammering, it might stop him from picking on smaller (and bigger!) blokes in the future. It also revealed to me just how vicious and how prehistorically savage *real* fighting could be. Blood and skin and bone and raw energy and hate all rolled into one violent moment. Although I was proud of my father that day and I knew there was no question of him backing down from that arsehole, the sight of Yates's bloody face, beaten to a pulp, stayed in my thoughts and dreams for a long, long time. It even popped into my head the night, many years later, when I stood in a cold, dark warehouse with several of Liverpool's hardest criminals and watched a bloke, probably no older than thirty, who'd committed the unforgivable sin of grassing on his mates, being physically crucified to the floor by a big ugly fucker with a massive great nail gun. The sort you see today being used by cheerful professional cockneys on DIY TV shows. Listen, forget *Changing Rooms* and *Ground Force*. This poor sod had been forced to the ground and was about to have his body changed.

This would have been in the very early 1960s. I was a very junior member of one of the toughest gangs in the Pool. The boss of the gang was the hardest man I've ever met. Even harder and braver than my father. To the majority of people he was the owner of a legitimate and highly successful nightclub. But to those who really knew him, he was among the top ten hard men in Liverpool. In my book, he was probably in the top five. Although he passed away in 1999, I'm not going to reveal his real name to you. What would be the point? I suppose I could lie and tell you his name was really Tarquin Lee-Groatspender or Gerald Knobfinder and you wouldn't know who I was really talking about, unless you lived in Liverpool in the early 1960s. So with or without your permission, I'll just call him B*****. Although I was obviously aware that B***** was a heavy-duty criminal, he was what the cockneys would call 'a diamond geezer'. In Liverpool, for me and for others to whom he was loyal and who were loyal to him, he was a bloody good mate, who would always keep his word – and would expect no less of the rest of us. For some reason, possibly because I used to make him laugh –

while making sure I never took the piss out of him or was even remotely disloyal at any time – he took to me when I was a young club entertainer and he started giving me occasional jobs to do for him, which paid well.

He also taught me to watch everything that was happening around me, make mental notes and say nothing; and always to make yourself small and anonymous. That way you could learn things, overhear conversations, pick up names and places which could be useful maybe six months or even a year later.

In return for being looked after, he sometimes asked me to make up the numbers when he had a job to do, usually when a show of force was all that was necessary to put the wind up one of his enemies or rivals. He wouldn't expect me actually to do anything nasty. He wanted me just to be there, looking tough along with his other gang members. But I wasn't there the night when B***** and half a dozen others were in a cold, dark Liverpool warehouse, standing around the walls. Because the room was badly lit, and they all wore dark clothes and said nothing, none of them could ever have been fingered as being part of this 'operation', except B*****, of course. But he didn't care. He was fearless. The toughest of the tough.

B***** stood over the victim, who was spreadeagled out on a filthy wooden floor, totally unable to move as his arms and legs were being held down tightly, and said very quietly, but with pure ice in his voice, 'Believe me, I didn't want this to happen. And I'm bloody well sure you didn't want this to happen either. But let's be honest, you brought this down on yourself. We asked you to keep your trap shut, but you couldn't. We warned you not to grass on us, and you did. I understand you go to church on Sundays, is that right?'

The guy, wide-eyed and very near the point of soiling his pants, nodded.

'That's good,' B***** said, 'because you've got to be punished for what you did, as you always knew you'd have to be, so we've come up with the perfect way to chastise a Godfearing soul like you.' He paused to light a cigarette. 'You're going to get just what Jesus got. Except we didn't have time to build you a cross, so this floor will have to do.' He knelt down over the victim and blew smoke in his face. 'You really should remember, that when I say I'm going to nail someone, I really mean I'm going to fucking nail them!' He stood up, nodded to a big fellah holding the nail gun and moved back against the wall. The man with the nail gun didn't mess around. There was no nervous hesitation. No prospect of his refusing to carry out B*****'s orders. He'd done this sort of work before. First the right hand, then the right foot, then the left foot, then the right hand. As each four-inch nail sliced into his flesh the victim wailed like a baby. Well, be fair, who wouldn't? Blood poured from each wound and those who were there almost felt sorry for the poor bastard until they remembered what had happened to good friends of our gang thanks to his over-talkative tongue.

The job done, B***** led the way and they all followed him out, looking back quickly before going out of the door. I heard they could just make out in the semi-darkness that the victim was desperately trying to pull both hands off the floor, but it's not easy when you've got four inches of metal nail pinning them down.

He didn't die, by the way. Not that time, anyway. B***** never said anything to me, but I learned a couple of days later that the police had got a call on the night of the crucifixion, telling them something dodgy was happening in that warehouse and they'd better get their arses round there right away to find out what was going on. They found the fellah and got him into hospital. I'm not sure exactly what happened to him, but he wasn't seen around Liverpool again after that. Nor anywhere else B***** could hear about.

So how did I meet this B*****? A man capable of ordering someone's crucifixion as easily as ordering a Chinese takeaway. A man capable of extraordinary kindness, generosity and warmth. Provided you didn't disrespect him. I've told you I'm hopeless at remembering dates, but we first met some time in the early 1960s. I was about sixteen or seventeen and working at various clubs around Liverpool as a solo singer. There were hundreds of clubs in the town in those days and if your act wasn't half bad, you could get plenty of work, although compared to today's wages, the money was a pittance. But when you're sixteen and having a ball, money isn't everything. One club I always went down well in was The Blue Angel.

The original owner of the club was, so I was told, a big fan of Marlene Dietrich and named the place after one of her old films. I'm so glad he wasn't a big fan of Katherine Hepburn or I might have been spending my evenings inside The African Queen. I think I'll leave you to make your own jokes up based on that fact.

Not so much today, because the nightclub scene has altered beyond recognition now, but in those days, the clubs always attracted villains and gangster types. It was often the case they owned clubs as well, and liked to be seen 'playing the host', especially when, in the case of some of the posher clubs, celebrities would sweep through the front door. Why they didn't employ cleaners to do the sweeping, Christ only knows. Then, nightclubs were places villains could hang out, just enjoying themselves before or after a job or even planning a job. The music was always sassy and loud so they couldn't be overheard. And if the coppers called in from time to time, all they saw were a bunch of well-to-do blokes having a night out.

So I've appeared at the Blue Angel a few times and B***** and his mates were usually there, all looking immaculate in expensive midnight-blue Italian suits and hand-made white shirts. I'm not going to say they looked the dog's bollocks because I've seen enough dogs' bollocks in my time to say here and now, they're not in the least bit attractive. Those two dangly things hanging down there *attractive*? I don't think so. And frankly, I'd be worried about anyone who said they were. Apart from a female dog, of course. And even then I'd be worried, because dogs can't talk. Now where the hell was I?

One night, after I've come off stage, B*****'s at the bar waiting to chat to me. He said something along the lines of 'That was bloody brilliant, Fred. What'll you have to drink?' and when I told him I fancied a lemonade, he thought I was joking. Even then I never touched booze. I eventually persuaded him I really did want a lemonade and I went and sat at his table with his well-turned out mates and we started talking, about nothing special really from what I remember. They seemed a friendly bunch and I didn't have anywhere to go, so I spent the rest of the evening with them having a bloody good laugh. Believe me, you don't need to get tanked up on sixteen pints of lager to enjoy yourself. No, fifteen's more than enough.

After that I'd bump into B***** down the Blue Angel and various other clubs from time to time and always had a chat. I didn't know it at the time, but B***** was a very well-known figure in the underworld. To me he was just a businessman, a nightclub owner with his fingers in lots of pies, who enjoyed my act and my company and liked a good night out. After I'd finished a show, we'd go to a casino. Me, B***** and usually ten or eleven of his mates and most nights we'd be out until dawn. It was on one of our casino nights, not very long after I'd met B*****, that I first got on the wrong side of him. And instantly regretted it.

While I was a professional singer and he was a professional criminal, I had done a bit of petty crime now and again and still kept my hand in occasionally. Nothing too dangerous. I always took from those who could afford a loss. Not old ladies or working-class families. You never stole from your own. To be honest, I did it more for the fun of it than for monetary gain. So, this particular night we're in the Odd Spot club in Liverpool and B*****'s engrossed in playing the dice.

After a while I got a bit bored watching him win a bit, then lose a bit, then win a bit again. During the evening, apart from eyeing up a couple of very attractive ladies, I'd noticed that all the money the punters were betting was dropped into wooden boxes attached to the underneath of the dice table. And I knew from visiting the club once or twice previously, that they only emptied these boxes at the end of the evening, which was usually around half past three in the morning.

I looked at my watch. Just after one o'clock. Those boxes must be bulging with money, I thought. The place was heaving, but nobody noticed me 'looking for something' around the bottom of the table. I quickly checked I hadn't been spotted and dived under the table, with the floor-length table cloth hiding me from view. I took out a penknife from my pocket and started to unscrew the bottom of one of these boxes I hoped would be full of money. One screw came away easily . . . then the next . . . then the next. But that fourth bastard was screwed in tight. I started sweating a bit. I thought, *What if they decide to empty the boxes early tonight because it's some special holiday like, I don't know, the . . . the . . . Chinese Hebrew Year Of The Well-Hung Horse or something?*

I kept working on that fourth screw, pushing and turning the pen knife with two sweaty hands. Suddenly, the box popped open and before I realised what was happening I was drowning in silver coins and pound notes and fivers and tenners . . . and the money was still dropping in from the game going on above me. Including some of B*****'s money too! Oh fuck! What would he have to say about that? But it was too late to worry. I had to move on to the next box and the next. By the time I'd emptied all the boxes, praying I wouldn't be discovered, I was stuffing money in my jacket, in my trousers, my socks, my underpants . . . every where!

Somehow, and I'll never know how, I managed to get out from under the table without being spotted and silently nodded to B***** to follow me outside to the car park. He must have thought I was having a fit or something, the way I was walking. But *you* try walking normally with fifty quids' worth of two-bob pieces jangling against your nadgers.

We got outside and B***** said, 'What the bloody hell's going on? I was on a winning streak in there!'

'I bet my winning streak was better than yours!' I said, and started taking fivers and tenners from my pockets and handing them to B*****. I decided to leave the two-bob pieces where they were as I didn't know B***** *that* well.

He was stunned. 'Where the fucking hell did you get all this money Fred?'

I was laughing as I kept handing him more and more money. 'Under the dice table! I used my pen knife and unscrewed the wooden boxes. It was a piece of piss! Half of it's yours, of course!'

I could tell from the way his eyes narrowed and his lips thinned out, he was not impressed by my money-making stunt. I waited for the bollocking.

B***** stood back and shook his head. I could see I'd upset him. He gave me all the money back in my hand, his head still shaking in disapproval. 'You are a little bastard, Fred. A right little bastard. You didn't think it through, did you? You did this on the spur of the moment, didn't you?'

I nodded, feeling like I did the day the headmaster called me to his study for fighting with cowshit.

'What you didn't think about was that people know you hang around with me. And if anyone saw you–'

I interrupted him, something I should never have done, I realise now. 'No one saw me, B*****, I promise! I was too quick!'

B***** shushed me with his finger against his lips. 'If anyone saw you,' he continued, 'and they tell the old bill, you'll get your collar felt.'

'But B*****, no one saw me, really they didn't.' Christ, why couldn't I just button my lip like I knew I ought to?

'Shut up Fred. Shut up and listen. Now, I've grown very fond of you in the past couple of months. You're a fast learner and I think you could be very useful to me. Because of your spur of the moment stupidity tonight, you could have ended up in the clink and then you wouldn't have been any use to me at all, would you?'

I had to nod in agreement. I was a prat of the first order and I was upset that I'd annoyed B*****.

'But,' continued B*****, 'I think you learned a valuable lesson tonight. You learned never, ever get caught with your fingers in the till while I'm standing right next to you. Because if I'd been implicated in any way, I'd be a very unhappy man. Very unhappy. Do you know *how* unhappy I'd be, Fred?'

'Very unhappy?' I answered in a voice that sounded like Mickey Mouse on helium.

'That's right,' he said. 'You do learn fast. But you still have to be punished for your stupidity. Don't you agree?'

Talk about mixed emotions. I knew I had to be punished, but didn't relish the thought. On the other hand, if I whined and cried and was unwilling to take whatever punishment B***** had in mind, I'd look a right wimp. 'Yes, I agree, B*****,' I said.

B***** walked slowly around me for a minute or two, considering what punishment he could dish out. I knew his car was parked in the next street, just a few yards away, with two of his heavy mob inside, waiting for whatever orders he'd give them. Like 'Take Freddie over to the moors. Put three bullets in his head and bring me back his ears!'

I was further up shit creek than anyone had else had ever navigated before and not only did I not have a paddle, I didn't even have a bastard canoe!

And then he looked at me and said, 'Yeah. I know exactly what I'm going to do with you, you stupid, stupid little bastard. Come here!'

What could I do but take my punishment? As I stepped towards B*****, my guts were churning and despite the cold night air, a thin film of sweat appeared above my top lip. He stood there in his long black overcoat, silhouetted against the light from a street lamp, his hands behind his back. I wondered if he'd slipped a gun out of his pocket without my noticing and was about to execute me. There was absolutely no doubt he was capable of severely punishing anyone who upset him. And boy, had I just done that! Because of his stone-faced appearance, it was always difficult to make out what B***** was thinking or feeling at the best of times, but in this semi-darkness it was impossible.

I stood about two feet from him for what seemed ages, but could only have been about four or five seconds. When he spoke, his voice was calm but nonetheless full of menace . . .

'Freddie, boy, you dropped a major bollock tonight and you know it. How are you feeling right this minute?'

'Shit scared.' What was the point of lying to the man?

'Yeah, I bet you are.' He walked towards me a couple of inches and placed one hand on my right shoulder and another on my left. Was he going to nut me? Break my nose? Jesus . . . did he have a knife in his pocket?

He brought both hands up to either side of my face and slapped me hard on both cheeks. I mean *hard*. So hard my brain seemed to rattle around in my skull. Then he did it again. And then a third, fourth, fifth and sixth time. Each slap seemed to be harder than the one before. My face was stinging like hell. B*****'s hands were as tough as a brickie's. Then he moved back and put his hands away in his overcoat pockets.

'Freddie, you're a little bastard. And I have no doubt that when you're 30 ... or 50 ... or 87, you'll *still* be a little bastard! But I know you'll never ever do anything as stupid as you did tonight again. Will you, Freddie boy?'

'N ... no, 'course not!' I was a bit confused. Had that slapping been my only punishment?

'Good boy. Because next time you behave like a twenty-carat pillock, you'll get more than a little tap!'

A little tap? Christ, my face was red raw.

'Tomorrow night, we're going back to the Odd Spot Club ...'

Was B***** crazy? Go back to the same club I'd just stolen several hundred quid from? He could see I was just about to open my mouth in protest and 'shushed' me.

Believe me, when B***** shushed you, you stayed shushed.

'Yes, Freddie. We're going back. Because if we don't, you, and more importantly *me*, being your friend and mentor, could well be under suspicion. So we'll turn up as per usual, and when they tell us what happened to them tonight, we'll be shocked and surprised that anyone would *dare* to steal their hard-earned cash from right under their noses. And I'll promise to put the word around that when we find the toe-rag who stole their money, he'll get a bloody good hammering ... just for starters.'

Once again, B***** was talking sense. If it had been up to me, I would have avoided the club for weeks, months maybe. But that would have been a really stupid thing to do. The club owners would have noticed that I wasn't a regular customer any more and might have asked some of their heavies to make enquiries about me and whether I'd been flashing more cash about than usual. And I'd have been in big trouble ... and B***** could have been implicated too. So that was some-thing else that made me realise just how stupid I was. The thing is, I was quite young, sixteen or seventeen. I had time to learn. I realised that there was a positive side to suddenly realising how stupid you are. It's an opportunity to tell yourself never to be stupid again. To try and think things through, if at all possible, before you do something that might be a bit risky . . . a bit dangerous . . . a bit *stupid!* Of course, everyone's stupid from time to time, but the older you get and the more life throws at you, the less stupid you become. That is, unless you're *really* stupid.

So, B***** grabs my arm and starts walking me towards the street where his boys were sat waiting in his car. My pockets are still bulging with notes and my underpants are rattling with the noise of silver coins.

'Freddie, you got off light this time. Think yourself lucky. You shouldn't have done what you did, but it's too late now. We can't go back to the club tonight and give 'em their money back. So, you and me will have a divvy-up. Fifty-fifty, straight down the middle, no quibble . . . right?'

I nodded. Three or four times. As far as I was concerned he could have all the bloody money. He hadn't killed me, so I was already ahead of the game. Who worries about money when they've narrowly escaped being executed? B***** suddenly stopped dead and looked me up and down. 'Why are you walking like Quasimodo with advanced haemorrhoids?'

I had to tell him straight. 'B***** . . . it's these silver coins in my underpants. There's hundreds of them and they're all rubbing up against my bollocks.'

He nodded. 'Hmm. Tell you what. Why don't we just go fifty-fifty on the notes. The silver's all yours, OK?' He started laughing and we walked around to the street where his car was parked.

It was a funny moment, but I still felt too stunned to join in laughing with him, although I was slightly more relaxed. That night I'd learnt a valuable lesson, had got off with a fairly mild punishment *and* might well have ended up with a couple of hundred quid for ten minutes' work. B***** put his arm around my shoulder and said, 'By the way, Freddie, has anyone ever told you that you're a little bastard?' *That* was the moment I started laughing with him.

Then we got in the car with two of his biggest, ugliest boys and drove off to the Jokers Club where we could sit at a corner table out of the way, have a bite to eat and divide up the cash between the two of us without attracting any unwelcome attention.

The Jokers Club was named after the big, muscular black fellah who ran the place. 'The Joker' was another of Liverpool's toughest guys – yes, there *were* a lot about in those days. He had to be tough, running a club like his, which was one of the most notorious joints in Liverpool at that time. It was also one of the most popular, despite the fact that the decor wasn't particularly attractive, the acts that appeared there weren't anything special and the only way the restaurant would have qualified for the Michelin Guide was because the meat in the curries they served had the texture of old rubber tyres. No, the only reason the Jokers Club was so popular was that there was no restriction on its opening hours. It was open 24 hours a day, seven days a week. People wandered in and out of the place all times of the day and night. Once you were inside, it was dark and smoky, loud music was always playing and there were no clocks on the wall to remind you that you had to go home.

If you were the sort of person who enjoyed a drink or three, after you'd spent an hour or so in the Jokers Club you lost all concept of time. It could be half past one on Easter Sunday morning or a quarter past three on Whit Monday afternoon. Then again, if you were the sort of person who worried about what time or even what day it was, then you didn't frequent the Jokers Club.

But if you were a man who'd just come off the nightshift at a factory and you didn't fancy going straight home to bed, you could wander into the Jokers at half past seven in the morning, order chicken curry and a beer, pick up a tired blonde, have a couple of dances to the chart hits of the day and go back to her place for a bit of rumpy-pumpy. Lovely! Of course, as far as your *wife* was concerned, you'd stayed on at work to do a double shift. If she questioned the smell of curry on your breath when you got home at two o'clock in the afternoon, you'd tell her you'd eaten in the works canteen. It was much less easy to explain away the bright red lipstick marks on the end of your old boy.

The police didn't mind the club being open 24 hours a day. It fact they actively promoted it. You see, a lot, though not all, of the clientele of the Jokers, came from the criminal world and criminals rarely work to set hours. They're usually opportunists who do whatever it is they do on the spur of the moment. So if a jewellery shop window had been smashed by a brick at two o'clock in the morning and a load of necklaces and rings taken, by three o'clock in the morning the boys in blue would be down the Jokers Club *with the offending brick* to see if the fingerprints on it matched up with any of the customers. Now not all criminals are geniuses. Some of them were dull enough to leave their fingerprints on the brick and have their ill-gotten gains in their pockets, while they waited to meet the 'fence' who would take the jewellery off them, for a price. And they'd be in the nick before you could say 'Dixon Of Dock Green'. And if you don't know who 'Dixon Of Dock Green' was, ask a policeman. Or an elderly relative.

Or an elderly policeman.

I liked visiting the Jokers Club because I knew whenever I went down there, I'd be entertained in one way or another. It was a very popular club with Norwegian seamen.

Was it because they liked the atmosphere of the place or the cheap drinks or the resident organist and drummer's version of 'The Yellow Rose Of Texas'? Or the fact the place was usually packed with wall-to-wall women of all ages, shapes and sizes, most of whom would give a sailor a good time, for a couple of notes. Usually these Norwegians were as nice as pie. The usual form was, they'd all turn up in a bunch, all laughing and joking and in a great mood. Then one by one they'd get plastered, pick up a girl and then bugger off into the night with her. No problem. But occasionally, things went a bit Andrew Lloyd Webber. They turned really ugly.

One night I was in the Jokers Club, having a soft drink and a chat with some of my mates, and I noticed this bunch of Norwegian sailors sat in the corner. Fifteen blond blokes and one with bright red hair. He must have been a Norse of a different colour. They didn't look very happy at all, for whatever reason I have no idea. Maybe it was because there weren't many girls in the club that night, or they weren't looking forward to sailing next morning or possibly because they'd all come straight to the club after being treated for some agonising, hideously deforming, pustule-exploding, wound-seeping, sexually transmitted disease by the local dick-doctor. Sorry, did that put you off your dinner? Well, it certainly put me off mine! Anyway, whatever the reason, they started arguing among themselves.

As I wasn't fluent in Norwegian in those days* I couldn't make out what they were arguing about. Perhaps Sven called Lars 'a stupid pickler-of-herrings!' or Ragnar called Erik 'a herring with no dress sense and the table manners of an albatross'. You know, one of the many popular Norwegian 'herring insults' you must have read about. Whatever it was, all of a sudden two of them stood up and knocked over the table they were sat at. Now these boys were *big*! Just a few centuries before, their relatives had invaded Britain, wearing helmets with horns sticking out from each side, wielding giant axes and generally putting the fear of God into everyone in their path. And as most people living here at the time were pagans who every full moon liked to set fire to giant wicker men and had never *heard* of God, you can imagine just how scary they must have looked!

As rough and as mean as the Norwegian sailors were, the bouncers at the Jokers Club were ten times as rough and as mean and they knew *exactly* how to put a stop to a fight quick as a flash. The bouncers (there were usually half a dozen or so on duty at any one time) had one advantage over the sailors, in that they were always stone-cold sober and the sailors were usually out of their skulls. This night, because they were having such a crap time, the Norwegians hadn't been knocking back one beer after another. They'd sat there, staring at their glasses, morose and introspective – which in everyday language means they were plain bloody miserable. So when the fight started, and all the sailors joined in, the bouncers initially found it hard to contain them because,

---

* I later obtained a degree in Advanced Norwegian at West Slough University and can now converse fluently in 137 Norwegian dialects. But I still hate pickled herring.

being soberish, the sailors' reflexes were faster. The bouncers knew that to get the incident over with fast so the club could get back to business, they had no choice but to reach for their secret weapons which they kept inside their jackets for emergency use only. Eighteen-inch long, two-inch thick iron bars!

Any doctor, physics professor or Liverpool-born comedian will tell you that not even the thickest sailor's skull can put up much resistance to an iron bar, especially when it's wielded by a seventeen-stone nightclub bouncer. In under three minutes, the dance floor was covered with unconscious herring-picklers. The bouncers opened up the back door leading to the alley and, one by one, dragged the sailors out. By the look of them, I wouldn't have been surprised if one or two of the sailors had dragged up before, but they'd never been dragged *out!* They were dumped at the far end of the alley and left there. Eventually they must have all come round with sore heads and bruised egos, with just enough time to catch their ship before it sailed on the morning tide. For the first day out at sea, they'd probably kept their doctor busy with the needle and thread. In fact, I worked out why the club was called The Jokers. Because so many customers left in stitches.

Liverpool was full of clubs in the early 60s and they were great places to work and enjoy yourself, provided you behaved yourself. Some of the clubs were run as legitimate businesses and then quite a few were run by characters like my good friend B*****. Of course on the surface, everything was legit. The staff got paid, the taxman got paid and at regular intervals, certain members of the Liverpool Constabulary got paid. Knowing B***** so well and being around his various business ventures, it was inevitable that I'd perform the odd errand for him eventually. When he knew he could trust me he gave me a semi-permanent job as his bag man. That meant, quite simply, that I carried a bag full of his money from one place to another, accompanied by one of his heavies, who was always armed. Either with a fuck-off knife or a shooter. When I first started being a bag man, I didn't know whether B***** sent the guy along to protect me or to keep his eye on me in case I fancied copping a few quid for myself. He needn't have worried on that score, as he soon became to realise.

The thing is of course, if you've got a pile of money, there's always some shit head who wants to take it off you. I'd heard about other bag men who had been stupid enough to take a handful of notes out of the bag and hope no one would notice.

Pillocks! They'd been punished severely because they hadn't respected the man who paid their wages and looked out for them. I always made sure I never came under suspicion.

B***** taught me to keep quiet, to watch, listen and learn. He was continually trying to test me, keeping me on my toes so I was always aware of what was going on around me.

Sometimes I'd walk into his club all smiles and in a great mood to entertain the audience and he'd look me up and down and say, 'Just look at the state of your shoes, Fred!' and as I'd automatically look down to check what was wrong with my footwear, he'd hit me hard across the top of my head. 'Wallop!'

As I rubbed my sore head, B***** would reprimand me for leaving myself open so easily. 'Never take your eyes off anyone you're doing business with on my behalf . . . or me! I could easily have shot you. Knifed you. Or punched you so hard in the guts you would have vomited up your Christmas dinner from two years ago! Because you let your guard slip for a couple of seconds, I could have taken your life away tonight. Remember that.'

Thankfully, that's the sort of life-lesson they don't teach in school, because most people today don't need to acquire that type of knowledge. Although we never discussed it too much, I assumed when B***** had been my age, he'd been taught the same 'lessons' long before we became pals. But when he was younger and his attention wandered for a second or two, he probably got more than a tap on the head from his 'teacher'. More than likely a knife or a bloody great axe had been aimed at him.

I know for a fact he'd looked down the barrel of a gun more than once – always a sure-fire way of stopping your mind from wandering. Unless the gun goes off and a bullet gets you in the head, in which case your mind will be found wandering all over the walls and ceiling.

B***** was well aware I had no intention of making crime my long-term career, and was hoping to make a living in showbusiness. Yes, I was spending a lot of my spare time hanging around with B***** and his boys and I did work for him occasionally at the same time as I was singing in the clubs. I didn't care what he and his boys did. I didn't want to know things that weren't my business. It was their genuine friendship and camaraderie, which I haven't found much of in show business, that I valued most of all. Does that sound weird? Me, wanting to be friends with the hardest man in Liverpool and his 'close business associates'? Maybe it does. But B***** and his lads were always great fun to be with and we all looked out for one another – and I don't just mean when one of them was holding up a post office!

I think B***** got a kick out of taking care of me, the kid who had distant ambitions of being a comedian, and making me tougher and more street-wise day by day. Which did me no harm at all when I did become a professional entertainer.

During the time we hung around together, he never once stopped showing me the right and wrong way of doing things, even though he realised that within a few years, all being well, I'd be leaving that sort of lifestyle far behind me. Looking back, around that time I did some incredibly stupid things without thinking them through.

When you're in your late teens or early twenties you think you know everything, but take it from me, you really know sod all! Your mind doesn't function clearly because you're always thinking about going out with girls, staying in with girls and enjoying yourself . . . hopefully with girls. Plus, if like me you're working the clubs for a living, you're always thinking about the gig you did the night before and the one you're doing tonight . . . and what girls you might meet. As you can see, there's not a lot of room in your head to think logically a lot of the time. Which can be dangerous as I found out one night, after I'd been B*****'s bag man for a some months.

I'd arranged to meet him and his boys early one evening, in a particular club. Let's call it the 'Poco-Poco'. Yeah. Very exotic sounding. I hadn't been there before but I'd heard it was a converted coal cellar with lights. I knew roughly where it was, and as I'm walking down this street, which is packed with dozens of different pubs and clubs, I see the sign outside a club, Pago-Pago. Well, it sounded a bit like 'Poco-Poco' so I thought it must be the club.

Beyond the doorway was a set of stairs leading to a basement, so I assumed this was our meeting place and that B***** had got the name of the club wrong. That was my first stupid mistake. To think B***** might possibly have mixed up the names of two clubs. My second mistake was not thinking that I might have made that first mistake! I went downstairs and walked through the bamboo curtain. The place was, as they all were, very dimly lit. This was for two reasons. It saved on electricity and it made the girls look prettier.

I ordered a fruit juice and looked at my watch. B***** and the lads were ten minutes late. As I sipped my drink and my eyes got accustomed to the gloom, I slowly made out three figures dressed in black standing against the wall. I couldn't see who they were straight away, but I knew they weren't the Beverley Sisters. Their beards and moustaches were much thicker and darker than the Bevs! Only kidding, girls!

Then the first three guys were joined by two more, all of them making no secret of the fact they found my presence in the club more than a little bit irritating. Then after five minutes or so staring at me, they all started to walk, slowly and menacingly, towards me. I've never been brilliant at mental arithmetic, but even I knew when it came to long division that five into one, especially when the five were built as big as these guys, meant I was probably fucked. Although I was quite prepared to go down fighting, kicking, elbowing and eye-gouging. My many afternoons at Sunday school weren't wasted!

I looked at my watch again. 'Come on, B*****, where the hell are you?' As the five fellahs got closer to me, I suddenly recognised who they were. Five brothers who ran a rival business to B*****'s. I knew there was no love lost between them and B*****. But why did they have a problem with me sitting there having a juice?

One of the brothers stepped forward. Christ, he was a big bastard. They all were. They probably worked out every day, lifting up two double-decker buses over their heads while balancing a third one on their dicks.

He poked a massive finger in my chest and snarled, 'What the fucking hell are you doing in our club?'

There was no point me trying to be clever. I could see two of the brothers were making their way around behind me to block off my exit. I calmly explained, 'I'm meeting some friends here. They're a bit late.'

The big bastard poked me in the chest again. One more like that and I'd have a permanent dent there. I thought about saying something like 'Get your big fat finger out of my chest or I'll tear your arms and legs off, and then do the same to your pansy brothers!' but I didn't want to frighten him!

'This is the Pago-Pago club,' he said. 'My brothers and I run this place and what we want to know is this. Why would your mob want to meet you here unless they were planning some sort of trouble? They all know full-bloody-well they're not welcome in here.'

'My mob? What are you on about? I'm a singer. Freddie Starr. I do all the clubs.'

'Don't fuck with me and my brothers. We know you work for B*****. He may think he's the hardest man in town, but as far as we're concerned, he's nothing but an arsehole. An arsehole who's been told that if any of his gang step inside this place they'll have their faces torn off.'

As I'm listening to this, three separate thoughts pop into my head. One, I'm definitely in the wrong club. Two, if I get out of this place alive, B***** will murder me for being stupid enough to mistake the Pago-Pago for the Poco-Poco. Three, I shouldn't be worrying about Two, because I'm not going to get out of this place alive. Then along came thought Number Four. I'd never be able to make a living as a singer with my face torn off. Except on the radio, perhaps.

As they all started closing in on me, using language and expressions that would make Chubby Brown blush, I really did think 'This is it. I'm done for!' They were taunting me and poking me and I knew it was only a matter of minutes before they really laid into me. I'd have had no chance. Then suddenly, they all stepped away from me and looked across at the doorway.

Despite the gloom, I could see B***** and seven of his lads had just walked in and were standing there watching what the brothers were doing to me.

Jesus! It was like the moment at the end of a Western film, when the cavalry arrives just in time! OK, B*****'s mob weren't on horses and they weren't blowing bugles, but you get the picture. See, what I didn't know was, as soon as I'd walked into this club, a place I didn't realise was totally off-limits to anyone remotely connected with B*****, some-one, I've no idea who, phoned B***** to tell him what had happened and that he should get down there right away. And B***** had wasted no time.

Without a flicker of emotion on his face, B***** walked straight up to the biggest brother and slapped him right across the face like a tart. He said, 'If you harm one hair of that kid's head, I'll come back here and fucking kill you! Are you receiving me? Touch him and I'll empty my gun into you and your cowardly fucking brothers. And when I've done that, just for the fun of it and because I fucking hate you, I'll reload and shoot the six of you all over a-fucking-gain!' He hadn't raised his voice much above a hoarse whisper so far, but the brothers had heard every word he'd said, clear as a bell. He lit a cigarette and walked up and down the line of brothers. None of them had said a word or even tried to move.

B***** hadn't quite finished. 'Boys, I realise that the five of you would be hard pushed to find half-a-brain between the lot of you, but I'd very much appreciate it if you could concentrate on what I'm telling you. Because it's important.'

He indicated to me that I should stand next to him and he put his hand on my shoulder. 'This lad, the one you were just about to tear apart, is not . . . I repeat not . . . one of my mob. He's got fuck-all to do with my business. He's a performer who happens to be a mate of mine. Because he's a mate of mine, you twats had better remember he's under my protec-tion no matter where he is and who he's with, 24 hours a day, 365 days of the year. And that includes bank-fucking-holidays and the first and last days of fucking Lent! Do I make myself abso-fucking-lutely clear on this point? Because I wouldn't want you big, tough, guys to misunderstand one word of what I'm telling you!' He paused. 'Do you really think if he was one of my mob he'd walk into this shithouse on purpose? Fuck off! He has no idea about who runs what club. He made a stupid mistake, wandered into the wrong club and for that you wanted to do him over! Fucking hell, you're so brave, aren't you? Five of you big fuckers against this lad. Jesus Christ!'

He took his hand off my shoulder and gently pushed me towards where his boys were standing by the door, which I did double-quick. B***** then went over to the brother who had been poking me in the chest and taunting me the most and said, 'Now, sunshine. I'm the arsehole you were just talking about and I've brought my gang with me. Would you like to be the first one who tries to tear my face off?'

The big fucker said nothing. He just swallowed and stared ahead. B***** laughed and brushed past him as he slowly walked out of the club. We all followed him and when we got upstairs to the street, my armpits were soaking with sweat. I'd been that close to being done in because I hadn't realised me, little Freddie, was now considered one of B*****'s 'mob' by his rivals. And once again, B***** had got me out of the shit.

I had some fantastic times with B***** and his mates. To be a young man in Liverpool in those days, mixing with characters like B*****, being in on a few dodgy deals, singing in the clubs for your bread and butter and going out on the town most nights of the week was unbelievably enjoyable. Far more enjoyable than anything that's ever happened to me in showbiz. And I'll include the 1970 Royal Variety in there too. Which reminds me . . .

A couple of days after I'd phoned B***** with the good news about my appearing on the Royal, he came to see me in my dressing room in Blackpool. The way he sat down and looked at me I thought he had some bad news. In a way he had.

'Freddie my son, you're on the verge of stardom. No, don't interrupt! I fucking hate this modesty thing of yours. Don't be modest! You worked hard to get where you are. Fucking hard. And you could go a lot further. Right to the top. There's nothing to stop you now. This Royal Variety could be your big chance. So . . . make sure you don't bugger it up!'

I looked right at him. 'You didn't come all the way from Liverpool just to tell me to not bugger things up, did you?'

'No.' He obviously found it difficult to put his thoughts into words and paused before he went on. 'You and me have had some fucking great times, Freddie. You sailed really close to the wind a few times . . .'

'Me . . . sailed close to the wind? Fuckin' hell. I've been hit by a Force Nine gale more times than I care to remember!'

'Yeah, but you're not a hardened criminal and you never will be. You found another way out of the streets. Another way to use your wits. You're a funny man. We all love you back in the Pool. The thing is . . .'

He stumbled over his words. I'd never known B***** do that before. He always knew what to say. He was the *man!* He lit a cigarette and sat forward in the chair.

'Freddie. From now on, you'll have stay away from us.'

My stomach went over. 'What do you mean, stay away from you?'

B***** sat back in the chair. 'Exactly what I said. If you do well in front of Her Majesty, you're going to lead a different life from the old days. You'll be mixing with a different class of people. Big stars. Television producers. Actors and actresses. West End agents. Who knows . . . more royalty? And if you want to stay a star in your business, you can't be seen to have any connection with me or my type of work.'

I didn't know what to say. B***** had been my friend for years. How could I stop seeing him just like that?

He stubbed his cigarette out in a saucer. 'I'm not saying we can't meet up from time to time. We'll stay in touch with you. When we see you're working a local club or theatre, we'll pop in and see you. But not mob-handed. Just a couple of us at a time. It'll be for your own good, I promise you. It was hard for me to come here today to tell you this, but it had to be done. You understand, don't you?'

'I thought we were mates, B*****. The best of mates. I can't drop you because I might meet a few poncey TV people.'

'We'll always be friends, Freddie. Always. We've been through too much together to throw that away and pretend those years never happened. But from today, we're living in two separate worlds. I'll be able to visit yours once in a while. But you'll never be able pay a visit to mine again. Never.'

'You're the boss, B*****,' I said. 'I'll do whatever you think is right.'

He gave me a hug, picked up his coat and left me alone in my dressing room. The entire meeting couldn't have taken more than five minutes. Just a few minutes. Yet my life would never be the same again. In those days I didn't know anything about the press and the way journalists can dig and dig and dig deep into the dirt and find stuff that was buried years before. I do now of course. But B***** was a clever fellah in many ways and by cutting our ties he was ensuring that if I did 'make it' in the business, and the press started getting interested in Freddie Starr and where he came from and who his pals were, they wouldn't find a single trace of B***** in my past.

Thus avoiding what newspaper reporters are so fond of – 'guilt by association'.

That's the sort of guy B***** was, and this applied to the others who ran Liverpool's underworld in those days. Cross them and they could arrange for you to disappear for ever. At the very least, you'd be hurt. Bad. But, respect them and they looked after you.

A couple of years ago I was told B***** had been taken to hospital in Liverpool. I was living in Berkshire at the time and drove straight to the hospital to see him, 250 miles, no problem. He was propped up in his bed, looking terrible. He'd lost a tremendous amount of weight and his skin was a sickly yellow. But there was still a trace of that spark inside him that refused to be snuffed out.

When I'd arrived, the doctors had told me he might not last the night. I sat on the bed with him and put my arms around him like I would my own father. I was determined not to be miserable or to make the situation any worse by saying the wrong thing. When you're in the same room as someone very close to you who's dying, however carefully you choose your words, they all sound so trivial and pointless. I didn't know what to say. So I started singing to him, very quietly. It was one of his favourites. The Righteous Brothers' 'You've Lost That Loving Feeling'.

As I held him, he felt so terribly vulnerable. Just skin and bone. But despite the fact he had very little strength left in him and was obviously close to death, this man whom I once thought of as a giant, a huge immortal giant, *started to sing the song with me*. He'd always been strong and even now, while his body was wasting away, he was refusing to give in to a painful death. That's how much grit that man had. Right to the end.

Somehow he survived that time but later, when he died, I went to his funeral, staying out of the way, at the back of the church. The place was packed, with family and friends and his many business associates from all over the country. They all came to pay their last respects. I was so upset I couldn't bring myself to speak. I watched his coffin being lowered into its resting place and my insides felt destroyed. This man, who had taught me so much . . . who had shown me such great times in the early days . . . and who was so smart he *knew* that when things started happening for me in showbusiness it would be in my interest not be associated with him . . . this man was gone. It hit me hard and I've not got over his death yet.

CHAPTER THREE

I remember my grandfather living with us when I was a child. What a cantankerous old bugger he was. Like my Dad, he'd also been a bricklayer and a bare knuckle fighter in his time and his knuckles were a twisted mass of scars. I was sure that for every blow he landed, he must have taken one to his head, because he was definitely, as I remember him, not the full shilling. In fact he wasn't even the full sixpence, so it wasn't easy for all of us who had to live with him, basically because he was a right pain in the arse. Alright, if you live to be 96 perhaps you're entitled to be a right pain in the arse. But from what I'd heard, he'd been causing people to clutch their buttocks in agony ever since he was born.

He spent a lot of time in his bedroom and if he wanted something, which to me as a young kid seemed to be every five minutes, he'd always bang on his bedroom floor with a big stick. I'd be sat there reading my *Beezer* comic or watching Robin Hood on the telly, and I'd hear that 'Bang! Bang! Bang!' coming through the ceiling. Then my mum or my dad would say, 'Fred. Go and see what your grandad wants!' and I'd drag myself out of my chair and climb the stairs to his room.

Most of the time he wanted a cup of tea. He drank lots of tea. Bloody gallons of the stuff. And because he wasn't able to run up and down the stairs twenty times a day to empty his bladder in the outside lavvy, he used to pee in a ceramic po which he kept under the bed. So one day, I'm sat downstairs and grandad starts banging on his bedroom floor with his stick as usual. Nobody else got up to see what he wants, so I go upstairs and into his room, which reeked of the unmistakable smell of stale piss, which as always was lapping over the top of his po, while it waited for some brave soul to empty it. He was sat up in bed and was pointing his stick at me.

'You were ages coming up here. Be a bit quicker next time. Now go and get me a bowl of soup and a cup of tea!' No 'Please Fred' or 'Thank you Fred' of course.

I thought, *Oh hell. His po's already full to the brim and now he's going to drink more tea* and *a bowl of soup!* I knew how long liquids took to pass through his system – about twenty minutes – so I made a mental note to fuck off out of the house as soon as I'd given him his tea and soup, in case I got landed with emptying his stinking po!

So I got the soup and tea, put them on a tray and start to make my way back upstairs. All of a sudden I feel what I thought was warm water on my head. I looked up and there was my grandad standing at the top of the stairs, laughing like an idiot with his shrivelled old dick in his hand, aiming at my head. What I thought was warm water was fresh piss. The old bugger was peeing on me! My hair was covered in warm piss. I shouted to him, 'You dirty bastard! You dirty, dirty bastard!'

I had the tray of soup and tea in my hand so I couldn't do anything but turn around and go back downstairs, while he's still pissing away.

As I disappeared into the kitchen, he shouted after me, 'And if you don't bring my tea quicker next time, you lazy bugger, I'll piss on you again!' and he was cackling away to himself like Walter Brennan in *Rio Bravo*.

Later on, when I was a bit bigger and stronger, there were times when he'd bang on the floor and shout, 'Fred. Take me to the toilet!' and I'd have to. But instead of him being a little embarrassed at what he was putting a slip of a kid through, or even a bit grateful for what I was doing for him, when he got to the toilet, he'd deliberately pee over the toilet seat and all over the floor. After he'd done that a couple of times, I used to lose my rag with him and say something like 'Oh please, Grandfather! You know that's an awfully naughty thing to do, passing water all over the floor in that unhygienic manner. Do try and behave yourself in future or I'll have no alternative but to inform mater and pater of your peculiar habits when they return from their visit to the vicarage!'

As I said, it was *something* like that.

And he'd stand there looking at me, with his ancient, fart-odoured, pyjama bottoms around his ankles, and say, with that mastery of the English language which is only acquired by the very best Oxbridge graduates, 'You cheeky twat! Why don't you go and fuck yourself, you turd-brained little tosser?'

Honestly, when I think about it now, Grandfather was *such* a brilliant wordsmith!

At the age of six I started having what they called 'hysterical fits'. No one knew why they started. I was always a shy child, but I started to feel withdrawn into myself and shortly after that I began finding it difficult to speak. I wonder now if it was because I couldn't cope with the fact that my big brother hated me. I was clamming up, although I'd been fine up until then. I started taking time off school because of these 'fits' and things got so bad my mother had to take me to a specialist. He recommended to my mother that I should go to hospital for six months. If I'd been able to speak I'd have recommended that he stuck his head right up his arse.

So I was taken to hospital and they started giving me all sorts of pills and medicines trying to bring me out of myself – I was even on phenobarbitone tablets. At six years of age! I even had to see a psychiatrist. I must have been in a bad way.

Despite all they tried to do for me, my speech was getting worse. To cap it all, while I was in hospital, while they were testing me for every known ailment under the sun, from ringworm to tapeworms and everything in between, the doctors decided my tonsils needed taking out. Something that was done regularly in those days whether they actually needed taking out or not. I was six for Christsakes. Having trouble communicating, cut off from my friends and family, in a great big ward lorded over by a hatchet-faced Matron. And someone decided I wasn't going through enough anguish – so I should have an operation for no apparent reason.

So as the doctors 'knew what was best for me', I had my tonsils removed and when I came around after the operation, an extraordinary change occurred. Before the op I could hardly speak. After the op *I couldn't speak at all!* I'd totally lost the power of speech. I tried to get the words out. Did I bloody well try. I knew what I wanted to say. I could hear the words and sentences and questions in my head. But they seemed to be stuck inside my chest and not a sound would come out of my mouth. If I wanted to communicate with anyone, I had to write things down and show it to them.

After further treatment in hospital, which was a waste of time, those wonderful doctors suggested to my parents that the only way, they felt, I could be cured was to be sent to a children's home for an indeterminate period. Today, if it was suggested to any loving parent that their child, who had no physical or mental disability, might be better off in a children's home, chances are they'd protest very loudly at such an idea and ask the doctor to find some other answer to the problem. But in the 1950s nobody questioned the authority of the medical profession. They were the new gods, untouchable and uncriticisable as they looked down from their gleaming white, stainless-steel, disinfectant-smelling Olympus.

I, of course, had no idea what was going on, I was just told I was going home from hospital. I'd only been home a short while when I was told I had to pack my little bag again. I was worried that I was going back to hospital, but Mum assured me I was going somewhere much nicer, where there were lots of other children I could play with all day. Being six and a right sucker for a good bedtime story, I fell for it.

The day I went to the children's home is as clear to me now as if it were yesterday. My Mum was taking me to the home by taxi and in those days a taxi in the street caused the curtains in every front room to flutter. Outside our front door my father picked me up and hugged me, saying 'Don't worry, son. The doctors will look after you,' and I can remember feeling so safe with his strong arms around me. I didn't want him to let go. I was already getting worried. He'd mentioned 'doctors' for the first time. And didn't mention all the children I was going to be playing with all day.

My Dad handed me to Mum and she put me in the taxi and came and sat next to me. As we drove off down the street, I looked through the back window as my Dad, my house, my street and my normal life disappeared. I still had no real idea where I was going. Mum held my hand and said, 'Freddie, you're going to a special place where children who are ill like you, get better. It may take some time. You may be there six months. But when you come out you'll be able to speak again. You want that, don't you, Freddie?' I nodded. But what I really wanted to do, but couldn't tell her of course, was to stay with my Mum and Dad. For ever. No more hospitals or 'special places'. Just stay at home and watch telly and kick a ball around in the street with my mates. That's what Freddie wanted.

When we got to the home (which years later I found out was in Hoylake – all I knew then was it had taken ages to get there) Mum told the taxi driver to wait, picked up my case and we both walked up the steps to the huge front door. The 'special place' didn't look very special to me. Just an enormous old house, dark and scary with no lights shining from its hundreds of windows. Mum rang the bell and a lady came to the door. Mum gave me my case and touched me on the shoulder. 'Freddie. Be a big boy and go inside with the lady. They'll make you better here.' She kissed me goodbye, the lady took me inside and the big front door slammed, locking out the world I knew. How could anyone do that to a confused, little mute boy of six?

I was led along a long, dark corridor and made to sit in a chair. The lady turned out to be the Matron and she told me that a doctor was coming to see me, but he was very busy and I should be patient. Fifteen minutes or so later – although I couldn't speak I was brilliant at telling the time – the doctor appeared. He seemed really tall, huge even. I started to feel a little frightened, but he sat down opposite me and talked softly and explained that he and the other doctors would do their best to help me regain my speech. By the time he gave me a glass of milk and a biscuit I was feeling a bit more settled. After an hour of talking to me, which I now realise was both his way of making me feel at ease, while at the same time enabling him to observe me for the first time – I remember he had a red notebook which he wrote in from time to time – he stood up to go. The door behind me opened and in walked the matron, smiling at me. You can't believe how lovely and how welcome that smile was to me. She put her hand out, indicating she wanted me to hold it with mine and we walked to what was going to be my own room. We went inside and there was a single bed and wooden chair. I put my case on the bed and looked out of the window. Despite the wire mesh covering the outside of the glass, I could see the vivid greens of lawns and the trees outside. It looked beautiful.

I didn't go home again for two years. And in all that time the only visitor I had was my mother. Who only visited me on four occasions.

The first six months were very tough for me. I missed Mum and Dad and felt very lonely. With all the time I'd spent in hospital and the home, I'd missed a lot of schooling. But the doctors weren't worried about this. They just wanted me to speak again. And by now I was fed up of writing everything down. I mean everything!

'Can I have a drink of water please?' 'This bread is stale' and by the end of every week, 'Have you got anything for writer's cramp?'

The doctors in the home used to strike a match and make me blow it out. It wasn't that they were too bone idle to blow it out themselves, it was part of my speech therapy. As I was blowing out the match, I had to form my mouth into a 'P' over and over again. Those doctors got through so many matches they could have used them to build a life-size replica of the *Titanic and* the iceberg. They were building me up to the point where I could get beyond just the 'P' sound and could say the name Peter. I don't know why. Perhaps it was easier to say than Freddie. Maybe they thought my name *was* Peter and I shouldn't have been in the flippin' place. Anyway, my days were full of this sort of speech therapy and my evenings were spent in my room, staring through the wire mesh at the world outside. If I was really up for the ultimate intellectual challenge to pass the time, I'd sit on my bed and count the squares on wire mesh. How many times did I do that during those two years? What? How many squares *were* there? 420! No, not really. How do you expect me to remember something like that?

The nurses and doctors were great to me, full of good humour and kindness, especially at Christmas time. They gave me the best Christmas I'd ever had. All the children had presents and home-made cakes and delicious Christmas pudding with custard. But naturally, I still wished I could have been with my family.

Slowly, month by month I made progress. After I was able to say 'Peter' clearly, they worked on dozens of other words which I was gradually able to pronounce. After that, my confidence being restored day by day, I was able to speak whole sentences.

One day Matron said to me, 'Freddie. You've done very well here. You're ready to go back to your family and your old school. Your mother will be collecting you first thing in the morning!' Fantastic news! I was going home! The very next day! I couldn't sleep that night. I had been six when I arrived at the home and now I was eight. Taking into account my time in hospital, I'd spent two and a half years of my young life away from my home and my parents.

When Mum arrived the next morning, she exploded out of the taxi and ran up the stairs to the front door where Matron and I were waiting. Mum kissed and cuddled me and she was crying and Matron was in tears and I had a little lump in my throat, caused by the knowledge I was going home and that I was leaving behind people who had been very kind to me during the last 24 months.

When we got home I had kisses and hugs from everyone, even Richard. When everyone had just stopped making a fuss of me, my Dad came in from work. He looked at me, picked me up in this huge arms of his and just said, 'Hello Fred! How are you doing?' Which I knew was his way of saying, 'I love you, Freddie lad.' I buried my head in his massive chest and those two years in the children's home melted away. It felt as if I'd only been gone away for a couple of hours. *This* was my home. I felt wanted and secure for the first time in my life.

My Dad's name was Richard Ernest Fowell and he was the fittest, strongest man in our part of town. Not only did he have his physical work every day on the building sites, he also kept fit at home with the aid of his 'apparatus' in the garden. It was just three long metal poles, two of which were stuck into the ground with the third hung horizontally between them. He'd stretch the muscles of his arms and legs by just hanging there from the middle bar, then pull himself up with either his arms or his legs. It was quite something to watch when you're a kid.

He also liked to run. Not jogging, in poncey trainers and track suits. He just loved running. He had this funny habit that involved running. Unlike the rest of us, he wouldn't queue at the bus stop down the road when he wanted to go into town. He'd always wait on our front door step until he heard the sound of a bus coming, then as soon as he caught sight of it, he'd slam the front door and run like hell up the road to catch up with it! Because of Dad's renowned strength and athletic ability, very few people got on the wrong side of him. One of my teachers did once and regretted it.

It wasn't long after I got back from the children's home and had returned to my old school. Between the time I got home and went back to school I'd been talking normally – although even at the age I am now, if I get nervous about something, I get an impediment in my speech. But when I walked into that old school and into the classroom I'd been allocated, all I saw were strange faces. All my friends had move up to higher classes, but I'd missed over two years' schooling so I had to start all over again. I found my new desk and sat down with all these kids I didn't know and immediately started to draw into myself again. It was if all the good work in the children's home had been for nothing. My teacher, Mr Brown, had been told where I'd been and what had happened to me and was told to go easy on me for the first couple of weeks while I settled in. What did he do in the first minute of the first lesson of the day? He made me walk to the front of the class, put a book in my hand and asked me to read out loud to the rest of the class.

I wanted the ground to open up and swallow me . . . or preferably him. I looked down at the book. The words were easy enough to understand . . . but . . . I . . . couldn't . . . seem . . . to . . . be . . . able . . . to . . . get . . . the . . . words . . . out! Mr Brown cajoled me for struggling over the simple words. What was wrong with the man? He knew I'd just had two years of intense speech therapy.

'Come along, boy! Read out loud and clear so everybody can hear you!'

I tried again. My mouth felt swollen. My tongue wouldn't work. I had a vision of me and Mum in a taxi, pulling up outside the children's home and her handing me my suitcase and saying, 'It's only for another two years, Freddie!'

I suppose Mr Brown might have been trying to help me get over my problem. Maybe he thought it would be good therapy for me to stand up in front of the class and read out loud on my first day. It *might* have been good for me if I could have got my mouth to work. But then again he *had* been told by my doctors to take things easy with me. So why should I give him the benefit of the doubt?

By now, all the kids in the class were laughing and pointing at me. So to that list of subjects that inexplicably make children laugh that we all know about, you can add 'other kids' misfortunes' to 'old people', 'toilets' and 'the disgusting bodily functions of humans'.

Having spent all that time in a children's home where I was treated with kindness and patience, the attitude of this pig of a teacher and the mob mentality of my classmates horrified me so much I just threw the book down and ran out of the class room, not stopping until I got home. My mother wanted to know what was going on and to my relief and surprise I was able to tell her. The words weren't struggling to make the journey from my brain to my tongue. They flowed easily! There'd be no going back to the children's home. Mum said, 'You stay here, Freddie. We'll tell your father what happened when he gets home from work tonight. He'll know what to do.'

I spent the rest of the day reading my comics and when my Dad came in and asked me how my first day back at school was, I was happy to tell him. As I was relating the story he'd nod now and then, and when I'd finished, he ruffled my hair and said, 'Don't you worry about Mr Brown, son. I'll walk to school with you tomorrow and have a word with him.'

Next morning, my Dad was good as his word and came to school with me. We both walked into my classroom where Mr Brown was addressing the pupils. My Dad looked at me and asked, 'Is this him?' I nodded. Without saying a word to my teacher, Dad walked up to him and smacked him bang on the jaw! He went down like a sack of soggy history books. Dad picked the dazed Mr Brown up off the floor and said, 'Brown. You were fully aware of my son's condition, and you deliberately humiliated him in front of all these kids!' As Dad looked around at the same scabby classmates who had been taking the piss out of me the day before, they nodded in agreement with him, all pretending to be my best friend.

'Don't you ever make my son speak out loud in front of the class again until *he* thinks he's ready. Is that understood?' Brown nodded as a trickle of blood escaped from his mouth.

'Uh . . . Uh . . . understood!' he replied, before Dad let him go and he collapsed on to the floor in front of the blackboard.

Dad put his hand on my shoulder and said, 'I'm off to work now, son. If you have any more trouble off him,' he nodded in the direction of Mr Brown, 'or any of the other teachers, you tell me. Now go and sit down and start learning.'

After that incident, with my confidence fully restored, knowing my Dad could sort out any problem that came my way, I didn't have any trouble speaking in front of the class. And I haven't shut up since!

My Dad used to say, 'If a policeman comes to this front door looking for you, I'll kill you!'

And of course, when I was in my teens, the day arrived when a policeman *did* come knocking on our front door. You need to know the circumstances that led up to this heart-stopping moment.

I suppose I was about fifteen. My mates and me sometimes used to hang around under a railway bridge not far from our house. No . . . I wasn't a trainspotter.

I used to play my acoustic guitar and sing along with the lads and the high stone walls and wide metal girders provided wonderful acoustics for us. Well, one day I was standing under the bridge, all alone, playing my guitar and singing to myself.

And no – I wasn't a sad little bastard because I was on my own. I was waiting for my mates. Right?

As I'm standing there, strumming and singing, I can see these five big fellahs walking towards me. I recognised some of them straight away. I'd seen them around town and knew they were detectives. I never had anything to do with the police if I could help it, but I knew them. They all looked very serious as they talked among themselves and because of the long, dark overcoats they were wearing, they reminded me of the characters in the TV series *The Untouchables*. Robert Stack as Elliott Ness in black and white, cleaning up crime in the 1920s. Brilliant stuff! As far as I'm concerned you can stick your namby-pamby Kevin Costner, Technicolor film version of the series . . . somewhere untouchable!

For some reason, as I saw these blokes walking towards me, the sight of them made me chuckle. I mean, to me it *did* look just like *The Untouchables* had stepped out of my telly and this amused me. So I'm standing there playing my guitar and singing between the chuckles and as they passed me, a couple of these fellahs obviously had the right hump with me because they thought I was laughing at them. They didn't know that in my head I was comparing them with my TV heroes. They thought I was taking the piss. And they didn't like it.

Two of them deliberately bumped into me as they walked past under the bridge. I mean a real hefty 'bang' from both of them. These were big mature men, who were supposed to represent law and order, and they were picking on a fifteen-year-old kid. They carried on walking past me, laughing and joking. Twats!

I wasn't going to put up with that shit so I shouted after them, 'Fuck off you stupid bastards!' and they all stopped in their tracks and turned around to look at me. Yes I know it was pretty dull of me to shout that out, but I was livid.

I had no idea why five detectives should be walking along together. Maybe they were the Liverpool CID Country Walks & Mountain Rambling Society and they'd got lost. But whatever it was they were doing couldn't have been very important because all five of them had time to pick on a fifteen-year-old lad who had been minding his own business until those big-headed sods had barged into him. One of the detectives, who must have weighed in at sixteen stone, walked straight over to me and went to hit me.

I'm five foot something and about eight stone dripping wet. I stood very little chance of causing him any major damage, but I wasn't just going to stand there and take it.

I raised my guitar in the air and hit him with it.

I didn't know it at the time, because I hadn't bothered listening my teacher during nature lessons, but a sixteen-stone, pug-ugly Liverpool detective wearing a long black overcoat is the natural enemy of a small, wooden, six-string guitar.

The guitar made contact with the detective's right arm, broke it in three places and he ran off crying like a baby. Seeing what I'd done to him, his big-mouthed mates were all too scared to tackle me and they all followed him down the road, scared to death of me.

Now come on! You didn't really believe that did you? This was *real* life.

What *actually* happened was, he deflected the blow and my precious guitar broke into a dozen pieces all over the road. I'd loved that guitar. What had I done? I'd pissed the detective off even more, *that's* what I'd done!

He came at me again and I managed to punch him on the jaw. I might as well have hit him with a party balloon for all the effect it had on him. But that didn't stop the four other brave lawmen charging at me. They must have been concerned about the welfare of Detective Shit-For-Brains being bullied by this fifteen-year-old serial killer. The five of them started to do me over. I mean they punched and kicked the crap out of me. And all the time I was thinking, if I'd learned to play the piano instead of the guitar, I wouldn't have been in this mess. Well, I could hardly have sat under a railway bridge playing Beethoven's Fifth on a piano as the 4.45 to Manchester steamed past overhead.

So they did me over good and proper, although I did manage to cut one of the bastards just above his right eye. This is the difference between the police then and now. Apart from the fact that you're not likely to see five detectives together at any one time – unless they're walking towards you and one of them is saying, 'I am arresting you in the name of the Law!' – the police today are a different breed. Then, they were happy to dish out instant punishment for my cheek and bad language. They were out of order in terms of *how many* of them wanted to teach me a lesson, but they dished it out and I took it. I could have reported it and it could have gone to court with me pointing the finger at them. But it would have caused more hassle than it was worth. Today, kids can shout and swear at a policeman and he won't do a thing. That's because *he's sat in his police car with the windows rolled up and can't hear what's going on around him.* OK. It's a harder, tougher world now and they have to adapt. But when you see police officers in their hundreds sat in motorway patrol cars, keeping their eyes out for speeding motorists, and just one or two constables, if you're lucky, walking their beat around town centres where the yobs and piss-artists cause a nuisance, I just find it puzzling.

Although I went home that afternoon without my guitar, I did take a few extra things with me. Like a swollen lip and a black eye. Dad looked at me and said, 'What have you been up to now?' I said, 'Fighting. But there was too many of them.' And that was it. I didn't want him asking too many questions because if he'd known I'd been swearing and coppers he'd have blacked my other eye.

My Dad used to mix with all sorts of people. He met them in pubs or clubs or during the course of his work. The great thing about being a builder (apart from showing off 75% of your arse-crack in public without breaking any laws) is that one day you could be building a wall for a retired docker, the next you could be laying a patio for the Lord Mayor.

You never knew who would come to our front door asking for him. One Saturday lunchtime a few weeks after my fracas with the five coppers, my dad was upstairs shaving, getting ready to go to a rugby match. He shouted down to me, 'Freddie! Some of my mates will be calling for me in a minute. Just let them in for me, will you?'

A couple of minutes later there was a knock on the front door. I opened it and standing there was a fellah I recognised straight away. He was the pug-ugly detective I'd broken my guitar on under the railway bridge. And his four mates were with him. It was 'The Revenge of the Untouchables'! I could tell straight away they remembered my face. I panicked because I thought they'd somehow found out my address and were going to cart me off to the police station. So after a pause of about three seconds, while I looked at them in total shock, I turned around and ran through the house, out of the back door, into the garden and over the fence into next door's garden – with Dad's words echoing around my head. 'If a policeman ever comes to this front door looking for you, I'll kill you!' There were five policeman. Would he kill me five times?

I looked around me and I couldn't believe what I saw. The five detectives had followed me through the house into the garden and they were leaping over the dividing fence, shouting, 'Get the little bastard!' Another second and they'd have me! I legged it over next door's fence and then over several other neighbours' fences. But as fast as I jumped over a fence, those coppers would jump too. And they were gaining on me. It was like a bizarre version of the Grand National.

Eventually, with them being much fitter and five times bigger than me, they caught me and dragged me back to the house. The back door was still open and my Dad, who had come downstairs to find out what all the noise was about, was stood on the back step, stripped to the waist, a white towel around his neck and half his face still covered in shaving soap. He looked at me with cold, cold eyes. 'What's going on?'

Two of the detectives stood each side of me, holding on to my arms. I looked up at both of them and said 'Ask these idiots!'

Dad said, 'Freddie. These *idiots* are my mates. The ones I asked you to let in. They're coming to the rugby with me this afternoon.'

These arse-holes were his mates!

One of the detectives said, 'He's the little sod we were telling you about. The one who gave us a mouthful down by the railway bridge a while back.' He ran a grubby finger over his right eyebrow. A strip of skin about a quarter of an inch wide, cut the eyebrow into two sections, like a tiny bridge across a furry little river. 'And he caught me in the eye with his fist.'

Poor baby! What about my swollen lip and all the cuts and bruises those bastards had given me? I was waiting for Dad to have a go at the coppers for picking on his son.

But instead he said, 'Lads, if he's been a naughty boy, you've got my permission to teach him a lesson!'

Teach me a *lesson?* When they were hitting seven kinds of shit out of me under the bridge, they'd already put me through college!

The five coppers didn't waste time and started to give me another good hiding. This time in front of my Dad, who, from the detached look on his face, might as well have been looking at a cat playing with a mouse in the garden.

The five gallant officers of the law gave me three broken ribs and a fractured cheek bone. In return for my fractured 'cheek' to them, you might say. Dad turned around and went inside to finish shaving, without even a concerned glance in my direction. In his eyes, I suppose, although they were his mates and he had asked them to call for him, I *had* brought the police to our door in a weird, roundabout way, by cheeking them a few weeks before. Mind you, and I'll tell you this straight. I can only be 'Mr Understanding' up to a point. I think they were way over the top to give two severe beatings to a young kid just because, quite rightly, he called them 'stupid bastards'. These days any kid dressed in that ludicrous Gangsta fashion wear (including the obligatory back-to-front baseball cap) who called a policeman a 'stupid bastard' might well get an award for being able to use words of more than one syllable.

Ten minutes later he and his mates went off to spend their Saturday afternoon at the rugby match, and I went to Casualty.

From what you've just read, you might have formed a picture in your mind of my Dad as a cruel, unemotional person. He was certainly a man who didn't like to show emotion, like the time I came back to the house after two years in the children's home. There were no emotional tears from him. Just a warm greeting and a hug. But I wouldn't have him called cruel. He was a strict man with Victorian values and if I or my brother Richard or our sisters were out of line, we would expect to be punished.

I wasn't aware that he knew I smoked, something I'd been doing for years. A lot of us did in the 1950s. We watched all the Hollywood movie stars (the ones without enormous bouncy hooters) on the big screen, like John Wayne and Humphrey Bogart and Burt Lancaster and they all smoked.

Naturally, as an eleven- or twelve-year-old sat in the one and nines, staring up at the screen, I was too young to appreciate the subtle, sophisticated, hidden meaning behind long, cool cigarettes . . . moist red lips . . . fluttering eyelashes and lingering stares between men and women. I just thought they wanted to shag each others brains out.

In war films, any bullet-ridden US marine at Iwo Jima who was about to kick the bucket was always handed a cigarette. Which I could never understand. If a soldier's full of holes and gasping for air, what's so compassionate about sticking a lighted fag in his gob as the poor bugger is struggling for breath?

So, wanting to be like the tough guys I saw at the pictures, I started to smoke. Not that there was any chance of me being shot at by a Japanese sniper – although there was a Chinese waiter I knew who didn't like me very much.

I didn't know that Dad knew I smoked until I was in my late teens. I came home one Friday night and instead of him being upstairs asleep with Mum, I was surprised to find Dad was downstairs in the front room, lying on what we called a 'Z-bed', a moveable lightweight bed that you could fold away when you didn't need it. I wondered if he'd had a row with Mum. That was the only reason I could think why he'd be sleeping downstairs.

He seemed to be deep in thought. I asked him if he was OK and he muttered something. Then he looked at me, held out a packet of fags and said, 'Have a cigarette.' I didn't know what to say. How did he know I smoked? I hesitated. He offered the ciggies again. 'Go on, have a cigarette. I know you like a smoke.' I smiled, feeling like a kid who'd been caught nicking toys from Woolworth's and took a cigarette from the packet and we both lit up. After a moment or two he said, 'I'm sorry I've been so hard on you over the years. But it paid off. You've got a bit of backbone to you.'

I didn't know it at the time, but he was very ill. Afterwards it hit me that this was his way of apologising for the harsh way he'd brought me up. It must have taken a lot for Dad to say this to me, although I didn't feel there was any need for him to apologise. Yes, he'd been hard on me at times, but he'd also been fair. I didn't, and still don't, have any ill-feeling towards him for my strict upbringing. I was taught right from wrong. Sometimes I crossed the line, always aware that if Dad found out I'd get a thick ear. There was no middle ground. If you did wrong, you expected to be punished. To paraphrase an expression used by our American cousins, even if you saw other kids nicking stuff from the grocer's shop, the golden rule I remembered at all times was 'If you don't want a smack . . . put those friggin' sweets back!'

And so we sat there, father and son, talking into the night, our cigarettes glowing in the semi-darkness of the room.

I was just starting out as a professional entertainer around that time. Television success was a long way off. The following night, I was appearing at the Empress Club in New Brighton. I didn't have a car in those days so I used to catch a bus from the house to the bus terminus and then take the ferry across the Mersey.

After I'd finished my act, I caught the 10.45 ferry back to the bus terminus. I jumped on a bus that would have taken me straight home, but after I'd been sat on it for a minute, something which I can only describe as a sort of sadness came over me and I got off the bus and sat down on a bench, knowing I could still catch the last bus, which left at 12.30. As I sat in the terminus, I was surrounded on one side by non-threatening, drunken old men, each of them singing an unintelligible lyric to a tune only they could hear in their befuddled heads, and on the other side, dozens of snogging couples, who'd spent Saturday night in the back row of the pictures, all of them praying their bus would be late, to allow them a few more minutes furtive fumbling and kissing. If you've never had a hurried, salt and vinegary, chip-flavoured snog under a bus shelter on a Saturday night, after a night at the pictures, you've missed out on one of life's great experiences. It's not too late. Try it next Saturday night. And if it doesn't make the blood rush to your head, write to me and I'll refund you the price of this book. No. Scrub that. I'll refund you the price of your chips.

Out of the blue, appearing as mysteriously as the sad feeling I had just experienced, my thoughts went to a girl I used to go out with a couple of years before. Her name was Angela Doreycott and I'd been very fond of her. But she became ill and tragically died of cancer before her life was really beginning. The last bus arrived and I got on it, along with a couple of drunken would-be Sinatras and half-a-dozen girls, tiddly from too many Babychams, waving through the dirty windows at the boys who had put them on their last bus home.

With Angela still on my mind, instead of getting off at the bus stop closest to my house, I got off a couple of stops before. I walked up the road towards the house where she'd lived and looked up at the window of what had been her bedroom. The room where she'd died. That feeling of sadness came on me again, this time even stronger, like the second wave that hits you when you're standing knee-deep in the sea and just recovering from the first wave that had taken your breath away.

When I got home a little later, I saw several cars parked outside our house, which was unusual. I knocked the front door and I could hear the voices of my sisters and other people coming from inside. I don't remember who opened the door for me, but I said to that person, 'My Dad's died, hasn't he?' and they nodded. He'd died three hours before. The house was full of relatives and I went into the front room where my mum was sat, sobbing her heart out, with several female neighbours consoling her. Our neighbours were always great in times of trouble like this, so they understood when I asked, 'Could you leave my Mum now?' They left the room and closed the door. I stroked my Mum's hand and did my best not to show how upset, how devastated I was inside. I wanted to be as strong as my Dad would have been under the circumstances. I put my arm around her and she cried and cried.

The undertakers had been called and Dad was lying in the coffin, with the lid off so people could pay their last respects before they took it away. I thought I should go and see him for the final time. It was the worst thing I could have done. I looked down at him and it wasn't my Dad. It was the shell of what had been my Dad. His soul ... his spirit ... whatever you want to call that mysterious life force ... had gone.

I kissed him on his forehead and touched his hand. He felt so cold. Ice cold. Mum walked into the room and I said, 'That's not my Dad. He's gone somewhere else. He's hovering somewhere. I can feel it. What we're looking at isn't my Dad.'

The undertakers arrived to screw down the lid of the coffin and I vividly remember the neighbours coming out on their front steps, as it was carried out of the house to the hearse.

Mum took his death very badly. On the day of his funeral she was hysterical. At the graveside I hung on tight to her, because I thought she was going to jump into the hole. My brother Richard was also affected badly. He used to go out drinking with our Dad, so he spent more time socialising with him than I ever had. He had a bit of a chip on his shoulder after Dad died. He'd say stupid, thoughtless things like 'None of you care that Dad's dead. None of you really care!' I felt like telling him to shut his stupid mouth, but unlike him, I respected my Mum enough not to start any trouble. Look, I was no angel in those days, believe me, but I knew not to shout my mouth off at such a sensitive time. I had to think about Mum and my sisters first. Richard, being seven years older than me, could take care of himself as far as I was concerned. I had to be the strong one. Keeping everyone together. I wasn't going to let the enormous feeling of loss and grief and terrible sadness that permeated the house affect me.

Two weeks after Dad was buried, it all hit me. My Dad was gone forever. I would never see him walk through the front door after a day's work on the building site again. Never see him exercising on his poles in the garden. Never be a victim of his daft practical jokes again. Never see him do his last-minute dash for the bus again. We'd never again sit there, father and son, talking into the night, our cigarettes glowing in the semi-darkness of the room.

I realised that it was true what people had said. Death is a part of life. It's going to happen to all of us and we have to accept that certainty. Of course, we shouldn't let it dominate our thoughts otherwise we'd be walking around like morbid, depressed zombies.

I'm not going to dwell on the great mysteries of life and death because, frankly, they're a mystery to me. But I do know that, however many millions you have in the bank, however big your house is, sometimes there's nothing you can do but accept what life throws at you. Death is one of those things you can't wave a cheque book at and buy off.

I'll always remember my Dad as a big man. Not just in the physical sense but in the way he conducted his life and expected us to lead ours. People put too much emphasis on how 'big' or 'small' people are. I'm the perfect example. I've been asked many times, 'Don't you wish you were bigger, taller?' but the truth is, I'm happy as I am. I don't look up at tall people and wish I was like them. I'm me and I'm happy with it.

I measure people by what's in their heart, not how tall they are. And I know that none of us is perfect. We all make mistakes. Make wrong decisions. Take a wrong turning at some point. End up with egg on our face. Sometimes we get things right and sometimes we get things wrong. If they generally balance out over a life time, that's not a bad deal, is it?

CHAPTER FOUR

My first performance in front of an audience happened when I was twelve years old and my mother entered me in a local talent competition. I've no idea what it was called. 'The Bright New Stars of 1955' or some such nonsense. I didn't want to get involved with it, but my mother insisted. She thought I had a good singing voice. In fact we all had good voices in our family. We had to. There was no lock on the toilet door! Now *there's* a joke that defines an age and a time!

Naturally Mum came with me on the day. The show was at a local theatre and when we got there we found out I was third in the running order. Someone who'd never performed on stage before would normally be bottom of the bill. I stood on the side of the stage and watched the first act go on as the orchestra played the opening bars of his song. He sang, took his bows as the audience applauded and walked off. A girl singer went on next and the crowd seemed to love her. *The crowd!* Hundreds of people who would be looking at me! My stomach was churning. Why had my Mum made me come here? I felt like running out of the building. The next few seconds were unreal. The girl singer came off stage and 'swished' past me in a cloud of perfume and nervous sweat. My mother put her arms around me, gave me a kiss and said, 'Go on son. Show them what it's all about!' and pushed me on to the stage.

The first thing that hit me was the powerful lights. They almost blinded me as I walked to the mike stand. This helped me in a way because the brightness stopped me seeing most of the packed house. Which, I learned later numbered 2,000 people! Me, a complete novice standing up in front of 2,000 people! I must have been nuts! My legs were like jelly. My mouth felt dry. A few nervous coughs came from various parts of the auditorium as they waited for this scared kid to start performing. Why hadn't the orchestra started playing my song?

The music started. I was singing a song called 'Long Lost John', an up-tempo number which had been recorded by Lonnie Donegan. Within a couple of bars, the audience started clapping along. My adrenalin rush started and I really got into it.

My performance seemed to be over in no time at all and the crowd went wild, clapping and cheering and whistling! I walked off stage trembling with excitement. It all felt very scary, but it also felt great.

After all the acts had done their thing, we all trooped back on stage for the judging. It was a bit of a cruel way to do it really. The host of the show placed his hand over the heads of each of the performers and the one who was cheered most would get the prize. The others were expected to slink off stage, with brave smiles on their faces until they got to the wings, when they would no doubt burst into tears.

Some of the acts got very little reaction, one or two had a moderate response. But when the host put his hand over my head, the audience went bananas! I was the lucky ... but talented ... winner! I received a silver trophy and five pounds! Five pounds! A small fortune for a schoolboy in the mid-1950s.

On the bus home, Mum kept saying, 'I told you you'd win, didn't I?' and 'That's my boy!' over and over. Yes, it felt good to have won – in fact it was amazing – but because of my mother's over-enthusiasm at my win, it was also a little embarrassing. To this day I still feel awkward if someone praises me or tells me how much they enjoyed my performance. It's not false modesty. I'm just not able to accept compliments about my work very easily.

After that memorable debut, there was no stopping my mother getting me started in show business. She immediately put me down for another talent contest and on the night I was just as nervous as I had been the first time. I didn't know then that it was quite natural to be nervous before you stepped out in front of an audience.

Christ, even when he was the leading light in British theatre, lauded all over the world for his film and stage work, Sir Laurence Olivier, arguably the greatest actor of the twentieth century, suffered terrible nerves for a time. Sir Laurence, at the peak of his career, while waiting in the wings of the National Theatre, had stage-fright.

After my talent show triumphs, Mum saw that I had potential to go a lot further as a performer and looked around for any venue I could gain more experience. I even spent three months as the bottom of the bill at a strip show at a theatre in Liverpool. Mind you, there were plenty of other 'bottoms' on the bill. All belonging to attractive young girls. This wasn't a seedy club. This was a theatre.

As television took audiences away from provincial theatres in the 1950s, especially when ITV arrived (giving us *two channels* to choose from!) impresarios and theatre managers would try anything to put bums on seats. One way was to put bums on stage. Strippers. Nude tableaux. Topless dancing girls. They were naughty but nice. Nothing mucky or disgusting. The girls all wore flesh-coloured sticking plasters over their hairy bits. And I don't mean under their arms.

So every night for three months I'd get the bus to the theatre and arrive an hour before I was due to go on stage. Strangely enough, this was about the same time that my Dad took an interest in my career and he'd come along to the theatre with me from time to time, 'to see how my act was improving'. I'd come off stage and he'd say, 'You were great tonight, Fred!' but I knew he'd only had eyes for the strippers who mingled and giggled and gossiped backstage and I told him so, which made him laugh.

After three months at this temple of female delights, which spurred my education on in leaps and bounds, mainly in biology, my mother heard about a dance troupe called the Hilda Fallon Roadshow, which I had to audition for – as a singer, not a dancer! I passed the audition and was with the Roadshow for five or six years, which was an invaluable experience for me, as I learned so much about performing from working week after week in front of audiences. There were sixteen kids in the show, 'a multitude of talent' as they say. Singers and dancers. We'd travel around in a bus to hospitals and community centres where our audiences would consist of wheelchair patients and pensioners, who all loved what we did. We even got a fee for every performance – a pound a time! I loved every minute of it. No that's not true. There was one thing that gave me the right hump. My mother would insist on coming along on the bus to watch her son perform and as before I found this embarrassing. Nobody in showbusiness wants their mother around them when they're working or preparing to work. I'd be on stage and I could hear Mum saying to members of the audience, 'That's my son up there!' and 'Isn't he lovely!'

I used to do a version of the Laurie London hit 'He's Got The Whole World In His Hands' and when Mum had a drink down her, she'd get up on stage and join in with me. As Chuck Berry once sang, 'Can you imagine the way I felt?'

Everyone on the Hilda Fallon Roadshow was expected to be well turned-out on stage. That meant neatly pressed trousers and clean shirts for the boys. One day, after seeing the Elvis Presley film *Loving You*, his first in colour, I turned up at the Roadshow wearing an outfit just like Elvis had worn in the film. A blue denim jacket and matching jeans. Did I think I looked great! I was dressed like Presley! I was bound to bring the house down just by standing on stage in my new gear! But when Hilda Fallon saw me, she went bananas! She laid in to me about how scruffy I looked and hadn't I learned *anything* about how important it was to look smart on stage? I tried to explain that the denim clothes were brand new and Elvis had looked smart in them in the film. but I got the impression that Hilda wasn't an Elvis fan and didn't often go to the pictures. Then she delivered the hammer blow. 'You're not going on stage tonight dressed like that!' I was horrified when she said that. But it was a lesson well learned. Since then I've always endeavoured to dress smartly on stage.

If you've seen me on tour, you'll know there are times when I walk on stage only wearing a large fig leaf. But let me assure you that the fig leaf has just come back from the dry cleaners, pressed and smelling as fresh as a daisy!

The Hilda Fallon Roadshow was great fun but at a pound a show it didn't pay very well. My Dad expected us all to bring a wage into the house, so when I was fifteen I left school and got a job at a factory called Leadco. Like everyone else who starts work for the first time, I felt very shy and awkward on my first day. My job was to clean dirty old oil drums that had to be stacked one on top of another, which took some doing initially. After a couple of weeks it became easier to pick up the oil drums and throw them ten feet in the air to allow my workmates, all of them very rough and ready, to stack them.

Eventually I got promoted to a different part of the factory. But my new job was very uncomfortable and potentially dangerous too. I had to work in a building that contained a large acid tank into which the oil drums had to be lowered to remove any heavily ingrained paint. I wore a thick rubber apron and gloves to protect myself from any acid spills, although my face was totally unprotected. One day I dropped a drum into the acid bath and the resultant splash went all over my face, including my eyes. The pain was excruciating, indescribable. I thought my face was going to be completely burned off. Next to the acid bath was a hose pipe which was continually turned on, pumping out water. I managed to grab it and let the cold water run all over my face and eyes and hair for ages. My face and eyes were sore for days afterwards, but I was very lucky. I'm sure if that hose pipe hadn't been there I would have been scarred and blinded for life. I should have gone straight down the hospital, but the lads I was working with looked after me.

Go to any factory in the world and the workers will tell you about the practical jokes they get up to. Factory work is mostly very boring and repetitive (a bit like Julian Clary's act which consists mostly of 'back passage' references) so it's inevitable that factory workers will occasionally let off steam to break the monotony. The trouble is, a practical joke has to have a victim, and when it's *your* turn, it doesn't always seem to be so funny. Two of the men who worked in the paint-spraying department at Leadco were Fred and Bert, both terrible pranksters. Their job, after the acid had taken all the crappy old paint off the oil drums, was to give them fresh new coats of paint, using big spray-guns. One lunchtime I wandered into the spraying department and I could see some of the lads talking among themselves as I went by, with grins on their faces. Suddenly two blokes grabbed hold of me and held me down while some of the other boys started taking my trousers off and then my underpants! Bloody hell! They hadn't even bought me dinner, the cheeky bastards! I'm on the floor, naked from the waist surrounded by a dozen or so fellahs, all pissing themselves at my predicament, when Fred and Bert appeared, each holding two spray guns in their hands – like two western gunslingers. They took aim at my exposed and rapidly shrinking privates, pressed the buttons and sprayed away. From my belly button down I was sprayed red, white and blue. Very patriotic. Then I was turned over and they sprayed my arse all colours of the rainbow. Big laughs all round of course. Except from my mouth. I was totally pissed off.

Apart from the fact it took me weeks to get that stuff off, you try walking to and from work and jumping on and off buses when your lower half is plastered in rapidly drying paint.

They say that 'revenge is a dish best served cold'. But my anger was still warm when I got my own back on the 'Spray Paint Kids'. A short while after the red, white and blue incident, Fred and Burt were working inside a big pit, about ten foot deep, which they'd gone down using a ladder. When no one was around, I walked over to the pit and looked down at the two of them. 'Hello Fred. Hello Bert.' They looked back at me and they could tell by the look in my eyes I was planning something. They both ran over to the ladder, but I was faster than them and pulled it up, dropping it on the ground beside me. They now had no way of getting out of the pit. 'You had a bloody good time with the spray paint the other day, didn't you? I could have reported the lot of you and there might have been a sacking or two, but I kept my mouth shut.'

Fred looked up at me. 'Yeah, well done for not snitching. Now let's have the ladder back, there's a good boy.'

'I haven't finished yet, Fred. You had your fun. Now it's time for me to have a bit of fun. Fairs fair, eh?'

Burt looked panicky. 'You're not going to paint us, are you?'

'No, Burt. I'm not going to paint you.' I showed them the hose pipe I'd been holding behind my back. 'I'm going to fucking drown the pair of you piss-taking bastards,' and I turned the water on full blast and pointed the nozzle at them. The water exploded all over them and although they kept trying, without the ladder there was no way for them to get out of the pit. They probably thought I'd switch it off when the water got ankle deep, but I just let it fill up deeper and deeper. They were frantic by now. Serves the bastards right. All they were getting was wet. My cock, balls and arse were red raw from where I'd tried to get the paint off with Ajax and hot water.

When the water was up to their waists, I thought that was about the time I should switch the hose off and I dropped the ladder for them to get out. They were absolutely drenched. As Burt put his first foot on the ladder to climb out, I vanished, hiding out at the opposite end of the factory for a couple of hours. As far as I was concerned we were equal. They'd had their fun at my expense. I'd had my revenge. End of story.

Wrong!

The next morning, as I walked into my department, Fred and Bert grabbed me, tied me up and held me over the acid tank. They didn't like the fact that I'd got my revenge on them and were now trying to scare me off ever doing it again. They thought they were the Leadco practical joke kings. Stupid twats! It didn't take long before the acid fumes started making my eyes water. Tied up and held down there was nothing I could do. I was choking on the fumes and feeling terrible. It was all too much and I blacked out.

When I came too, someone was splashing water on my face. My eyes burnt like hell and I struggled to open them. Through a mist I could see Fred and Burt staring at me. They were shit-scared now that they'd gone too far. They and the other lads had been worried by the fact it had taken me twenty minutes to come around. I was as white as a sheet and felt like shit. I could taste the acid. My mouth, my tongue, my saliva tasted of those terrible fumes. Eventually I tried to stand up and they lifted me to my feet. But ten minutes later I blacked out again, totally fucking up their plans to keep the whole incident quiet. They knew they had no choice but to call an ambulance and once they did that, all the factory would find out what had happened, including the bosses. They were going to be in deep, dark, doo-doo. The ambulance arrived and I was taken to hospital, where they sorted me out and released me later in the day.

A note here to anyone thinking about pulling a practical joke on someone in the near future. Think it through. Really think it through. If it's a harmless prank, then do what you want to do. But don't expect your victim to take it lying down. He or she will eventually have his or her revenge. Don't dish it out if you can't take it yourself, my friend.

But if the practical joke, set-up, prank or whatever you want to call it, has even the slightest possibility that it could bring even the tiniest amount of physical harm or discomfort to your victim, here's my advice. Forget it! Are you listening? Fuck-ing for-get it! The couple of seconds' fun you have when your victim realises he or she has been had ain't worth the hassle. If you do insist on going ahead with it even though you've read what happened to me at Leadco, fair enough. But don't be surprised if you get a letter from the victim's solicitors soon after, claiming damages etc. This is the twenty-first century. People will sue you up the arse for anything if they think they have a chance of coming away with a couple of grand.

Or you might even get a visit from some of the victim's bigger friends or relatives who, quite rightly, are eager to smash your face in.

As I said, you really should think it through.

A day or so later when I returned to Leadco, the bosses asked me who had tied me up and held me over the acid tank. I pretended I didn't know, saying they'd come up behind me so I didn't get the chance to see their faces. Had I told them who the stupid buggers were, all of them would have had instant dismissal. If they'd done the same sort of thing to someone outside the factory gates, they could have gone down for aggravated assault or even affray, because the act was pre-meditated. But I have never grassed any one up. That's not my way. So when I went back to the factory, the fellahs were grateful I hadn't named names and after that they didn't pull any more of their daft tricks on me.

While I was at Leadco I used to sing along with my co-worker Jimmy. We'd harmonise like the Everly Brothers and got so good at it, practising every day, the other fellahs would ask us to sing requests at lunchtime and give us lots of applause.

I already had some stage experience, I would have been around sixteen by then, so we started singing together at a local youth club. Every night we'd clock off from the factory, go home to have our tea, get changed, and sing with a small group who played at the youth club.

From that Jimmy and I formed our first band. It must have had a name but I can't remember it. We learnt lots of Buddy Holly and because even then my singing voice was similar to Elvis's I was always asked to sing Presley numbers.

A new dance hall opened in Liverpool where new groups were invited to play on Saturday nights – for nothing. But we loved playing so we'd go along and go right through our repertoire of rock 'n' roll and Buddy and Chuck, but it was the Elvis songs the girls in the audience seemed to go for. I don't suppose there were any Elvis impersonators anywhere in Britain at the time – not that I was consciously impersonating him. I loved Elvis's voice and I was just singing exactly like him, which isn't quite the same thing in my book.

I'd be on stage, singing 'Stuck On You' or 'Teddy Bear' and there'd be hundreds of fourteen- and fifteen-year-old girls in the audience all screaming at me and I couldn't understand why. I mean I *enjoyed* it, I just didn't understand it! That was a regular gig for us and we got better and better. After a gig we'd be surrounded by girls who all wanted to meet us, and now and then we'd strike lucky and have a little snog and a feel off one of the older ones. Ah . . . stocking tops! Much more fun than dropping dirty oil drums into an acid bath at Leadco.

We then progressed to paying gigs, including a venue in Dingle, Liverpool called the Wilson Hall. It was a racially mixed crowd, Liverpool in those days being a multiracial society long before some clever-dick resident of Hampstead invented the expression. But as racially aware as it was, Liverpool could also be rough. At the end of most nights a fight would break out between the black boys and the white boys, usually over girls. Men have been fighting over girls in dance halls since the beginning of time. I wouldn't be surprised if Attila the Hun had the odd fist-fight with Genghis Khan over some dusky slave girl at their local Palais de Danse on more than one occasion. They don't tell you this sort of stuff on The History Channel, do they?

So we'd carry on playing and singing during these fights, just like the old saloon piano players in cowboy pictures, ducking to avoid bottles and the occasional chair. This was always a nightmare for the promoter, who could see all his profits being spent on repairs and higher insurance premiums. One night sixty police officers arrived to break up the fight – sixty of 'em! This didn't help matters at all. In fact the situation did change, because when they saw their uniforms, the black boys and the white boys all joined forces to kick the shit out of the boys in blue! At one point they were throwing *the coppers* into the Black Maria (a large, solid police van). It was a battlefield. The police never again responded to any requests to sort out Saturday night trouble at the Wilson Hall.

Not long after that I left the group and met Howie Casey, another resident of Liverpool. He invited me to play in his group, who were an excellent bunch of musicians, but sadly, everywhere we played, trouble broke out. We would never stand for any nonsense, would never ignore catcalls and insults shouted by arse holes in the audience. Then someone would try and pick a fight with one of the group, or one of us would be flirting with a girl and her boyfriend would come back from the gents and see us, and that caused more problems.

A fight would start, and we'd always get the blame for starting it. This was a shame because we built up a reputation as troublemakers and it stopped us from getting work eventually. All we wanted to do was play music and entertain people.

We used to travel up and down the motorway to gigs in an old van without windows in the side or back. I think it was used by a butcher to hang pigs' carcasses in when we weren't using it, because it stank. And it was worse when we were in it, mainly because of our bass player 'Spread'. By Christ he could fart. I have never in my life smelt farts that came anywhere near as stench-loaded as his. It wasn't as if he dropped the odd one or two during a journey. It was like one long expelling of noxious air from his anus. I'm not exaggerating when I tell you that there were occasions we'd bang on the metal between us and the driver (the lucky bastard who was far away from the smell) and ask him to stop the van so we could open the back doors and jump out into the fresh air for a couple of minutes. Spread was totally unconcerned with his personal problem or the effect it had on the rest of us. To him, farting was as natural as breathing. Trouble was, when he farted, no one else fancied breathing. I'm not sure which were worse. His deadly, silent ones that our nostrils slowly discovered in the middle of a conversation. Or his deafeningly loud trumps that reverberated around inside our metal prison on wheels. I'm not sure where Spread is these days, but I'm sure he had something to do with opening up the hole in the Ozone Layer.

I was also singing with lots of other groups around Liverpool, gaining experience all the time. I had a regular gig with the resident band in a club in New Brighton called the Empress and when I was on stage singing I used to notice a pretty girl looking at me. She looked a bit older than me and she'd deliberately dance in front of the stage, where I was standing and every now and then she'd look up at me. I was seventeen by then and was able to tell when a girl fancied me – and she definitely fancied me. I let it go a few weeks, playing it cool, then one night between sets I casually started talking to her. She seemed very nice, although face to face with her, I couldn't tell how interested she was and apart from finding out her name was Betty Black, that's about all I could get out of her. We danced a few times, but I couldn't see any great romance starting between us, not even a one-night stand, basically because she was always accompanied by her friend June, who didn't like it when I was talking or dancing with Betty because that meant she'd be alone on the side of the dance floor, looking pissed-off.

We started seeing each other on a casual basis, and after a while I started feeling very emotional about her. But she would confuse me at times because I couldn't tell how she felt about me even after we'd been out on a few dates. She blew hot and cold. One day very loving, the next day remote and uncaring. I'd see her at the Craftsmans Club in Birkenhead. One night I'd be talking to her and she'd be chatty and laughing at my silly jokes, the next night she'd hardly bother speaking to me. On one occasion she walked in and didn't even acknowledge me. I didn't know where I was with her and told her so. She didn't like me being so blunt and didn't talk to me for weeks after.

Then one night we met up and started talking and we were friends again. It was when she told me her age, I realised what her problem was. She was 27, a good 10 years older than me, which concerned her but didn't worry me at all. It was only after I'd taken her home to meet my parents for the first time that her age became a problem. My Dad didn't approve of me going out with someone ten years older.

He said, 'Whatever you do don't make her pregnant' and 'You're too young to settle down with a woman that age. Go out and enjoy yourself. There's plenty more fish in the sea.'

But Betty and I got closer and closer and I fell in love with her. We went out for a few months and I asked her to marry me, although I didn't want to cause a family row. I waited a decent while after dad had died and Betty and me got married at the registry office, with the reception laid on at her mother's house. All our friends and relatives were knocking back the booze, but as always I stuck to tea or Coca Cola.

We moved in with her mother and her four brothers. It was very rare back then for newly married couples to move straight into their own house. They would rent a flat or 'rooms' from a landlady, or if they didn't have much money, they would move in with the bride's mother. Big mistake. But a lot of us made it.

At this point, I would like to defend that much maligned rib-tickler known as 'The Mother-in-Law Joke'. I'm well aware that to any smartarse young comic who started his comedy career in university revue and was talent-spotted at the Edinburgh Festival by an executive from Channel 4 who wouldn't recognise great comedy even if it clamped itself on the end of his knob and bit down deep, the mother-in-law joke is the very height of naffness. It personifies all that the new breed of comedian despises in mainstream, working-class comedy.

In response to which I say, with all reasonableness, 'knickers! knackers! knockers!'

What the trendies need to be reminded of is that the mother-in-law joke is not just something that old, north country comedians used in their act to get easy laughs. It's a valid socio-economic statement that resonates throughout our recent past.

Stick with me, will you? The most serious bit's nearly over.

Just because the period of our history in which the mother-in-law was a fearsome figure may (and I stress *may*) be over, it doesn't lessen the validity of the joke and its source. Today it's normal practice for a young married couple to move into a new home straight after the honeymoon. There's no sitting around in some grotty rented flat for them. Only a brand spanking-new, paint-fresh, mock-Tudor semi in Badgers Meadow or Foxes Hollow is good enough for the twenty-first century newly-weds, and bloody good luck to them. If you can afford it, buy your own place as soon as you can. You'll still argue, but only with each other.

The mother-in-law gag was a cathartic release for many couples who, in the 50s, 60s and 70s were forced to move in with their mother-in-law for financial reasons while they saved up for a deposit on their own house or flat, or waited to get to the top of the council house list. It was purgatory living in your mother-in-law's house because she never let you forget it was *her* house. Which was a constant cause of friction between the new husband and wife, because the wife, still living in her childhood home, would invariably take her mother's side in any argument.

Thousands and thousands of couples lived with their mothers-in-law and it was difficult most of the time. If a man and his new bride moved into *her* mother's house, her mother would find fault with everything he did, and if they moved into *his* mother's house, as sure as eggs is eggs, the mother-in-law would find fault with her, whether it was her lack of culinary skills or the fact she didn't iron her new husband's shirts the way mother always had. Every day there'd be niggles and arguments and rows and stony silences. That was no way to start a marriage. So when the couple listened to the radio or watched TV and a comedian who knew what he was talking about took the piss out of mothers-in-law, then, for a few minutes at least, they'd feel they weren't the only couple with the same problem. Their laughter made their life a little more bearable until they could get a place of their own.

Social history lesson over.

It soon became apparent that living with Betty's mother wasn't a good idea so we moved out and rented a flat in Birkenhead, which was a right dump, but it was *our* dump. Although there wasn't a lot of dosh about in the very early 1960s, jobs seemed to be plentiful. If you got fed up in one crap dead-end job, you could leave on the Friday and start another crap dead-end job on the Monday. So around the time I married Betty, apart from singing in the clubs at night and getting involved with other 'work' and certain people that Betty needn't know about, I was also working at Cammell Lairds shipyard during the day.

If you thought Leadco sounded like a madhouse place to work, it had nothing on Cammell Lairds. It had a huge dock wall going all the way around it and once they clocked in, some of the lads would do an hour's graft, then slip over the wall and go into Liverpool for a few pints or to the pictures. Then they'd slip back into Cammell Lairds and clock off with the rest of us. I did it a couple of times myself.

I was still at the shipyard when I was playing with a group called Howie Casey And The Seniors, who were one of the first beat groups on Merseyside. Their leader, Howie, a brilliant sax player who later played on the Wings album *Band On The Run*, was a member of The Roy Young Band in the 1970s and is now a much in demand musical director. They already had a brilliant lead singer with the group, Derry Wilkie, a good-looking coloured guy and in fact as Derry And The Seniors they were the first ever British group to play a residency in Hamburg.

Once they were established there, Howie is reported to have complained to their manager, Allan Williams, about the quality of another group he'd sent over there. 'They're bums!' he said. 'Those Beatles are just bums!'

The first night I went to see the Seniors play, one of his guitarists was acting like a prat and Howie told him to pull his socks up or he'd be out of the group. Well, he kept acting the prat so he had the sack. All the musicians in Liverpool knew each other in those days, and Howie had heard me singing somewhere and asked me if I'd like to join the Seniors. I could sing all the Little Richard and Elvis songs and even if I say so myself – well this is my book – you couldn't tell my version from the original. I had an ear for voice impersonations. I also had a voice for ear impersonations, but that didn't impress people so much. My singing talent, coupled with my sense of humour, my sense of the ridiculous which I've always had, pointed the way to what I wanted to do. Make audiences laugh. But for the moment I was happy to be part of a band I thought were going places.

So I joined Howie Casey And The Seniors and my real adventures in showbusiness really began. Before we split up a couple of years later we recorded an album called *Twist At The Top*. Its sales completely bypassed silver, gold and platinum and went 'aluminium'. We also put a single out, 'Double Twist', which had nothing to do with the then current dance craze. It was all about a painful hernia I'd just had an operation for. It had lots of airplay by the pirates. Not the pirate radio stations. *Real* pirates in the China seas. They played it all the time to torture people into revealing where they'd buried their treasure.

When we split, Howie joined Kingsize Taylor And The Dominoes, another combo that should have been massive stars. But there's no logic in the music business. If there was Status Quo would have had to learn a fourth chord by now.

CHAPTER FIVE

So much happened when I was with Howie Casey And The Seniors, particularly during our residencies in Hamburg, that it could fill a book. But you'd only be able to buy it under the counter in one of those establishments you find in the sleazier parts of Soho. You'll get more than just a flavour of those totally immoral times in the next couple of chapters.

We were called 'groups' then. At some point in the early 1970s 'groups' became 'bands'. To us rock 'n' rollers at that time a *band* was a twenty-piece unit with five trumpets, half a dozen trombones, a grand piano and Ronnie Hilton or Denis Lotis standing at the mike, in a white tuxedo. Or big Billy Cotton shouting 'Wakey! Wakey!' It didn't mean three guitars and a drum kit.

I think the transition from 'group' to 'band' occurred when rock music became more progressive and self-indulgent. If you recorded a simple pop song like 'In The Summertime' you were a group. If you made a concept album about a far-off fairy kingdom where spacemen from Atlantis rode purple unicorns across rainbow bridges to the seventh dimension, you were a 'band', man! Bands smoked dope, groups played practical jokes on each other.

Take the time the Seniors had a residency at a club called the Inn at the Top in Ilford, Essex. We didn't have a lot of money to spend on our digs, so we all had to share a room together and that's when I discovered that the other singer with the group, Derry Wilkie, was a heavy-duty snorer. A real buzz-saw which kept us all awake. I'd turn over and shout all sorts of abuse at him: 'Shut the fuck up you noisy bastard. And give me back the blankets!' He might wake up for a second, the snoring would stop, and then he'd fall asleep again and the terrible noise would continue until breakfast time. Which for us was around noon. I'm someone who needs his eight hours' sleep, so after a couple of nights of this, I was a wreck during the daytime. This couldn't continue, so I decided to have my revenge on him.

Derry was very fond of his thick, black hair which he was always twiddling with, using an Afro-comb. I think it was the Wednesday night, after we got back from the gig and we're all huddled under our blankets and Derry's snoring away like a fog-horn, that I struck. I'd been out that day to buy a bottle of peroxide and an eye-dropper. I got out of bed, stood over Derry and dipped the eye-dropper into the peroxide.

While he was buzz-sawing through the night, I used the eye-dropper to drip peroxide on to his hair. It must have taken me about half an hour to complete the job, but the noisy bastard was sleeping so deeply he had no idea what was going on.

Next morning I watched him get up and walk into the bathroom. Two seconds later I heard him scream, 'Fucking hell! My hair's covered in fucking orange spots! Which one of you fucking twats did this to me?' Did I tell you Derry couldn't take a joke?

He ran back into the bedroom and made straight for me. He knew it was my sort of stunt and he was ready for a scrap. 'You twat. Look what you've done to my fucking hair! It's covered in orange spots!'

I looked at it and said, 'They look more like a subtle tangerine colour to me!'

He was pissed off in a major way. 'You think you're so fucking funny, you twat! We've got a gig to do tonight. How can I go on stage looking like this?'

I said, 'Just put some black shoe polish over the orange spots. No one will notice. Look, I'll help you.' So before the gig I applied some black polish to the dots and although they didn't look that great close-up, on stage I didn't think it would be noticeable.

That night, we're on stage, the place is packed and we're about three or four songs in. We've both started to sweat, as we did every night. But Derry didn't usually sing with his hair full of black shoe polish.

I could see that the polish was slowly streaking down the side of his face and he obviously wasn't aware of it. We were both singing in front of the band, and because of the noise they were making he couldn't hear me say, off mike, 'Howie, the polish is running down your face! Howie!' He just kept on smiling and singing as his face got blacker and blacker. The only way I could think of to bring it to his urgent attention was to sing into the mike. I sang, 'Howie . . . the polish is running all over your face. Howie . . . the polish is running all over your face!' to the tune of Chuck Berry's 'No Particular Place To Go'. It works. Try it.

He suddenly twigged what was happening and, still singing, took out a hankie from his back pocket; calling me every bad word under the sun, he started to wipe the streaks off his face. And *that*, ladies and gentlemen, is the first time anyone streaked in public!

At this point, my early musical career starts to become a little complicated. I was with the Seniors for a while, but I was also with The Midniters and then my final group before I went solo, The Delmonts. But the music scene in Liverpool around that time, as the Merseybeat explosion happened, was very fluid. Singers, drummers and guitarists would move from group to group, either permanently, semi-permanently or just for the odd gig. It was a bit like being a footballer and changing teams, but mostly without a transfer fee. You'd be in a band and someone from another band might be on the look-out for another singer because their front man might be more interested in shagging than singing and they'd have a quiet word with you. 'Psst! Wanna be in our group?'

You could fall out with one group and be playing a gig with your new group the following night. This was before John and Paul started writing their own material. We all sang, basically, the same songs, so there was no trouble in learning your new group's repertoire.

After we'd played together for a few months, Howie Casey approached me and asked if I'd like to join the Seniors in Hamburg. I'd been married to Betty for about three or four years, so I would have been around twenty. The magic of being married had worn off, as it does, and besides, at twenty, a man doesn't have the maturity to take marriage too seriously. I still wasn't convinced a trip to Hamburg was going to be worth my while. I was happy singing around Liverpool and Manchester with The Delmonts. But when Howie said, 'If you come out to Hamburg with us, I guarantee you'll always be shagging your brains out,' something – I have no idea what it was – made me change my mind. I was overjoyed. Being a serious musician, my baton was immediately raised. It was also doing leapfrogs; handstands and somersaults at the prospect of performing to a whole new audience. And singing on stage.

Betty wasn't happy. But she knew whatever she said wouldn't hold me back. I suppose she would have been thirty by then and it must have gone through her mind many times, 'Why did I marry a kid of seventeen?'

Carrying all our own instruments and equipment, Howie, the other Seniors and me sailed over to the Hook of Holland and caught a train to Hamburg. I was actually in Germany. The place Adolf had called home. The war had ended just seventeen years before. It was hardly ancient history, so it was difficult for me to get images from all the war films I'd seen out of my head. To me, the Germans wore leather coats, monocles and jackboots and marched around shouting things like 'Achtung!' and 'Schnell!' at each other and 'Shtupid Englander!' at John Mills. And the men were ever nastier!

We went to the Star Club on the first night. Famous now of course, but just one of hundreds of such places at the time. We went in to check the place out and see what the groups who played there were like. The first thing we couldn't miss seeing as we walked in were loads of enormous bouncers. I'm not talking about ladies' breasts here. Please! The bouncers were all built like brick shipyards. They worked for the owner of the Star Club, Manfred Weichleder who, apart from employing dozens of British beat groups, also owned several notorious sex clubs which would feature such educational acts as 'The Lady And The Donkey'. Yes, quite.

So we're in the Star Club this first night and there was a group playing on stage and standing in front of the group, looking up at them with glossy lips and smoky eyes, were a bunch of the most attractive women I had ever seen in my short life. I mean they were stonking! Howie and the boys, who had played Hamburg several times, had already told me that free love was the rule not the exception in Hamburg. He looked around the club and said, 'If a girl fancies you tonight, she'll buy you a drink.'

'You're joking!' I said. 'That wouldn't happen back home!'

Howie looked at the gorgeous girls in front of the stage and said, 'As you can see, Freddie, we're a long way from home now.'

Well, I stayed in that club until four in the morning waiting for a German beauty with long black hair and leather trousers to grab me and take me to bed with her. I wouldn't have minded if a German beauty with *no* hair had grabbed me. But I didn't get so much as a glance from any of the girls. They totally ignored me. I thought Howie has been pulling my plonker about the free love situation.

The next day me, Howie and the boys met for lunch at a cafe where all the British groups hung out. The Beatles, Gerry And The Pacemakers, The Big Three etc. We all knew each other and as the weeks went by, I found it a great place to chat and trade gossip and dirty jokes. I complained to Howie that I hadn't been ravished the night before and he just smiled and said, 'You saw the way those girls were staring at the group on stage. It'll be our turn tonight.'

That night Howie Casey And The Seniors opened at the Star Club and we had the place rocking! I looked down and all along the front of the stage were dozens of fantastic-looking girls. I was so excited, so eager to get off stage I'm sure I sang every song at twice the normal speed. Sure enough, when we finished our first set, as Howie had predicted, a beautiful German girl who spoke excellent English came up to me and said, 'Can I buy you a drink?' I looked at her long black hair, her hazel eyes and red lips . . . the wonderful curve of her breasts and that soft, silky white neck and said softly, 'Why don't you piss off, you ugly old trout!' No! I'm kidding! I didn't say that at all. I said, 'I'll have a Coca Cola.'

She looked concerned and said, 'Are you sick?'

I didn't know what she meant then, but at the time, the clap was rife among the groups and the girls and if you were taking medication for it, you weren't allowed to drink alcohol for the six or seven days it took the tablets to work. She thought I'd caught a dose and that nearly put the kybosh on our potential bonking session.

'No,' I said, 'I'm not sick. I don't drink alcohol!' – which she was relieved to hear. She bought me a coke, then I bought her a drink and so it went on until I had to play another set with the boys. She stayed in front of the stage all through my performance, smiling at me.

I came off stage and sat next to her and she snuggled up to me and said, 'I like you. Would you like go to bed?'

'No thanks,' I said. 'I'm not in the least bit tired.'

'No, silly boy,' she said. 'Would you like to go to bed with me and make the love?'

So. It was true. These frauleins weren't backwards in coming forwards. As it turned out some of them liked coming backwards too, but I won't go into that here.

I took her back to where I was staying, the annexe adjoining a big hotel. It wasn't much, but it had a bed and a bathroom. The two essentials for a night of sweaty sex.

I wish I could remember the German girl's name, because she was spectacularly built and a real stunner. I got to know many more of the frauleins and they were all beautiful. I swear to you that in the time I was there, I didn't see one ugly German girl. Even the Donkey who worked with The Lady was quite presentable!

That first time, I thought, I don't know how many Germans she's bonked, but if I *am* her first Englishman, I can't let the side down. I must keep the British end up and fly the flag. When this wonderful creature stripped off, you could have flown a full-sized Union Jack from my personal bell-ended flag pole and let it flutter in the breeze of her sensuous perfume. She was amazing. Have you got the picture yet? She made Jennifer Lopez look like Bella Emberg. No offence, Bella! A lot of European men such as the French and the Italians, have reputations as great lovers. Bollocks! When it comes down to it, you can't beat a British swordsman!

In the afterglow of our passion, my lovely fraulein's legs were still shaking as she slipped her shoes on. 'Englander. You are goot fucker, ja?'

I sat up in bed, indignant and said, 'I've never fucked a goat in my life, you cheeky bitch! The odd sheep, yes, but only in an emergency!'

'*Nein!*' she said, sitting on the bed and running her long fingers over my bare chest. 'You are goot at fucking!'

'Oh, yes,' I said, 'I am very goot. The thing is, love, when it comes to fucking, us Liverpool lads don't fuck about. Well, we fuck about, but we don't fuck . . . about. So . . . when will we fuck again?'

I put my hand out to touch one of her magnificent tits, now tucked away safely beneath her black T-shirt. She laughed and backed away from me. Standing up and putting her leather jacket around her shoulders she said, 'I don't know. We shall see. *Auf wiedersehn!*' and blowing me a kiss, she left.

That was my first encounter with the sexual revolution. In Britain, I hadn't even been wounded. One of the reasons people married quite young back then was, unless you knew a local good-time girl who was more than happy to bonk and didn't tell tales afterwards (such girls *were* about then, but their diaries were usually full until the end of the year and she wouldn't drop 'em until you'd slipped a rubber johnnie over your knob first), if you wanted regular sex, you got married.

So to any British lad visiting Germany in 1961, especially if you were in a pop group, it was a sexual wonderland. They didn't seem embarrassed by sex or sexuality like the British. It was all up-front. But obviously not so up-front that children would have access to any of it. In Hamburg you could go into any bookshop and next to a copy of, say, *David Copperfield* or *The Collected Wisdom of Bertrand Russell* there'd be *Lesbian Nurses in String Vests* and *The Filthy Fraulein's Bathtime Romp*. As you can tell from those examples, the bookshop owners of Hamburg may have known a lot about sex but they knew nothing about displaying books in alphabetical order.

I was barely out of my teens and it was one of the most exciting times of my life. If you're a man, put yourself in my place for a moment. You're young, you're working in a foreign country for the first time in your life, you're singing with a pop group, you're away from your wife and surrounded by amazing women who don't act coy when it comes to copulating. They like sex and most nights they want to have sex with *you*! I mean, how lucky was I?

My eyes were opened by so much out there. The second-in-command at the Star Club was Horst Vascher. He made sure the police stayed away from the club by paying them off regularly and generously. He was a no-nonsense guy, always treated women with respect and woe betide any man he saw mistreating a lady. But he wasn't a squeaky-clean do-gooder. He was into everything illegal. Drugs, prostitution, the protection racket, the lot. Horst had worked with so many Liverpool bands, his accent was half German, half Liverpool, which cracked me up when he came out with things like 'Know what I mean, like, *mein herr*?' When you're in the sort of business he was, you have to be a tough-nut and he'd been a professional fighter some years before and looked like it. I heard that he'd killed a man with his bare hands . . . or had he killed a bear with a man's hands? . . . either was possible. Anyway he'd been done for manslaughter and I'd been warned he was a dangerous man. Maybe I'm drawn to these dangerous characters, I don't know, but I always got on well with him and used to make him laugh at my daft jokes and impressions. Believe me, it's hard work for a British comedian to make a German laugh!

When I wasn't performing (on stage or in bed) he'd take me around the city with him as he did his daily 'errands'. He'd say, '*Come mitt me, Freddie. I haff somezink I must do today zat I zink you vill find interestink!*' Oh, I speak fluent German, me.

And we'd get in his car, a big black thing which I think German High Command had left behind with the engine running and the keys still in the ignition when they ran out of Berlin, pissing their neatly pressed pants.

I'd never know where he was taking me. One morning we pulled up outside a big apartment building not far from the city centre and he pointed at a window on the third floor and said, '*I am just goink to check on somezink up zere! Unt zey do not know zat I am cummink!*' and winked. I followed him up three flights of stairs and we came to a door, which he banged on with a leather-gloved fist, twice. The door opened and he barged right in as if he owned the place, with me right behind him.

We were in someone's living room, with a three-piece suite, a TV set and a coffee table. Nothing unusual. Except for a nervous-looking man standing next to a 16mm camera, who stared at us in an annoyed fashion, 'harrumphing' to himself because his work had just been interrupted and behind him was another man holding a small arc lamp, which was switched off. Spreadeagled on the sofa was a well-built guy who looked about thirty, wearing nothing but a big grin. The reason for his good humour was obvious. Kneeling over his erect penis was a blonde girl (I couldn't see her face so I don't know how pretty she was) wearing black stockings and suspenders and at the other end of the sofa, with her bare arse perched a few inches above his beaming face, was a beautiful dark-haired girl wearing white stockings and suspenders. All three of them were sweating from their interrupted activity and I think they were glad to have a bit of a breather. I was on the set of a blue movie.

I looked behind me and the person who had opened the door was standing there. A small ferret of a man with bottle-thick glasses. Horst spoke to him in German for a couple of minutes. Now I defy anybody in those circumstances, however shy they might be, not to stare at the three people sharing the sofa. My eyes kept being drawn to the three of them, naked and sexually aroused, certainly in the guy's case, but all totally relaxed in front of a stranger.

Horst finished speaking to the human ferret who, scowling as if he wasn't happy with what Horst had said to him, walked over to the cameraman and lighting guy. He nodded at them and they switched on their equipment. Then I realised. The ferret was the director! I didn't know blue films had to have a fucking director! That's a fucking director, not a director who fucks, by the way. He then nodded at the guy and two girls on the sofa, which was his subtle way of saying 'Action!' and as if a still photograph had suddenly come to life, they started fornicating frantically and, may I say, very inventively. The blonde went down on the guy's giant willie and jerked her head back and forth, while the brunette lowered herself on to his face and started moaning loudly and not very convincingly. We watched this for a while, then Horst touched me on the arm and indicated that we should leave, which we did, quietly closing the door behind him.

As we walked down the stairs, Horst said, '*I was finding out for Manfred how many films zey haff made today. Zey are all paid well and we expect zem to giff us, how you say, our money's worth. It is my job to check up on these guys from time to time, know what I mean like?*' That Liverpool-German accent again.

'So how many films *have* they made today?'

'*Only ze three!*' Horst said.

I looked at my watch. It was almost ten past eleven. 'But it's only just gone eleven o' clock,' I said. 'Three films in one morning isn't bad, is it?'

Horst shook his head. '*Nein. Not goot! Zey haff been here since haff pest eight! Zey are behind schedule. Zat is why I was not pleased with the director. He must deliver eight films a day. Zey are only twenty minutes long. Zey are not fuckink epics!*'

I was intrigued. 'So that bloke with the girls is expected to come eight times a day?'

Horst shrugged. '*Zat is not hard work. Fucking pretty girls all day. You could do zat standink on your head!*'

'No, I've never tried it that way, Horst,' I said, which made him laugh.

He explained that Manfred financed and produced the blue films, which he would then sell to distributors all over Europe. This was twenty years before video cassettes were invented, flooding the world with triple-X films. Anyone who wanted to see a mucky movie in 1962 would have had to buy an expensive and bulky 16mm projector or its smaller, cheaper brother, the 8mm projector.

Every couple of days I'd discover something new in Hamburg. Like the time the boys in the group took me to the Herbertstrasse. That was a pedestrianised street where dozens of very attractive female prostitutes sat in shop windows, dressed in not very much at all, all trying to attract customers (mainly male, I assume!) by beckoning them with a red-nailed finger or a sexy pout. If a girl successfully interested a customer, he'd go into the back room of her establishment and if she was giving him a blow job, she'd leave a sign on the chair she'd just vacated that said 'Gone to Munch' or if they were actually having full sex, she'd leave a sign that said 'Closed! Legs Open in Ten Minutes'.

I'm kidding.

There was little chance of customers catching a dose from these girls because they were checked for infections by government doctors every week. And for this service to the community and the tourist trade, the government would take a small slice of the action from the girls. So everyone was happy. I remember asking one of the girls, 'Helga. Have you had a check-up this week?' and she said 'Ja! And I have also had a Russian up . . . a Pole up . . . and several Swedes!'

I'm kidding again.

So the boys took me to the Herbertstrasse this first time and as we entered the street, they warned me to behave myself, because these brothels were all run by madams, fierce dragon-featured German women who kept their eyes on the girls and the customers and they wouldn't put up with any nonsense by visiting Liverpool pop groups. I looked in the first window and there was a beautiful girl sat there with her legs crossed, revealing just enough of herself to interest me, mouthing 'You come inside?' and blowing kisses in our direction. By the way, I don't want to give you the impression the street was only open to Howie Casey And The Seniors.

There were loads of people walking up and down: groups of tourists, looking for a bit of local 'colour' so they could disapprovingly tell the folks back home about the 'disgusting things' they'd spent half an hour ogling; there were couples, young and old; men of all ages and sizes on their own or in pairs, daring each other to go inside. And us.

Every window was full of goodies. Very attractive ladies who would have sex with you for a few deutschmarks. We weren't going to bother because we were getting our ends away every night for free with girls equally as pretty. Although the boys had told me to behave, half-away down the street, after passing about twenty or so shop windows, I thought to myself, if we can look at the girls for a cheap thrill, why can't the girls have a look at *us*? I got the devilment in me and while the other lads were preoccupied by what was on offer, I dropped my trousers down to my ankles.

I was walking around behind the boys and waving at the girls in their windows. The girls started laughing and pointing at me, which made Howie and the lads turn around. When he saw me, Howie went pale. 'For crying out loud, Fred. You can't do that here. They'll have us all behind bars! Pull your trousers up right now!'

I just smiled at him and said, 'No, don't worry. I'm just giving the girls a look!'

Well, Howie and the boys all had a real panic and did their best to get my trousers back up but I resisted. I was having a laugh and I wasn't going to let them stop me.

All of a sudden, an enormous fat woman stormed out of one of the buildings and made straight for me. She was one of the madams who protected the girls and she was not happy at what she was witnessing. She looked like a walrus in an ankle-length black leather coat and, I swear this is true, she carried a big, thick, leather bull whip in one hand, giving the impression she knew how to use it. She started shouting harsh words at me in a harsh German accent which came out of her harsh German mouth.

I didn't understand much German then, and pretended I had no idea what she was saying. Although it was obviously something along the lines of 'Get your friggin' trousers on, you naughty bastard!'

Every time she spoke I'd say, 'What did you say? No speaken ze German!' which would make her even angrier. The boys were trying to apologise on my behalf and doing their best to persuade me to get dressed, but I was enjoying the ludicrousness of the situation. As the madam got closer to me I could see she had the build of an all-in wrestler, the skin of an old trout and the suspicion of a moustache. If she wasn't actually a walrus herself, she was obviously related to one.

As she towered above me, I decided to take things to another level. Most people would have had enough by then and pulled their trousers on, the joke over. But I'm not most people. I wanted to prolong things and as the evening breeze caught my bare arse, I'd had an abscess on my bum which was clearing up, but still visible. At its worse it had been just like a tax inspector who's reluctantly had to gave you a big rebate – nasty, sore and a right pain in the ass.

So I pointed at my buttocks and said to the madam, 'Nasty abscess on my ars-en bum-en! My doctor . . . are you listening . . . my doc . . . tor . . . he say to me . . . you need lots of fresh air on your ars-en bum-en. The air must circulate around your ars-en bum-en. Do you understand? Cir-cu-late? So, that is what I am doing. Is that alright?'

She glared at me and held up the whip as if she was going to unfurl it and give me a whack on the backside. 'No. No, that is not the way to cure my sore ars-en bum-en!' I said, pointing at the whip. 'That would make things much worse. Air! Fresh air is the answer to my ars-en bum-en abscess!' She was going bright red with anger now, so I tried one more ploy.

'Herr doctor . . . he say to me . . . to . . . me . . . "Ars-en bum-en inside trousers . . . no goot! Ars-en bum-en outside trousers . . . very goot!" Ja? You understand that, can't you? Arse in . . . bad! Arse out . . . good!' and I pointed at my abscess.

The boys were doubled-up crying with laughter by now and a small crowd of curious passers-by had collected around us and they were giggling and pointing at my bare ars-en bum-en.

Her eyes narrowed and she bent forward to get a closer look at my arse and the abscess. After what I thought was far too thorough an examination, she nodded and said something to me in fluent walrus that I took to mean, 'Take your ars-en bum-en down to the hospital!'

I said, 'Ja! Ja! It is so painful. I go to hospital!' and picked my trousers up and started to walk off towards the end of the street, immediately dropping them again. I daren't turn around or she would have seen I was wetting myself, tears of laughter falling down my face as, trousers around my ankles, I walked the quarter of a mile to the end of the street, the rest of the group following me at a discreet distance.

It only took me a few weeks to find my way around Hamburg (I worked the German clubs for three years, off and on) and sometimes I'd take a new group who'd just arrived on a walking tour of the city. We'd invariably end up in the Herbertstrasse and I'd always make sure they knew they had to behave themselves. One evening a month or so after I'd dropped my trousers in the strasse, I'm looking in one of the windows with some new group members, fresh in from Liverpool, and who should come out of the front door of the building but the walrus with the whip.

She looked me up and down slowly and said in perfect English, 'Young man! Your arse. It is better now? *Ja?*'

'Yes,' I said. 'It is very much better now. The fresh air worked wonders. Thank you for asking!' And she nodded and went back inside.

The group were all open-mouthed and one of them said, 'Why the hell did she ask you about your arse?'

'Well, just between us, boys,' I said, 'that woman is the best spanker in the city. If you like to have your botty smacked, she's the lady! Last week I paid her fifty marks to give me my first-ever spanking and she went to town on it with a cheese-grater, a rubber washing-up glove and three Brillo pads and she was worried she might have hurt me too much!'

Howie And The Seniors were very fond of playing practical jokes on each other. Liverpool people do have a very quirky outlook on life and a wicked sense of humour and in Hamburg in the early 1960s, the wilder the joke the better. Unless you happened to be the victim. A lot of the jokes involved drugs, which were easily available. They seemed to be an almost compulsory with rock musicians. Pills, pot, LSD. Even cocaine.

Some of the guys drank lots of alcohol *and* took loads of drugs which must have really fucked-up some of them mentally and physically over a period of years. I wasn't a drinker, but the pranksters around the scene would spike people's drinks with LSD and think it was hysterically funny. Twats!

Just so you know. Although we had some laughs, we *did* work hard while we were out there. The Star Club was open 24 hours a day, seven days a week and there was always a group playing on stage. We'd play for an hour solid, get off to let another group on, have three hours off, go back on for another hour, let the next group take over and so on. It was a conveyor belt of loud and raunchy rock 'n' roll. We were all fairly young and fit and during our breaks we shagged ourselves senseless or partook of mind-bending substances.

Sex, drugs and rock and roll anyone?

But as the captain of the *Titanic* once said, 'It isn't all plain sailing.' The sex wasn't entirely free. The price tag was the occasional dose of VD. I knew there was always the chance of me catching it but the odds were lessened because if a girl was infected, she wouldn't hide the fact. She'd tell you right out. 'I cannot make love with you at the moment. Wait two days. In two days, all clear!' So that prevented a lot of lads catching it. There was a clinic in the city where you paid fifty marks for an injection and seven days' worth of tablets. After seven days it cleared up, and you were free to catch it all over again. In Hamburg, it seemed, an infected willy was no more bother than an infected toe.

We did have contraceptives out there, but we hardly ever wore them. They were called King Kongs and they had a funny-looking shape to them, with little rubber spikes and bits hanging down. When you had one on your old boy, it looked for all the world like you were balancing a cockerel on the end of it, complete with a beak.

It looked bloody ridiculous. It was hardly a turn on for your lover if she saw you standing there proud and erect with a chicken's head on the end of your willie. I did try them a few times but they just made me and the ladies I was with laugh, spoiling the moment. Us lads, and the girls we were having carnal fun with, didn't ever worry about catching diseases or possibly getting pregnant. It was totally irresponsible of us, I know, but that's how it was then. I won't say it was a more innocent time, because it wasn't 'innocent'. Just a lot freer and easier, thirty years before AIDS put the willies up people.

Yes, all this time, my wife Betty was at home, working hard. I did send her money home when I could, but we didn't write that often. It's easy to forget your responsibilities when you're several hundred miles away from your grotty little Birkenhead flat, lying on your back in a Hamburg hotel room while a powerful brunette fraulein bounces up and down on your bell end.

As for my musical career, the months went by and the group was on the musical treadmill of three hours off, one hour on, day after day. Naturally, being together all the time, things started becoming a little fraught between me and the rest of the group. We'd have rows and it always seemed to be them against me. Then it would blow over for a while until the next time. And all the time, we had to be wary about who would be the next victim of a practical joke.

I owned two pairs of round-toed cowboy boots in brown leather, which were my pride and joy. I had one pair for everyday use, which might get cleaned occasionally, and another pair which I only wore on stage. I would always keep my stage boots highly polished, much to the amusement of the other lads, who loved taking the piss out of me when I'd shine my boots in the dressing room.

I was hardly ever late for a gig, always preferring to be at the club early, but one night I arrived at the club about fifteen minutes late because the taxi taking me there had overheated and ... well ... I ended up being late. I saw Howie and the lads standing by the bar, and we still had ten minutes before we were due to go on, so I dashed into the dressing room for a quick shower.

I dried myself off and put on my stage jeans and some clean socks and slipped my left boot on, then my right boot. Something didn't feel right. There was something soggy in each boot and it felt horrible. I took my left boot off and as I pulled my foot out I could see it was coated in a smelly, brown liquid. I took the other boot off and *that* foot was covered in the stuff too. Human shit. Possibly made up of a digested vindaloo curry, eaten the night before. The stench was terrible. It only took me a couple of seconds to realise that someone had taken a massive dump inside each of my two best shiny boots, thinking it was a big joke.

With my socks slimy and stinky and my best boots full of shit, I had no doubt the boys were at the bar congratulating themselves on a successful wind-up. I thought, *Right you bastards! I'll have you!* Because if anyone declares war on me, with practical jokes, they'd better be prepared for massive retaliation. Whatever they do to me, I'll always go one better

. . . and bigger. The twats had tried to ruin my wonderful cowboy boots which were now lying on the floor, looking like a couple of tabloid reporters – both of them full of shit.

I ripped my socks off and binned them, because they would be no good to anyone ever again. I soaped and washed my stinking feet under hot shower water, before washing my boots inside and out. They were expensive so I prayed the leather would be OK.

I scrubbed every last piece of pooh off my boots and while they were both drying, I sprayed them with underarm deodorant and splashed aftershave inside them, hoping to get rid of the smell, which was still lingering inside my nostrils. I was thinking, *Those dirty bastards! Of all the filthy, disgusting tricks to play on me. And to use my best boots is unforgiveable! I'll get my revenge, you bastards!'*

But before I could revenge my honour . . . and my shit-filled boots . . . they had me again. The bastards!

I'd not mentioned the cowboy boots incident to the lads on the night it happened. I'd worn my ordinary boots on stage that night and wouldn't give them the satisfaction of knowing I'd fallen for their shitty trick. A couple of nights later, all pals together, we went to a place called the Roxy Bar. Once again there was a beautiful girl sat at the bar who appeared to be staring at me. I drank my coke and ignored her, but Howie soon started to comment. 'Freddie, that girl at the end of the bar fancies you. Her name is Rose and she was asking about you a few nights ago at the Star Club.'

I took a sip of my coke and looked at her again. She had a firm Germanic jaw, high cheekbones and long, blonde hair that fell down to her well-developed bare shoulders. 'She is *very* attractive.'

Howie and the other lads went and joined some German girls at a booth at the far end of the club, set back from the dance floor with a circular table in front of it. I followed the boys down, but there were only enough girls for them, and I was in danger of being a spare prick at an orgy.

By the way, don't you find an orgy's an embarrassing social occasion? Well, you never know who to thank when it's all over, do you?

I sat on the end of the seat and was thinking of going back to the annexe after I finished my drink. Then Rose appeared in front of me and smiled a seductive smile Obviously she had the right horn for me. Being a man of the world, I smiled back. Then she winked at me . . . I winked at her. And there we both were. A right pair of winkers. 'My name is Rose,' she said, 'may I sit with you?'

I stood up and she sat on the end of the seat next to me. Howie sat next to me with his arm around a girl and winked at me as if to say, 'I told you she fancied you!'

Rose put her drink down on the table and said, 'I saw you at the Star Club. I think you are a very sexy man.'

What could I say but 'Really?' I wasn't going to get suckered in. I wasn't!

'Yes,' she said, 'I think you are very, very sexy.'

'Well, that's very, very nice of you to say so,' I said, looking around the club.

Rose put her arm around me and I was suddenly aware that her other hand was touching my knee under the table. The touching became a stroking, which travelled up my thigh towards my privates. What was I going to do. Run screaming from the table? The music was so loud and the crowd so noisy, I don't suppose anyone would have heard me. Rose's right hand was now touching my knob. She expertly started un-buttoning my fly one-handedly, while gazing into my eyes. Here we go again.

I was trying to get Howie's attention, by nodding in the direction of Rose's hand, so he knew something was going on under the table, but he was deep in conversation with the girl he was with. Rose then got my knob out and was manipulating it in a rather pleasurable way. Howie looked over at me and instantly saw what was going on, giving me the thumbs-up. He shouted in my ear, above the sound of the rock 'n' roll band on stage. 'We've all been after Rose for months. You've only been in town for five minutes and she's all over you, you lucky sod. I can't believe it.' He nudged the girl next to him, she nudged the Senior next to her and eventually everyone around the table knew what Rose had in her hand.

She downed her drink in one gulp and slid beneath the table. Was she pissed or what? Whoops! One second my cock was in her hand . . . next it was in her mouth. She was giving me oral sex under the table in this crowded club. Although only the people around our table knew what was going on. The lads were all egging me on, telling me I was 'The Man' because they'd all failed with Rose, but I'd succeeded.

I lay back in the booth in ecstasy. Thankfully, she had some sense of decorum and didn't go all the way to bring me off, but she got bloody close! Her head appeared from under the table and she started French kissing me. Some of the kisses actually started out as English ones before she translated them into French. God, she was good at snogging! I could hardly breathe, so I gently pushed her away from me while I gulped some air into my lungs. She started rummaging in her handbag, looking for her purse as it turned out, and she said something I couldn't quite make out because of the loud music pulsating around the club.

'Sorry, love,' I said. 'What did you say?'

Still looking in her handbag, she repeated what she'd said, a little louder this time, but I still couldn't hear her.

I shouted, 'Rose, love, I can't hear what you're saying!' She took her purse from out of her handbag, put her mouth next to my ear and shouted, in a voice that sounded like Frank Bruno with laryngitis, *'Do you vant anuzzer drink?'*

I thought, *Fucking hell, she's got a helluva deep voice for a girl!* Then I saw that Howie and the lads were doubled-up laughing. What was so funny? Why were they looking at me and Rose? The girl with the deepest voice I'd ever . . . Oh no! It was obvious now. That firm jaw. Those well developed shoulders. And that Adam's apple! Christ almighty! Rose wasn't a girl. She was a fucking fellah! And he'd just been sucking my sweet!

I jumped up and pushed past Rose or Fritz or Helmut or whatever his name was and ran to the gents toilet. You know the song 'I'm Gonna Wash That Man Right Out Of My Hair'? Well, I just had to wash that man right off-a my cock! I got completely undressed, I mean completely stark-bollock naked, and started running the hot tap in the sink, which was quite large, certainly large enough to accommodate my arse when I sat in it. Five inches of hot water just about covered my cock and balls. Men were walking in and out of the toilet for a slash, and I was sat in the sink washing my bits and pieces with a little bit of soap, looking up and saying 'Evening!' They tried not to catch my eye, because they thought I was some crazy Englishman who liked to bathe in public. I kept running more and more hot water in an effort to clean myself, until the gents was like a Turkish baths. Steam everywhere. I had a mental image of the transvestite nibbling my knob under the table and I wanted to wash it all away. I also used the same piece of soap to wash my mouth out.

Look, don't screw your face up because I was washing my privates with the same tiny piece of soap I used on my mouth. This was an emergency! I could taste that fellah's horrible tongue in my mouth and I wanted to get rid of it fast. I also started plotting a brilliant revenge on Howie And The Seniors. They were going to pay for this latest outrage.

I mean, how much is a man supposed to take before he explodes?

I knew that the boys would expect me to think long and hard about ways I could get my own back, so instead of stewing things over for weeks, planning my retaliation, I decided I'd get my own back that night. And I knew exactly how I was going to do it. It's amazing how you can work things out in your mind when you're sat in a sink in the gents toilet of a German nightclub.

In a couple of hours we had to be back on stage, so I got dried and dressed and slipped out of a side door back to the Star Club and when I got to the dressing room I picked up an acoustic guitar that one of the lads cherished. It was lovely looking, with a brilliant tone to it and he always took great care with it. But then, my best leather cowboy boots were special to me too. I loosened the strings of the guitar, dropped my trousers and . . . I know this will sound disgusting to you . . . I sat over the sound hole of the guitar and emptied the contents of my bowels inside it. When I'd finished, I shook the guitar so the contents would be spread inside to give the maximum effect at the appropriate time, tightened the strings up and placed the instrument back in its case.

I hadn't started all this – they had! War had been declared on me and this was my very first skirmish with the enemy. When the rest of the boys arrived I kept the owner of the acoustic guitar talking as he was getting ready, hoping he wouldn't open his guitar case until the last minute. Eventually it was time for us to go on and I 'kindly' opened the guitar case, gingerly took out the precious guitar and handed it to the guy who quickly strapped it on and took in on stage with him. Within a couple of minutes we were playing in front of a large, enthusiastic audience and the heat from their bodies and the stage lights above us speeded up the time it took for the distinct aroma of shit to fill the air. I'm singing away at the mike, watching my fellow group-member with the acoustic guitar looking around to see where the foul smell was coming from. He checked the soles of his shoes . . . sniffed his armpits . . . sniffed me and the other lads . . . but he had no idea he had a guitar full of shit in his hands. He just couldn't work out where the smell was coming from. We've all heard of shit guitar players. He *really was* a shit guitar player.

We finished the first song and he said, 'Freddie. Can you smell something horrible?'

I sniffed the air and pretended I couldn't. 'What sort of smell?'

'Well . . . like someone's just shit!'

I shook my head and we got right into the next number. We were starting to steam up by then, really sweating. The smell was getting worse. How the audience hadn't got a whiff of it I don't know.

In the middle of the song, I sidled up to the guitarist and said, 'This smell . . . is it like the smell a cowboy boot might make if someone took a crap in it?'

He looked at me suspiciously. Was he starting to twig that something was up?

'I think I might know where your smell might be coming from,' I said.

'Do you? Well, for fuck's sake tell me!'

'It could be coming from inside there!' I pointed at his guitar.

'Why would my guitar smell of shit?'

'I'm not sure. Maybe it's got something to do with the fact that I crapped in it about an hour ago!'

'What?' he said, and looked inside the guitar. With his nose just inches away from the offending material, the full blast of the stench hit him. 'Fucking hell. You really have shit in my guitar!'

'Yes,' I said. 'And one of *you* lot shat in my best cowboy boots the other day. You arranged for a transvestite to suck my cock. So unless all this bollocks stops *tonight*, I'll shit in your guitar every night . . . and your shoes . . . your stage suits . . . your beds . . . the fucking lot. And when I've got no crap left inside me, I'll hire someone with the screaming squitters to do it for me. Understand . . . twat features?'

He looked inside the guitar again and then at me. 'Yes . . . yes!'

The audience was too drunk or too stoned to know what was going on and as long as the music was playing they kept dancing. That is, until the moment the guitar player could no longer stand the smell, turned the guitar upside down and emptied its disgusting contents all over the stage. The audience couldn't believe what they were seeing and all the girls in the front quickly moved back. The other fellahs in the group saw this stuff pouring out of the guitar in a nasty, smelly cascade and stopped playing.

I walked off and remember how quickly the bouncers managed to find a bucket and a mop to clean up the stage. Ten minutes later, the air now smelling of disinfectant and the German version of carbolic soap, we got back on and finished our set.

We called a shaky truce after that night, although we did still pull the odd joke on each other. But none of them was as disgusting, degrading or humiliating as the ones I've described.

CHAPTER SIX

I've mentioned before that apart from all the non-stop copulation that went on in Hamburg, a lot of music was being played 24 hours a day, mainly by British groups.

The Beatles first went out there as early as August 1960, invited to play the Indra Club by its owner Bruno Koschmider, who booked them for 48 nights between 17 August and 3 October. They were a five-piece unit then, with Stuart Sutcliffe on bass and Pete Best on drums along with John, Paul and George. They completed their contract and were immediately banned from the Indra Club for playing too loud (!) and on 4 October they started playing at the Kaiserkeller, also owned by Herr Koschmider. According to Pete Best, the non-stop slog of playing seven nights over several months turned The Beatles into a charismatic powerhouse!

The Beatles were playing Hamburg for the third or fourth time when I went out there. I already knew the lads, especially John Lennon from the Liverpool music scene. The Beatles used to play gigs at a club I used to go to called the Grapes.

Gerry And The Pacemakers played there, as did Billy J. Kramer (before he teamed up with the Dakotas), The Fourmost, Rory Storm And The Hurricanes . . . loads of them. Liverpool was bursting with groups. A city full of talent. Why it should all happen for that city at that particular time, who can say? It wasn't just the music. There were poets like Adrian Henri and Roger McGough and cheeky young comedians like Jimmy Tarbuck and Johnny Hackett too.

Brian Epstein was always down the Grapes, not just to have a night out, but to suss out who the most popular groups were. I have a tale to tell about Mr Epstein a little later.

Later on I regularly saw The Beatles perform at the original Cavern club (the one that visiting Beatle fans are taken to see in Liverpool now is only a reconstruction) during their famous lunchtime sessions, which were always opened by the resident DJ Bob Wooller, in the same way. 'Good afternoon, cave dwellers! Welcome to the Cavern!' He'd put on the first record and the place would erupt. The Cavern Club wasn't, as some people think, a place that had opened in the wake of the Mersey Boom in the early 1960s.

Many years before its brick walls echoed to the 'Liverpool Sound', it had once been a basement warehouse beneath Mathew Street. During the mid-1950s it had been transformed into a jazz club, where intense young men with goatee-beards would play interminable saxophone solos. The guy who owned it, an ex-accountant called Raymond McFall, was someone who liked to keep ahead of the trends and when jazz stopped packing the place out, on certain nights of the week and at lunchtimes, he'd feature up-and-coming local beat groups. Clever man. He must have been clever to entice audiences, first jazz fans and then pop music fans, to pay money to visit what was basically just three large, smelly, brick-walled tunnels.

Office boys and girls, shop assistants, schoolkids, sometimes there'd be a couple of hundred people in the place, dancing away their lunch hour to the local groups or just enjoying the music while they ate a 'Cavern lunch', soup and a roll washed down with Coca Cola. Once a group started playing, the walls would be dripping with condensation within ten minutes. But the atmosphere was amazing.

All the Liverpool groups eventually met up socially or we'd find we were sharing a dressing room when there were several of us on the same bill. Which is how I got to know The Beatles. John always came off stage with the adrenalin pumping through him, shouting 'Whooooo!' at no one in particular, still full of energy as if he had taken a couple too many purple hearts, while the other three would just relax, smoking and laughing.

I toured with The Beatles, you know! Oh yes! But wait. I'm getting ahead of myself. I'm still in Hamburg with Howie Casey And The Seniors at the moment.

In 1961 The Beatles were just another group. They'd gained fans in Liverpool but they didn't stand out from all the other Merseybeat combos. They were covering the same songs as the rest of us were, classic rock 'n' roll covers.

Then they started listening to R&B records that were brought in from America by friends and relatives in the Merchant Navy who went back and forth across the Atlantic and they took that influence on board, eventually blending it in with their unique blend of raw rock 'n' roll and melodic harmonies to create their own distinctive sound. One thing that made them stand out visually in the early 1960s, before the success of 'Love Me Do', was the fact they ditched the then still popular 1950s 'Tony Curtis quiff', swept back hairstyle that most lads were still happy with, plastered in Brylcreem.

While they were in Germany they had their first 'Beatle cuts', styled by Stuart Sutcliffe's girlfriend Astrid Kirchherr, which I thought made them look like Larry, Moe and Curly Joe, the Three Stooges, whose short comedy films I'd seen at the pictures. Their image subtly changing under the influenced of Astrid: they started wearing black leather jackets, black denim jeans and matching polo neck sweaters.

The fact that John and Paul were brilliant songwriters with a wonderful sense of melody and harmony is indisputable, but I've no doubt that their 'look' was an enormous help at the time that 'Love Me Do' came out. Their early publicity pictures, moodily shot, showing off their trendy 'moptops' and dark jackets and shirts, certainly put them apart from the Cliffs, Billys and Hanks in their shiny mohair suits and greasy quiffs.

When we were all working in Hamburg, Howie Casey And The Seniors would be playing the Star Club and The Beatles would be down at the Top Ten Club and when our shifts permitted, we'd all go and watch each other play. One night John Lennon came out on stage with the others, wearing a lavatory seat around his neck. What made it funny was, in the hour they were performing, none of them made a reference to it. I've seen John walk on stage and say, 'Good evening, you German bastards! I'd just like to remind you that my country, Great Britain, won the Second World War, two-nil away from home! And now I hope you enjoy "Long Tall Sally" . . . you bastards!'

While I was between hotels in Hamburg, John let me stay in his hotel room with him. When he wasn't playing on stage or writing songs with Paul, his way of relaxing was to keep on working. He had so much creative energy. I'm not saying he didn't indulge in all the delightful recreational activities on offer in that sleazy, seedy, wonderful city like the rest of us randy sods, but he seemed happiest when he had a pen and a notebook in his hand. He would create surreal Goon-type poems (he was a huge fan of the original Goon Spike Milligan who created alternative comedy in the early 1950s) getting through pages and pages. When he ran out of paper, he'd write his poems on the wall of his room and sign them. I don't have many regrets, but I sometimes wish I'd had the foresight to strip the wallpaper off when I left and hide his poems away for forty years! Think what they would have fetched at auction at Christie's or Sotheby's!

His room of poems featured quite a mixture of styles. Edward Lear-type nonsense rhymes; anti-German tirades, referring to the Gestapo; and wickedly scathing, satirical lines aimed at political figures of the time. Lennon was quietly creating his poems in that grubby hotel room, pre-empting by a couple of years the British satire boom which arrived in the wake of the Profumo–Christine Keeler scandal. Just three years later the poems he'd written in Hamburg later turned up in his published collections such as *John Lennon in His Own Write* and *A Spaniard in the Works*.

John and I had a similar sense of humour, that sense of the absurd which he worked into songs like 'I am the Walrus' (although there's a lot of hate in that song too, aimed at his old schoolteachers) and which I channelled into my stage and television career years later. We were on the same wavelength. But, unlike John, I didn't want to change the world. He was dissatisfied with the way things were being run in Britain, where there was much more awareness of what 'class' you were then. The upper and middle classes who ran the country and the factories and central and local government tolerated the working classes because they needed them for factory fodder or to keep their parks and streets neat and tidy and to service their Rolls Royces and Jaguars. I think John and The Beatles *did* change things a little, by helping to break down the class barriers once they were world stars.

When they were at their peak, almost everyone would have at least one Beatles record in their collection, whether they were dukes or dustmen. Which I'm sure amused John.

He was more than just a rock 'n' roller, or a songwriter. *Much* more than that. There were so many things going on that he didn't think were right, so much unfairness and injustice and he'd get wound up about them, frustrated that he couldn't do anything about putting them right. During these early years he developed a healthy cynicism which never left him. This must have helped him during the time he was vilified for saying The Beatles were more popular than Jesus.

Even if you weren't around at the time, you'll be aware that he was criticised for that comment. The Americans in particular took offence and on the news we saw film of ministers in various States overseeing the burning of Beatles records and books.

But these religious fanatics hadn't actually heard what John had said. They'd only picked up his comments second- and third-hand and acted impulsively, and gone ludicrously over the top in my opinion. The comments which inflamed so many intolerant people were taken from an interview he'd given in which he'd pointed out The Beatles were just a bunch of musicians who had millions of followers, like Jesus once had, but that as the churches were empty and people were becoming less and less interested in religion, maybe The Beatles *were* more popular than Jesus.

He didn't mean it in an arrogant anti-religious way. It was just one of his many observations on the world as he saw it. While he was a Beatle, he'd be totally candid with interviewers and whether the public agreed with him or not didn't concern him. But it stirred up a hornets' nest for a while which affected the sales of their records in various parts of the USA.

After I left Howie Casey And The Seniors, and with my Hamburg experiences behind me, I went back to Liverpool. During the Merseybeat explosion, with the charts on both sides of the Atlantic full of records by The Beatles, The Searchers, The Swingin' Blue Jeans and so many others, I was in a group called The Midniters and we were talent-spotted and signed up by the brain behind The Beatles, Brian Epstein. Before he became The Beatles' manager he hadn't any previous experience in showbusiness apart from spending three terms (which he is on record as saying he hated) at the Royal Academy of Dramatic Art in the late 1950s.

The first time he saw The Beatles at the Cavern was on 9 November 1961. At that time Brian was running the record department of his family department store NEMS (North End Music Stores) in Whitechapel, central Liverpool, and because a lot of kids had come into the shop asking for a record by a local group called The Beatles, and he didn't have it in stock, he thought he ought to check them out. The record in question was 'My Bonnie', recorded while they were in Hamburg. He was impressed by their performance at the Cavern and became their manager in December 1961, although until he consulted a solicitor, he had absolutely no idea what went into a contract between a manager and a performer. The Beatles took a gamble that he would take them where they wanted to go. 'To the top . . . to the very top!'

So, after the success of The Beatles, he signed up Gerry And The Pacemakers. Once they had records in the charts, he looked around for any band he thought had potential. Liverpool was *the* place for young pop bands. Throw a stick into Lime Street and you'd hit ten of them. Brian saw The Midniters working, liked us and within a few weeks he arranged for us to join one of the touring pop packages which were very popular in the 1960s. Made up of six or seven pop acts, they went to all the theatres and cinema-theatres around the country for two, sometimes three, months, playing each city or town for one night only (two shows, one at 6.10, the other at 8.40). Each show had a comedy compère, who had the hardest job of all, trying to make himself heard above the screams of the teenage girls. No one wanted to hear his jokes, but he had to go on in front of the curtain for two or three minutes at a time, in order to give one group time to get off stage and the next one time to get on stage and plug their guitars in. It was manic. When they were starting out, both Des O'Connor and Jimmy Tarbuck had the dubious pleasure of compèring package tours.

Some of these one-nighter tours had an odd assortment of acts on one bill, their only connection being they all happened to be signed to one particular record label or management company.

So, Epstein got The Midniters, featuring me, on one of these crazy package tours. But this one was something special, because the headliners were The Beatles! This was 1963 when they were well established with several hit singles and albums under their belt and Beatlemania was at its highest. Don't ask me where we played because every theatre and cinema we played looked the same to me. Just getting in and out of the venues was a nightmare for The Beatles and also for their support bands. Our vans and cats would pull up outside the stage door, or any side door we could be let in, and as soon as we finished in the evening, we'd dash out the same door to get back on the road to the next town, sleeping in some remote layby or, if we could afford it, some cheap bed and breakfast.

We were on the show to promote our Decca single, 'Who Told You?' which was produced by the 'Telstar Man', Joe Meek (of whom more later) and which thanks to the airplay it got, actually got as high as Number 10 in the charts in May 1963. Doing two shows a night meant we could stand in the wings and watch The Beatles close the first show.

It was always pandemonium. The screaming from the crying, sobbing, hysterical audience drowned out everything else. The Beatles might just as well have saved their voices and mouthed the words – thus anticipating the musical trends of the early twenty-first century. You could just about hear the 'thump' of Ringo's drums and the low notes of Paul's Hofner bass. But as for the lyrics, forget it. To the girls and guys in the audience, it was exciting enough just being in the same building as their idols, to see them in the flesh, in their town, in their local Granada or ABC or Hippodrome, 'live' and in colour and not just as four-inch high figures on a black and white TV screen.

After the tour, because of the usual group in-fighting and bickering, The Midniters were on the verge of breaking up. I knew that Brian Epstein was planning another massive pop tour, this time headlined by Gerry And The Pacemakers (the first British act ever to have their first three records reach the Number 1 position). As I didn't have much work lined up, and because I needed to prove to Betty that I could be continually successful in showbusiness and not just sporadically, I wanted to talk to Brian about the possibility of The Midniters appearing on the Pacemakers' tour so I phoned Brian's secretary Beryl Adams at NEMS Enterprises Ltd (he retained the initials of North End Music Stores) in Moorfields, near Exchange Station. She set up a meeting with Brian, which, as always, I was a little early for. I was a bit nervous, as I was there primarily to ask him for a job – never a pleasant experience whatever business you're in – and it didn't help that he kept me hanging about for what seemed ages in the waiting room. I suppose that's why they call them waiting rooms.

Eventually I went in to see Epstein. We chatted for a while about The Beatles' UK tour which I'd recently been on, traded some showbiz gossip and, feeling a little more confident, a little more relaxed, I asked him about the possibility of The Midniters being part of the upcoming tour by Gerry And The Pacemakers. I didn't mention that me and The Midniters all hated each other and we might fall apart mid-way through the tour. I was very young but not stupid. Brian suddenly sat up straight in his chair and took on the persona of a cold, clinical business man, the same persona which had helped him take on the British music industry and turn The Beatles from a pop group to a phenomenon. He bluntly told me that he hadn't made his mind up who was going on the bill with Gerry, that he'd been approached by dozens of groups who would give their eye teeth to do the tour and he'd have to think about it. I was about to say 'Thanks' and leave, when he relaxed a little and said 'I'll try and work something out about the tour. But we need to talk about other things too. You and the boys have a bright future in the business, but you'll need my expertise to help you. I'm going to be very busy all day today so why don't I pop round your place tonight and we can have a longer chat?'

I said, 'Yeah, that'd be great,' and I wrote down my address on a piece of paper for him, shook his hand and left the office.

It was common knowledge among the groups in Liverpool that Brian Epstein was a homosexual. The national papers in those days wouldn't have mentioned it, even if they'd known. Today they'd put it on the front page whether it were true or not, then if it was proved they were wrong, they'd print a tiny, half-inch square retraction on page 56.

I was a young lad, not bad looking – no, bollocks to that! – I was damned handsome and hung like an Arab stallion. I hadn't realised Brian had taken a shine to me.

I was still living at my mother's house then and at eight o'clock Brian turned up driving his Rolls Royce. I walked out to meet him, aware of all the neighbours staring through their net curtains and instead of switching off the engine and coming into the house, Brian beckoned me to sit in the passenger seat next to him. I got in and we drove off very slowly down the street and headed out into the countryside.

Hmm, I thought, I'm off for a ride in the country with a homosexual man. The term 'gay' didn't have any connotations then. But we had plenty of other, cruder words to describe men who fancied other men. We made small talk along the way and after half an hour or so, he pulled into a layby and we started talking about The Beatles and what a great future The Midniters had if we were handled properly etc. I lit a cigarette and sat back to listen to what he had to say, hoping that he would finish with 'Congratulations! You're definitely on the tour with Gerry Marsden and the boys.' We sat there for over an hour and he talked about nothing but business. It seemed odd that he'd chosen to hold a meeting in a layby, rather than my front room or even one of the many country pubs we'd passed on our drive, but who was I to argue? I needed the work. Epstein could supply it.

Brian suddenly leaned forward and put his hand on my right leg and started rubbing it up and down. I didn't know what to do. I was in his car in the middle of nowhere. I could hardly open the door and run off. Before he went any further I had to tell him that I was straight. 'Brian, don't do that. I'm not into that sort of thing.'

He ignored my protest and started to put his arm around me. I looked right into his eyes – a very bad move on my part as it happened, because it could have made him think I *did* fancy him – and I could see he was getting turned on. What the fuck was he going to do next? He pushed his face towards mine and tried to kiss me full on the lips. I kept saying, 'Brian, please get off! Get off! Brian. I'm not a homo!', but Christ, he was so persistent, grabbing at my arms and legs and still trying to plant a kiss on my lips. He seemed determined to have his way with me and was getting excited at the prospect. It was horrible, especially as I couldn't make him understand I just wasn't interested. He was deaf and blind to the fact that I was repelling his advances.

Some people won't take 'Fuck off!' for an answer and Brian was one of them. I mean he was one of them as well as being one of *them*. I started to lose my temper and instead of just pushing him away, I started punching his upper arms, which startled him, because it bloody hurt. He quickly backed off and composed himself. The ardour ebbed from his body and he started the car and pulled out into the road, heading back for the city. He ran a shaking hand through his dishevelled hair and apologised to me several times. I said, 'It's alright Brian. Don't worry. I won't tell anyone about what you tried to do.' Had I been the type to exploit such a situation, I could have threatened to tell the papers what had happened unless he made sure me and The Midniters were on the Gerry And The Pacemakers tour. The press would have lapped it up. Imagine the headlines if I'd grassed on him! 'Beatles' Boss Epstein In Homosexual Attack On Innocent Young Pop Singer!' It would have ruined him and could have potentially damaged the Fab Four's career, by association.

But on the journey home I wasn't planning to get my own back on him. I just felt embarrassed. Had I given him any sign during previous meetings that I was homosexual or even bisexual? Had I fuck! He'd seen me with Betty and other women too. All that was going round inside my head was 'Why did he do it?' and 'How many other lads has he tried it on with who were too shit-scared too fight him off?' Consequently, we hardly spoke two words on the way back to my house. We pulled up outside my front door and as I went to get out of the car, he said, 'Come and see me at my office in two days!' I slammed the door and he drove off down the street.

Two days later I turned up at his office and sat facing him across his very expensive desk. He looked immaculate as always, but his body language wasn't as business-like or as confident as the last time we'd met in the same office. He looked at me, but not directly into my eyes, as if he were trying to avoid any look of disgust or pity I might throw in his direction. But as far as I was concerned, his assault on me (because clearly that is what it would have been described as if the matter had gone to court) in his Rolls Royce was ancient history to me. Finished and done with.

We had a cup of coffee and chatted about the Pacemakers' tour and he went through a shortlist of groups he was considering as supports for Gerry. But he didn't include The Midniters on that list. Was he building up to it? Out of fairness, I thought it was time to put my cards on the table. 'Brian, me and The Midniters have fallen out. We're breaking up.'

He put his cup down and flashed me an insincere smile. 'Yes, I'd heard.'

He already knew the group was splitting! Fuck! Bad news certainly gets around quick, especially among showbusiness people. I continued, 'But it's no problem because there's another group who want me to join them. They're great lads, very talented. You should come and see us when we've rehearsed together a few times.'

He just stared at his empty cup and said, 'Freddie, you've been all around the houses for the last ten minutes. So, tell me the bottom line. What is it you want?'

He knew exactly what I wanted, but the cruel bastard was sticking the knife in me and twisting the fucker. He was playing the power game with me.

'OK, Brian, the bottom line is, I would love to appear on the Gerry And The Pacemakers tour with my new band. A fifteen-minute spot on the tour would be perfect for us. What do you say?'

He looked me right in the eye for the first time and I could see his lips forming a faint smile. Was he happy to be able to put me on the show or just gloating that I wouldn't be on it?

At least ten seconds went by before he said 'No!' and from the triumphant expression on his face, you'd have thought he'd just won a world championship fight. He must have been getting his rocks off, talking down to me as if I was nothing. My mind was racing and my stomach was churning.

I tried another tack, hoping to rescue the situation. 'If you don't want to take a chance on my new group, let me do a solo spot! You sometimes have a band on these tours to back people, don't you? I can sing with anyone, me!'

Brian looked me in the eye again. 'Freddie. You're not doing the tour.'

I didn't say it to his face, because I didn't want to give him the satisfaction, but I knew that he'd turned me down for the tour because I'd turned *him* down a couple of nights before. Had I allowed him to seduce me, I would have been on the tour. No doubt about that. The whole situation was very unfair, because Epstein knew I was desperate for work and that whatever new band I'd be joining would have been as good as, if not better than, any of the shortlisted names he'd mentioned to me. But in reality, he wasn't that worried about the support acts. He knew the show would do well with Gerry And The Pacemakers headlining. All he cared about was satisfying his predatory cravings. And slamming doors in the faces of the boys who wouldn't give in to them. From the amused look on his face I was under the impression that if I'd offered there and then to unzip him and suck his cock while he sat at his desk, he might change his mind and put me on the tour. Fuck him! There are some things in showbusiness can make your skin crawl.

I could feel the anger building up inside me and, at the risk of completely ruining any future I had in pop music I said, 'I understand what's going on here, Brian. I know why you've done this. So I'm going to leave quietly now without losing my temper.' I made my way to his office door and opened it. 'Just before I go, would you do something for me?'

He looked at me as if I was a piece of dog dirt.

'What?'

'Go and fuck yourself! Then go and fuck Gerry Marsden And The Pacemakers and if you can still manage it, go and fuck John, Paul, George and fucking Ringo! Goodbye!' and I left, slamming the door behind me and walked out into the street, not knowing what the hell I was going to do next.

Brian Epstein was found dead in his flat in Belgravia, London on 27 August 1967. He was taking the tranquilliser Carbitrol and had overdosed. I didn't send a wreath to his funeral.

Epstein wasn't the only Big Cheese in the music business who tried to get his end away with me. Joe Meek, that tortured genius of a record producer whose composition 'Telstar' gave The Tornados a Number 1 single in Britain and America in the autumn of 1962, produced the Freddie Starr And The Midniters debut single 'Who Told You' in 1963, which was written by Geoff Goddard (with 'Peter Gunn Locomotion' on the B-side for any music anoraks out there). And it was *my* B-side that Joe Meek was after. As with Brian Epstein, the facts about Meek's homosexuality only came out after his death, which coincidentally also occurred in 1967. On the morning of 3 February, plagued by paranoia, insecurity and mounting debts, Joe Meek killed his landlady, Mrs Violet Shenton, with a single-barrelled shotgun before reloading, pulling the trigger and blowing his own head off.

Committing suicide is one thing. But taking another human being with you, especially a harmless middle-aged lady, when you go is unforgivable. You've got to be a pretty fucked-up individual to do that. Joe was an innovator, a genius at creating new sounds for the 1960s. But he was convinced his house was bugged by 'them', people from other major record companies, trying to steal his secrets.

Joe didn't have what could be called a 'normal' recording studio. He produced his hit records and many more that failed, in his house, a three-storey flat at 304 Holloway Road, North London. He'd have cables and wires all over the house, with a drummer in the living room, two guitarists in the kitchen and the vocalist and his microphone in the bathroom.

Unorthodox, yes, but it worked. The Midniters, with yours truly, recorded another single produced by Joe Meek, which didn't do well chart-wise called 'It's Shaking Time', which was released in November 1963 and I recorded a solo single for

Joe that no one remembers called 'Never Cry On Someone's Shoulder'/'Just Keep on Dreaming', a double B-side which escaped in October 1964.

This being the time when homosexuality was illegal, like a lot of gay men, Joe would go 'cottaging', a quaint description for the sordid practice of picking up men in public lavatories and having sex with them. That wasn't an anti-gay statement. It would be equally as sordid if straight men tried to pick up women in public lavatories for sex.

Being a famous producer, with Top Ten hits under his belt, hundreds of groups wanted to make records with Meek. This meant that his house would be full of slim young men in tight jeans either making records or just hanging around waiting their turn. Joe must have thought his ship had come in! But when it came to trying it on with me, he hit the rocks.

A singer called Dave Adams, who was a good friend of Joe Meek, saw me and The Midniters at Streatham Ice Rink – playing not skating. They had groups playing while people skated around the rink or fell flat on their arses. Anyway, Dave thought we were great and arranged for us to audition for Joe. Joe liked us (although I didn't know exactly how much he liked me, initially) and according to the publicity stuff he put out about us, he thought, 'Freddie is one of the most talented artistes I've ever worked with. He's going to be a big star because he's got that extra something!' Yeah, and he was after it!

Joe didn't seem to have much of a sense of humour. If the recording session was going on too long, I'd get bored and drop my trousers while I was singing. Joe would go ape-shit that I wasn't taking things seriously. Then there was the time he thought something was wrong with the microphones because he couldn't hear my vocal. He was downstairs at his controls and couldn't figure out why no sound was coming through from me, two storeys up. Again he went nuts when he found out the reason he couldn't hear me. I just wasn't singing! I was just mouthing the words. I should have known better I suppose, but I enjoyed a giggle at his expense. He had a very soft-spoken West Country accent and when he got angry it sounded funny to me.

He had loads of spare rooms in his house and if a recording session went on until the early hours, he'd let group members crash out on beds and sofas. After one late session, about one o'clock in the morning he said, 'Go and get your head down in there, Freddie,' pointing at a bedroom door. 'I'll bring you a cup of tea in the morning.'

Now I didn't know he was gay then, I just thought he was a little eccentric, and none of the other lads around the house who knew of his sexual preferences, or even suspected his leanings, had the common courtesy to tip me the wink that he might try to wink my tip! So the fact that there was no lock on the inside of the bedroom door didn't set off any alarm bells. A soft-spoken man I hardly knew had invited me to sleep in his spare bed with the promise of a cup of tea in the morning. What was wrong with that?

Yes, yes, I *know!* Look if you're so bastard clever, why didn't *you* warn me?

I got undressed, slipped under the sheets and switched the bedside lamp off. I was exhausted and soon fell asleep. I was rudely awakened by something hard sticking in my back. I thought someone was pointing a gun at me. But it didn't feel like cold metal. It felt warm. And from the way it was moving along my back, alive!

A hand touched my bare arse. What the fu . . .! I jumped up, switched on the lamp and looked down to see Joe Meek, naked as the day he was born, laying in bed next to me.

He smiled and threw back the sheets to reveal his very excited-looking, blue-veined member. (That's his prick, in case any of you weren't sure.) It had been his big stiffie and his probing hand that had woken me up! I leapt out of bed and said, 'What the fucking hell d'you think you're doing, you great poof? Fuck off for fuck's sake!' It wasn't very eloquent, admittedly, but I wanted to make it clear to him that I preferred girls.

Joe just lay there, smiling. 'Come on, Freddie,' he said in his Gloucestershire burr, 'let's have a bit of fun!' He may have been Meek by name but he certainly wasn't meek by nature. I'd just caught him trying to give me one up the jacksy and he didn't look the least bit embarrassed.

'Fun? For fuck's sake, Joe, I'm not a fucking queer!'

That's right. I used the word 'queer'. In 1963 we hadn't heard of political correctness, but at that moment, at 304 Holloway Road, I didn't think it was socially acceptable for a strange man to get into my bed with the intention of sticking his knob somewhere that was used exclusively for one-way traffic.

Joe looked as if he was making himself comfortable in my bed, which really pissed me off. 'I'm warning you, Joe. Fuck off out of the room now, or I'll beat seven kids of shit out of you!'

Joe shrugged, got out of bed and left the room, stark naked, his knob still very much erect. He didn't even say 'Good night!' He was in too much of a hurry. There were another half a dozen musicians, at least, asleep in the house that night, so I assumed he was taking his hard-on from room to room, in the hope that someone might relieve him of it.

In the absence of a lock, I propped a wooden chair up against the bedroom door just in case Joe thought about trying again.

By the way. The bastard never did bring me a cup of tea in the morning.

The next day we started recording about ten o'clock and carried on well into the evening as he endeavoured to produce that special Meek sound he thought the major record labels wanted to steal from him. Neither he nor I mentioned what had happened during the night. Despite his faults and tantrums, you couldn't help but like the old poofter. While I was recording my songs at Holloway Road, it was impossible for me to forget that he was the man who wrote and produced 'Telstar', his first massive success which sold millions of records worldwide. He never tried to come on to anyone while he was producing them. He was always 'Mr Professional' when he was tweaking knobs in his recording studio. Stop that sniggering! If you want any cheap 'knob tweaking' jokes, you can make your own up.

Joe Meek was buried in his home town of Newent, Gloucestershire. I hope he found the peace in the next world that he failed to find in this one.

CHAPTER SEVEN

After being rejected by Brian Epstein for the Gerry And The Pacemakers tour, I bummed around Liverpool doing all sorts of jobs to earn a few quid. I wasn't afraid to try my hand at anything. One of Betty's brothers, George, owned a scrapyard full of wrecked cars and I worked there for six months, dismantling the old bangers. By the time I left the job, I was shit-hot at taking a car engine apart. A skill I never had any further use for. But you never know . . .

The 1950s was a time when people didn't really care what they had to do, as long as it put food on the table. Sometimes this would mean crossing the line between right and wrong. When I was fifteen or sixteen I used to hang around with a gang of older boys, five in number, and whatever they got up to, I'd string along, trying my best not to reveal I was crapping myself that a copper might come along and nick us. On one memorable occasion, as the junior member of their gang, I got roped in when these bigger, but definitely not brighter, lads thought it was time they moved on from petty theft to safe-cracking. They must have sat through too many black and white British crime movies as they spent a month choosing which building they were going to break into and several more weeks planning the method of entry, the precise amount of explosives it would take to blow the safe open and what the two escape routes would be. There was always a second escape route.

Being a good few years younger than my partners in crime, I thought they knew what they were doing. As they crouched over the table, planning and discussing jemmies and detonators, they sounded like professionals who had planned for every contingency. On the night, the five of us broke into the building easily enough (no, I'm not going to reveal *which* building, even forty-odd years later) and the explosives 'expert' went about his work. As we kneeled in front of a massive steel safe, which was illuminated by our torches, I whispered to one of the lads, 'That seems a lot of explosives just to open a safe. Does he know what he's doing?'

Without turning around, the safe-cracker said, 'Of course I know what I'm doing, you little toe rag. Just keep those torches on me and shut the fuck up!'

Criminals and their bad language, honestly!

He took a couple of blankets from a hold-all and started placing them around the safe. That started me off. 'Are you going to blow that safe or sing it to sleep?' It was partly nerves and partly the fact the situations seemed a little bit ridiculous, that made me say it. It actually felt like we were in a British B-movie, all trying to look tough.

Mr Safecracker finished his work and told us to hide around the corner as, although the explosion would be quite small, we didn't want to be standing over the safe when the door flew open. So we hid around the corner, about 20 feet from the safe, he set off the explosives and then ran over to hide with us.

I don't know what I expected, but it wasn't the enormous 'BANNGGG!' that followed. I am talking ear-splittingy L.O.U.D.!

I thought the whole roof was going to collapse as chunks of plaster and dust fell from the ceiling. There was smoke and the smell of burning everywhere and the safe door hadn't just flown open – it had flown *off* and landed at the other end of the room.

We ran over to look inside the safe, conscious of the fact the explosion would have been heard for miles around and we only had a minute at most to grab the money. There were thousands of pounds in the safe, alright, maybe three or four thousand, a fortune then. But it wouldn't do us any good because, thanks to our 'expert', the explosion was so fierce it had set light to the fivers and tenners. The largest pile of money any of us had ever seen in our lives was going up in flames. Our dreams of wealth literally turning to ashes.

Well, it struck me as bloody hilarious, all that effort for bugger-all return. I started laughing, which annoyed the other lads, especially the safe cracker. One of them started hitting me and telling me to shut up, but I couldn't stop. I was doubled-up but they couldn't see the funny side. Still peeing myself at what had happened, I ran outside, taking one of our escape routes. As I made my way home, a couple of fire engines, sirens blasting, were travelling in the opposite direction, heading towards the damaged building I'd just left. Before I went into my house, I made sure there wasn't a speck of plaster or dust on my clothes or my hair. It was unlikely I'd be accused of being part of a safe-cracking gang, however incompetent they'd been, but I didn't want there to be any evidence connecting me to the explosion. The fact we'd come away with nothing wasn't important. The fact we'd probably caused thousands of pounds' worth of damage, and given the insurance companies a headache, was.

I was much better as a young singer than I was as a would-be criminal. Just over a year after I'd left The Midniters, I still wasn't performing with one particular group on a regular basis and one night I happened to be walking past a club in Liverpool. I remember it was wintertime and bloody freezing. I happened to know the doorman of the club and started chatting to him. He said, 'Why don't you come in out of the cold, Freddie?' I asked him which group was playing that night and he said The Delmonts, whom I'd met while I was working in Hamburg. So I took up the doorman's offer and went upstairs into the warmth of the nightclub.

The Delmonts were already on stage and one of them spotted me and asked me up on stage to sing a couple of numbers. The crowd liked the sound we made together so they asked me to join them. Just like that, as one of my favourite comedians used to say. The money I earned from gigging with them kept the wolf from the door. Betty liked to make sure all my stage clothes were freshly pressed and laundered and even made cufflinks out of button for me. She really was a great girl, except when she made sandwiches with meat straight from the freezer! She didn't seem to realise there had to be a period in which you allowed it to defrost and more than once I'd be sat in the house with friends eating sandwiches and I'd suddenly bite down on a lump of ice in between the slices of bread. Hardly something that would get mentioned in a divorce court, I know, but it showed her naive, unsophisticated side.

Me, the fellah who once took a malicious dump inside someone's guitar, calling my wife unsophisticated!

The other members of The Delmonts were Alan, Kevin and Kevin's brother Terry who usually drove the van, which was a horrible green colour and full of great big holes which let in icy drafts of wind when it went any faster than 20 miles an hour.

We played dance halls, working men's clubs, rock venues . . . anywhere. One night, I was singing on stage in front of a packed dance floor and I thought, 'When this song ends, I'm going to do a couple of impressions. And if the kids like it, I'll keep them in the act.' I had no idea how the other Delmonts would react.

I'd been listening to an album by Sammy Davis Junior in which he said something along the lines of 'You know, it seems to me that a lot of movie actors want to be singers and a lot of singers would just love to be movie actors! Let's see how Marlon Brando shapes up as a singer!' and he'd go into a perfect singing impression of Brando or John Wayne or whoever, tackling a standard. So with that idea in my head and not being 100 per cent sure what I was doing, before the next number I said, 'Ladies and gentlemen, I went to see a Vincent Price horror film last night and as I watched it, I couldn't help thinking, how would Vincent sing "Tutti Frutti"? So let's find out, shall we?' and I nodded to the group to start playing Little Richard's 'Tutti Frutti', which was the next song on our list. They didn't have to play it any differently, but they looked slightly pissed off, even though I was singing it in my normal key, using Vincent Price's voice. I got the feeling straight away that the other Delmonts didn't like me doing anything different from our nightly repertoire. Anything that would single me out from the rest of the group. I've always been able to pick up 'vibes' from people, and on the whole they were always right.

I finished that song and because I sensed the audience had liked what I'd just done, I kept the fun going by cracking a couple of jokes. Then I went into a spot-on impression of Elvis, singing, as I remember it, 'All Shook Up'. When I finished, the kids in the audience gave me a great round of applause. I felt fantastic, but didn't milk it too much, and to keep the group happy, carried on the rest of the set as normal. I'd always done impressions, like Jerry Lewis and Bogart and James Cagney, but not with a group. Even though The Delmonts weren't impressed with my humour, I thought it would be good for me to build on that first night's 'experiment', so I went out and bought a flat cap and the next night we played, I performed a rock 'n' roll song as Norman Wisdom, who was huge at the time. If he had a new film on release, there'd always be a queue outside the cinema waiting to get in. So his popularity, coupled with the fact that I knew I could do an accurate impression of him, gave me the confidence that the audience would enjoy it. And they did. Another big round of applause when I finished the song. I did a Tommy Cooper impression and one or two others and the kids stopped dancing and started coming towards the stage, laughing at my take-offs and gags as they tried to get a closer look at me.

I hadn't told the boys about the flat cap, I'd kept in inside my jacket. So they were as surprised as the audience, but gave me a different reaction. I could hear them muttering behind me, 'What does he think he's doing?' Kevin in particular disliked my impressions and wasn't very keen on me either me. It didn't take long for me to understand he didn't like anyone to take the limelight from him. But although he could sing and play, he couldn't do impressions. So I really couldn't let someone with such a negative attitude worry me.

He was happy to be like all the other groups around, but I had the feeling that if we injected more comedy into the act, we would become sufficiently different and have the comedy/music market to ourselves in Liverpool.

It didn't take long for someone to give me advice about what to do next. A club-owner named George Block had booked us a few times and had watched the audience reaction to my comedy. One night after a show, while The Delmonts were taking their gear out to the van, George beckoned me into his office.

'Freddie,' he said, 'you're a talented boy and the audiences are warming to you. I could see that tonight. But you won't get anywhere without some guidance. Go and see a guy I know who can help you. He manages lots of good acts. His name's Mike Hughes.'

I said, 'Thanks, George, but I won't bother. See, what I really want to be is a disc-jockey. Any vacancies?' He was trying to help me get on as a performer and I was telling him I wanted to be a disc jockey!

George shook his head. 'You'll be wasting your time and your talent if all you do is play records for a living. Go and have a word with Mike Hughes. What harm can a friendly little chat do you?'

I spoke to The Delmonts about George's advice but they weren't interested in having a manager. Kevin said, 'What do we need a manager for? We're doing alright as we are.'

We were doing alright on one level, but we just played the same tunes in the same clubs in rotation. But they obviously loved the rut they couldn't see they were stuck in. Despite all the aggravation I was getting from Kevin, something inside me, another one of my 'feelings' told me that everything would work out for the good and I just had to be patient. So we carried on playing the clubs, carried on travelling around in an old van and carried on arguing. It wasn't a case of 'bolshie' Freddie having ego problems. Just let me explain the sort of thing that went on and then decide who was being a pain in the arse. Kevin's brother Terry did some of the driving and whenever he took us to or brought us from a gig, he would get a little bit of extra dosh out of our fee. We'd all divvy up for him. Fair enough. But whenever I drove us to gigs and dropped everyone off at various points around Liverpool in the early hours of the morning, did the lads offer me a little bit of extra dosh? Did they bollocks.

It wasn't that I especially did the driving just to earn a couple of quid extra, although I could always do with it – it was the principle of the matter. Why was it when Terry drove, he got paid, but when I did, they wouldn't offer me a penny more? It was never mentioned by them and I wouldn't ask for the extra money.

I used to bite my tongue all the time. I didn't want to come across as antagonistic. That might sound strange, not to say untruthful, to anyone who's seen me on stage or on TV during the last thirty years, I'm sure I've always come across as supremely confident. That confidence only comes with experience.

People in and out of the business may have heard that I've thrown the odd tantrum or two or had a stand-up row with a TV director or a producer when I wasn't happy with the way rehearsals were going or if I thought the material they expected me to perform was sub-standard. Which is fine. I found out that you have to raise your voice once in a while, otherwise you get deafened by the egos of lesser talented people. But sometimes I wish I had a videotape that I could show people of some of the humiliating experiences I went through in those early days, before I became a household name. Like the many miserable nights I shared a dressing room with The Delmonts. In those days I let too many people shit on me. Then one day I wiped it from out of my eyes and decided there was no point holding back what I felt inside.

What was the worst that could happen? The Delmonts might sack me. So what?

I was out there every night fronting the group, helping to make us money and they were too mean, too hateful to pay me for driving. When Terry drove I was supposed to smile and hand over my money to him. We had a gig at a venue 85 miles from Liverpool one night and I drove us there. That's a long way to travel in a battered old van. I can't remember where the gig was. I do remember how knackered I was when we arrived and when we'd set up our equipment on stage and went into the dressing room to get changed I came out with it. 'Look lads, is there any chance of me being paid a few quid for driving us here tonight? Whenever Terry drives, he gets paid. Why not me?'

Well, you'd have thought I'd called them all a bunch of ponces. They went berserk, especially Kevin. He really laid into me verbally. To be honest, it was him who always stirred the shit. Terry was an OK sort of bloke, but sadly he had an arsehole for a brother. Alan was a very kind man and compassionate too. But both he and Terry always seemed to do what Kevin wanted.

The row cleared the air for a while and we carried on playing the clubs and dance halls. I didn't let up asking them to consider getting a manager and they finally relented and agreed it would be worth having one meeting with Mike Hughes just so we could see if he was the sort of fellah we could trust. We phoned his office in the famous Liver Building, but we found out it wasn't that easy to set up a meeting. He had to see what we were like in front of an audience first and if he liked us, *then* he'd consider seeing us. So we gave his secretary a list of dates and said Mr Hughes was welcome to come along to any of them to see us working. As it turned out Mike couldn't come to see us, so he sent an assistant down to a club we were playing. The assistant reported favourably back to Mike the next day and told him he could see we had potential. Within a couple of days we received a letter telling us we were signed to the Mike Hughes Organisation, even though we hadn't actually met Mr Hughes.

Some agents and managers are no better than licensed pickpockets. At that time it was common for them to take 25 percent of your earnings as their commission. A quarter of your earnings! Which isn't chicken feed. Mike worked differently. He put us on a sliding-scale contract. If we didn't earn much, neither did he. Once our money started going up, he started earning more commission.

But Mike Hughes was like the Scarlet Pimpernel, a dark mysterious figure who lived in the shadows, and just when you think you'd get to see him, he'd vanish in a thick cloud of smoke. Or a big black taxi. We never saw him! For a time we were convinced he didn't even exist. We'd get letters signed by him and phone calls supposedly from him, but we never met face to face. Ricky McCabe, Mike's right-hand man, was brilliant at fending off enquiries about him and it would always be Ricky who came to see us playing at night. I used to say to him, 'Why doesn't Mike Hughes ever come to see us playing or want to meet us in his office?'

Ricky would say, 'You know how busy Mike is' and change the subject.

I suppose Mike could well have been busy. We knew he looked after lots of artistes, like the great Freddie 'Parrot Face' Davies (now acting in films and TV); Ken Goodwin and Mike

Burton who went on to become two of Granada Television's *Comedians*; Mike Newman (who appeared in hundreds of editions of the game and variety show *3–2–1* which still keep turning up on certain satellite and digital channels); and Johnny Ball, who was a stand-up comedian then, years before he started hosting those excellent science shows for children on television.

We started building quite a reputation for blending comedy with music and gathered momentum, through word of mouth. People would say, 'You want to go and see The Delmonts. They've got this fellah with them called Freddie Starr . . .!' and everywhere we went the audiences loved the music and especially my comedy impressions. Which drove Kevin up the wall with jealousy, even though he must have realised that if we'd just stayed a normal pop band, it was hardly likely we'd be so busy or have someone like Mike Hughes interested in managing us.

We did eventually get to meet Mike Hughes at the Liver Building and the act retained The Delmonts' name for about a year after we'd been with him. Then I got a phone call from Ricky asking me to call around to see Mike at his office the following morning, without the other boys in the group. Mike was a very soft-spoken, shy man who, I thought, didn't like confrontations or having to crack the whip with his acts. Did he want to fire me? I couldn't understand why he didn't want to see the other boys at the same time he saw me.

I walked into his office and he said, 'Freddie, I've had an idea. I think it would be better for business if you change the name of the act!'

'I agree,' I said. 'Why don't we call ourselves The New Beatles. We could make a fortune!'

'I was thinking you should change it to Freddie Starr And The Delmonts. What do you think of that?'

I knew what the other lads would say. No chance! 'Why don't you ask the rest of the group?' I said.

'I'm asking you,' he said. 'What do you think? After all, it's *you* people are coming to see. You and your comedy act.'

I didn't even know I had a comedy act! I was just pissing about on stage in a Tommy Cooper fez and Norman Wisdom cap.

I told Mike that a decision about changing the group's name had to be discussed with the boys. Why hadn't he asked us all into his office and then suggested the name change? Now it was me who was going to create the hornets' nest.

I went back to the boys and told them about Mike's suggestion that we change our name. I stressed that it wasn't my idea, and that if Mike thought it was better for business and we started earning more money as a consequence it had to be good for al of us. What I was thinking, but didn't dare say to the lads, although they may have thought it too, is that Mike was looking to the long term. He knew that at some point groups eventually broke up and if the name 'Freddie Starr' was already linked to comedy, it would be easier to get me started as a solo act.

So what did they think about being rechristened 'Freddie Starr And The Delmonts'?

They hated the idea, and who hated it the most? That's right. Pain in the rectum Kevin. I could have bet money on what he'd come out with first and I'd have won.

'Who the hell do you think you are?' He spat the words out at me.

Was he deaf or stupid? I'd explained to them all clearly and word for word what Mike had said. It wasn't what Freddie Starr wanted. It was an idea from our manager. But all they could see was the green mist of jealousy and they called me a big-headed bastard etc. All the usual insults. They found it easier to shoot the messenger than go up to the Liver Building and confront the man whose idea it had been.

I didn't want to cause any more friction than there already was between us. When it's just four fellahs sharing a van, a stage or a dressing room day after day, it's hard not to get on each others' nerves. When you've got a Kevin among you too, you'd better watch out!

Mike Hughes had obviously made his mind up that we were going to be Freddie Starr And The Delomonts because a couple of days after he'd called me into his office, we'd turn up at venues and the group's new name was already on the posters. He'd already printed them and sent them out to the promoters! So it wouldn't have mattered if the lads had refused the name change. Mike Hughes had decided and that was that! We were now Freddie Starr And The Delmonts and Kevin wouldn't let me forget it, constantly trying to rile me with niggling comments and insults. He was always saying, 'It was you who wanted the name changed', and I'd say, 'Oh piss off. It was Mike's idea. If you don't believe me go and ask him yourself.'

And Kevin would come back with, 'He's bound to say it was his idea, *now*, isn't he? Just to keep the peace. But I know it was your idea originally.'

And we'd go round and round in circles. Can you imagine how boring and annoying this would be night after night? Seeing my name featured so prominently on the posters really got up the boys' noses, mainly because 'FREDDIE STARR' was printed twice as big as 'And The Delmonts'. The resentment between all four of us was simmering away like a volcano waiting to erupt.

We were playing at a working men's club one evening and Kevin walked in to the dressing room, made straight for the full-length mirror and started combing his hair. I was sat on the sofa behind him and when he saw my reflection he said, 'What are you doing sat there? Get off your arse and get those amps in!'

'I tell you what, you prick,' I said. 'Instead of poncing about in front of the mirror combing your hair, why don't you pull your finger out of your arse and bring the fucking amps in yourself . . . twat!'

Kevin turned around and gave me what he thought was a menacing look, but which in reality gave him the appearance of a man suffering with advanced piles. He'd always thought he was a bit of a hard case, but he would have been useless in a fight, far too concerned about getting his face marked. I'd always let him think he was a tough guy because it made for a quiet life. He kept up the stare and now he looked like he had constipation and piles. I'd taken enough of his shit. Besides I'd hung around with real hard men and he didn't frighten or intimidate me one bit.

So I just laughed at him, which made him even angrier. He said, 'It's not fucking funny. I'm going to smash your head in!'

'Kev, don't even think you can take me on,' I said quietly, without any anger in my voice. 'There's no way you're going to smash my head in. You can try if you like. I wish you would. But you'll never do it, believe me! Now go and get the amps in yourself.'

I'd learned a lot from B***** about handling an angry man. Besides I could have made a phone call and half a dozen of Liverpool's hardest bastards would have been round to tear Kevin apart. But that wasn't my way. I was quite capable of sorting out a loudmouth like Kevin myself. He was so dull he thought I was chickening out of a fight so he kept goading me. He really was a prat.

'I'm telling you again,' he barked. 'Get those amps in!'

'I'm not going to bring the amps in, Kevin,' I said. 'I've driven the van here and I'll be driving it home tonight. You won't pay me any extra for doing that, but when your brother Terry drove it he had another twenty quid in his hand. That's something that's never been sorted despite all the times I've mentioned it. And one more thing. Take another look at the poster outside. It says "Freddie Starr And The Delmonts". I'm not proud of getting top billing over you, but that's life. I'm Freddie Starr, you're a Delmont. So you can get the bloody amps in!'

He just stood there in his 'tough guy with piles and constipation' stance. Alan and Terry walked in and could see we were having an argument.

'What's going on with you two again?' Alan said.

I told him what had started the row off, but they seemed to side with Kevin as usual.

'Kevin does fuck all because he's too preoccupied with looking at himself in the mirror,' I said. 'And you two don't have the backbone to stand up to him. I'm telling you now, all this has got to stop because I am not putting up with the way he talks to me. Let's face it, I'm the one out front. The one they've come to see to do the impressions and the jokes. Yes, I can see by your faces you don't like it, but that's the truth and you know it.' I was off and running now and wouldn't let any of them get a word in.

'I'd let you all try to do what I do, but you'd be pissing useless at it, because none of you have got a funny bone in your body. Not one of you. Which really sticks in your throats, doesn't it. Look, if you think Freddie's getting too big-headed, then I'm quite willing to let you go out in front tonight, all of you, one at a time. You can borrow my props and you've all heard my jokes and impressions enough times you could do them in your sleep. I'll just sing in the background. How do you fancy that?'

They all looked at each other. Maybe one of them was going to say something, but I didn't give them the chance.

'And by the way, Terry, you used to get twenty quid a week extra for driving, but when I do it I get fuck all. Is that fair, Terry? Eh? Not one of you bastards has slipped a fiver in my hands and said, "Thanks for bringing the amps and instruments in the van tonight, Fred." Not one of you!'

At that stage of The Delmonts' history, the van was only used to carry our gear and me. The others had cars, Kevin having bought himself an MG sports car which he drove around with the top down in all weathers to impress the girls.

'You've all got motors and I drive the shitty old van and I'm always the first to get to the gigs. By the time you turn up, half the gear is on the stage, put there by me. So here's what's going to happen. From now on, you three bring the gear in, or I'll fuck off out of the group and we'll see if The Delmonts without Freddie Starr can pack out every fucking club for miles around.'

They all started to crowd around me. It was an epidemic! Now I was looking at *three* men with piles and constipation!

'Boys,' I said, 'don't start on me because I am *fucking mental* and if you get me going I'll have each of you on the floor. Now back off!'

They all thought about it for a second and quietly backed away.

The gig that night went off without a hitch, I got big laughs and lots of applause and the audience had no idea how fraught the atmosphere was between us.

The very next morning I went out and bought myself a white mini from a garage in Birkenhead. The garage had a little bit of work to do on it and said they'd have the car ready to pick up at two o'clock So I walked home, where I'd left the old green van the night before and drove it over to Terry's house, parked it outside and when his wife came to his front door, I handed her the keys to the van and said, 'Would you please give these keys to Terry?' and caught a bus back to Birkenhead and picked up my new mini. Two nights later I turned up at our next gig in my new car. I hoped it would give them the clear message that the days of me driving the old green van to gigs and humping amps on stage were over. That was one major argument settled.

Almost a year to the day after Mike Hughes had told me about the group's name change, I had another call to go and see him.

'What is it this time, Mike?' I joked. 'Am I having a pay rise and a Christmas bonus?'

'You're not far wrong there, Freddie,' he said. 'I've been watching your progress and you're getting better every time I see you perform. You've all been splitting your money evenly between the four of you since you started with me. I think it's time you should be on more money than the rest of them.'

'Now hang on a minute!' I said. 'I'm not going to tell them that. I told you about all the shit I got off them when I told them we were changing our name. How the hell are they going to react if I tell them I'm going to be earning more than them? Mike, I don't want any more money. It'll only cause more problems between us.'

'Freddie,' he said. 'You're having more money and *I'm* not going to tell The Delmonts. *You* are!'

CHAPTER EIGHT

I didn't tell the lads straight away. How could I? There was already enough tension between us when we'd meet at a gig or when we rehearsed. I wish Mike Hughes could have seen what was going on, he might have been able to sort them out. Give them a pep talk along the lines of 'all work together with Freddie or piss off!'

He wasn't there on the nights when, for example, we'd be in a big dressing room and I sat on my own at one end of the room and they sat at the other end, reading their papers or just ignoring me. If we had a cup of coffee at a transport cafe they'd always try to sit as far away from me as possible. And not because I wasn't using the right deodorant. They were enjoying totally excluding me from their little circle, until we went out on stage. Three months had gone by before I told them that Mike Hughes thought I deserved more money than them.

We were very popular around this time, 1966, 1967, and we were out playing five or six nights a week. I was quite content with the money I was earning as a professional singer and didn't want more cash. It sounds daft I know, because we can always do with a few quid extra, but even if Mike had put me on an extra hundred notes a week, it wouldn't have been worth all the hassle I'd have to go through. Despite the problems I was having with the others, being an entertainer was much better than working in a scrapyard or cleaning the paint off oil drums with acid.

Out of the blue Mike arranged for us to fly out to Bahrain to entertain the troops. We went down great. Not in the plane . . . on stage. While I was out there I bought 200 duty-free cigarettes. We were playing a club and these cigarettes were, I thought, tucked safely away in my bag which I'd left in our locked dressing room. When I came off stage I was going to meet some friends of mine, so I went into the dressing to get the cigarettes and they weren't in my bag. The Delmonts came in to get changed and I said, 'Who's taken my cigarettes? I had 200 cigarettes in here!' Alan, Terry and Kevin all looked down at their shoes and I could see Kevin had his usual smirk on his face.

'What the fuck are you smirking about, you twat?' I said.

'I wasn't smirking and we haven't touched your cigarettes!' Kevin said.

He wasn't very convincing. Terry and Alan looked sheepish.

'Kevin, do you think it's really possible for someone other than us to come into a locked room and have the luck to only open one bag . . . mine . . . and see 200 cigarettes inside it? That's bollocks! You think it's funny stealing someone's property, don't you? Well, let me tell you something that might just take that smirk off your face. Mike Hughes told me months ago that *he* felt I should be earning more money than you. I didn't think so at the time, but I fucking well do now!'

All three of them visibly tensed when they heard this. They'd hated me for months, but now I wouldn't have been surprised if they'd tried to kill me. Kevin gave me his musician-with-piles stare, so I picked up a heavy glass ashtray and held it above my head.

'Come on then you arseholes. You've been waiting for this haven't you? You've been dying to take a pop at me. Come on and do your worst. It'll just show you up for the unprofessional bunch of tosspots you are!'

'You're lying again,' Kevin said. 'I bet you asked Mike for more money and he just agreed with you.'

I could easily have smashed the thick, glass ashtray into his angry little face. He wouldn't have been so eager to look in the mirror then.

'You're totally wrong as usual, Kevin. Check with Mike. Phone him at the office now. He'll still be there. Fucking phone him and he'll tell you exactly what he told me. But whether you phone him or not, this is the last time you three try and threaten me and I'm not going to be ridiculed, isolated and ex-communicated by you because you're jealous of me. The way you treat me is disgusting.'

They were standing there, still trying to look menacing. I continued, 'And there's a good reason why you should start treating me like a human being for once. I'll bet you one hundred quid in readies that if the compère of this club went out on stage tonight and announced that Freddie Starr wouldn't be appearing because of illness, there'd be a roomful of disappointed people out there. But if he told them that Freddie Starr's backing group couldn't make it and Freddie would be using another band, they wouldn't give a flying fuck. And that would apply to any club we play. That's the truth of the matter. That's why you're all eaten up by jealousy. Because I'm very good at what I do. It's taken me years to learn how to be funny on stage and it's paying off because people are coming to see me. Me, not you fuckers. I could book any group to back me and I guarantee they'd have more enthusiasm, more commitment than you lazy idle bastards. Call yourselves musicians? I've got more musical talent in one of my farts than you have in your whole bodies. Just remember, with me we can go places. Without me, you lot are going fucking nowhere!' and just in case they hadn't got the message, I threw the glass ashtray over Kevin's head and it smashed against the wall.

A week later, The Delmonts requested a meeting with Mike Hughes to have it all out with him about my wages rise. Why they hadn't arranged to meet him months before, I have no idea. That shows you how dull they were. Anyone with a bit of something about them would have set up a meeting with him as soon as the group's name changed. They explained their grievances to Mike and, from what he told me later, this is what he said to them in his soft-spoken but blunt manner.

'Freddie Starr fronts the group. The audiences like Freddie and without him, lads, frankly you wouldn't be working. You certainly wouldn't be with the Mike Hughes Organisation.' I did say he was blunt. 'I can pick up that phone and get him another four-piece backing group within ten minutes, so count yourselves lucky that you're working with a guy like Freddie – who, incidentally, didn't want to change the name of the act when I suggested it and didn't want more money than you when I suggested it. Am I making myself clear?'

They all realised they'd just shot themselves in their big toes by setting up such a confrontational meeting with Mike and by doing so they'd completely run out of ammunition. They must have come across as a bunch of whining, complaining, whingers, which is precisely what they were. Mike gave them the ultimatum: either that they behaved themselves or they were history. But while Mike had them in the office, he had more to say. 'You've got a summer season to do in Rhyl as Freddie Starr And The Delmonts. Every day of the season you will treat Freddie as a human being. You won't pick on him, try to humiliate him or be jealous of his success. If you do, I will know within a minute of it happening and it won't be because Freddie snitched on you. I have people working for me who keep their eyes and ears open. Any trouble and The Delmonts will be out on the street. Your contract is entirely separate from Freddie's and I can tear it up any time. I can tear it up now if you like,' and he reached into a desk drawer.

They almost shat themselves. They hated me but they didn't want to miss out on a long lucrative summer season and told Mike they'd tow the line.

Mike had one more thing to say. The final knockout punch. 'After you finish your season in Rhyl, Freddie Starr And The Delmonts, as an act, will cease to exist. Freddie will be going solo and you can if you wish continue to perform under your current name. It's irrelevant to me because I shall not be representing you. Goodbye.'

And they shuffled out of his office.

Freddie Starr And The Delmonts were a very popular act at that time. We even went on ITV's hugely popular talent show *Opportunity Knocks*, hosted by Hughie Green. He came to see us in a club in Manchester and we hoped he'd like us enough to offer us a spot on the show. In that unmistakably rich, mid-Atlantic accent that impressionists have imitated for years, he said, 'Yes, boys, I like your act tremendously! I'm going to give you a three-minute spot on the show and the rest is up to the Great British viewing public!'

We were going to be on TV and be seen in 18 million homes! Consistently, *Opportunity Knocks* was, despite what some critics thought, one of the biggest shows on television and ran for many years. The 1960s and 1970s were a golden age for TV variety shows, whether they were showcases for up-and-coming performers, like *Opp Knocks*, *New Faces* and *Search for a Star* (I even hosted a very popular talent show myself for the BBC in the 1980s called *Freddie Starr's Showcase* from the massive Harrogate Centre), or big Saturday night shows featuring star names. *Opp Knocks* came back in the 1980s with Bob Monkhouse hosting, as *Bob Says Opportunity Knocks* and revived again a couple of years later with Les Dawson as the host, which was ironic because Les, as a struggling young comic, had appeared on the series when Hughie was in charge!

Any act that went on *Opp Knocks* had to have a 'sponsor', someone who knew you and thought you could do with a break on TV. The sponsor's brief chat to Hughie before you performed provided a short interval between acts and allowed Hughie Green to come out with terrible gags and raise his famous eyebrows to the camera occasionally. Our sponsor was another one of Mike Hughes's acts, Freddie Davies, by that time an established performer with lots of TV and stage appearances under his belt.

We performed well and at the end of the show, when we waited for the audience reaction, the famous hi-tech, state of the art, top of the range 'Clap-o-meter' (a strip of cardboard manipulated by a man off-camera) gave us the highest audience applause. We then had to wait for the viewers' votes to arrive to see if we were coming back the following Monday. Hughie had this way of talking to the viewers as if they were all deaf, senile 120-year-old maiden aunts living in Eastbourne. He'd say things like, 'If you want to vote for the Ukrainian Over-60 Women's Tractor Juggling and Bull Wrestling Troupe, and you can't spell their name, just write "Ugly Bearded Women" on your card and we'll know who you mean! And remember, it's your vote that counts!'

When the cards came into Thames Television that week, we were the viewers' favourites and we went back on the next show. In fact we won for six weeks on the trot, which gave us fantastic exposure, helping us to get lots of gigs, including summer seasons. We might well have won a further six appearances on *Opp Knocks* but the series came to an end. One of the great things that happened to us, as a result of winning the show six times, was being invited to play in Canada, at Expo 67 in front of thousands of Canadian teenagers. What an experience. We were doing well and if the other lads had had any common sense they wouldn't have tried to give our golden goose a right stuffing.

We got a summer season at Blackpool from appearing on *Opp Knocks* and at the time Betty was pregnant. We'd been married about eight years and I can't remember if the birth was planned or not but we were both delighted when we found out. But we started drifting apart soon after, which can easily happen when you're away from home night after night and weekends when most couples can relax together or socialise with friends. A long summer season like the one we were doing in Blackpool (I think it was for eighteen weeks) can drive a huge wedge through a relationship. When Betty went into the hospital in Liverpool to have the baby, I was on the phone to the maternity ward all the time, anxious to find out what was happening and how Betty was doing. This went on a for a couple of days and then, sod's law, I forgot to ring one evening, between shows and went straight to bed after we'd finished. Two shows a night can be knackering. Next morning I got up late and made my way to the payphone in our digs, to phone the hospital. As I ran down the stairs, one of the Delmonts said, 'Did you get the message?'

I said, 'What message?'

'Someone phoned from the hospital. One of Betty's relatives. She had a baby boy last night. Congratulations!'

What was going on? Why hadn't anyone had the courtesy to phone me and speak to *me*, the baby's father, instead of just leaving a message? She must have had the baby while I was on stage. Christ! Why had I forgotten to phone her? I got into my car and drove over to Liverpool. When I arrived at her ward, a nurse stopped me at the door. 'Mr Starr. Your wife doesn't want to see you. I'm sorry.' I could understand why she was annoyed with me for not phoning the night before, but not why she wouldn't she see me, or let me see our son, whom we later christened Carl. I drove back to Blackpool crying my eyes out.

We often appeared in clubs on the same bill as acts who had achieved success in the pop charts some years before and

Left My mother and stepfather with my daughter, Donna

Left Freddie Starr And The Midniters. Girls screamed wherever we played. So we put our trousers back on.

Freddie Starr &
The Midniters

Top left What a smoothie Prince Philip was. He said to Tina, 'Your palace or mine?'

Bottom left Las Vegas – and my name in lights!

Right Here I am with my son Jody on stage …

Below … and with my daughter Donna on horse-back

Above Here I am with Donna, Sandy, and my great mate Russ

Left The great day when Miinnehoma won the '94 Grand National – with trainer Martin Pipe

Right Tommy Cooper's magic was comical. And his comedy magical

Above Before I met Mr Faith, I didn't know him from Adam

Left Oliver Reed – what a man! Even when he baked cakes at home, he used hell-raising flour!

Above I threw soup, melon and prawn cocktail all over Antony Worrall Thompson. And that was just for starters!

Left And this was my special Master class

Below Bouncy Elvis. He may not have had a wooder heart but he did have a rubber bum

Above Bruno being Frank with me

Below Magic moments: with Engelbert Humperdinck, Jerry Lewis and Sammy Davis Jr

Above Muhammed Ali and me on Parkinson. The conversation didn't stop all night – Michael couldn't get a word in!

Right With Tom Jones. He sings 'It's Not Unusual'; I've seen it and it is!

were no longer packing out theatres. Such a performer was Karl Denver, whose Karl Denver Trio had four Top Ten hits between 1961 and 1962, including 'Wimoweh' which got as high as Number 4. But by 1967 he was on the cabaret circuit, no doubt still earning good money, but no longer the big name he'd once been.

I'd seen him on TV loads of times and he had a face that, shall we say, was easily recognisable, so when I saw him backstage at the club, I walked over to him, put out my hand and said politely, 'Hello, Mr Denver. My name's Freddie Starr' and with absolutely no expression on his face, he looked me in the eye and spat on my stage jacket! A great big ball of spittle dripped down my front! And he just walked right past me. I was flabbergasted. Karl Denver, once top of the pops, was now a twat of the first order! He wasn't going to get away with it. Remember, you start something with me, my friend, and you'll get it twice as hard!

I guessed he would be heading for a drink in the bar, so I sneaked into his dressing room, picked up his acoustic guitar and began to take out my revenge on the horrible bastard. No. I didn't do *that* again! How disgusting do you think I am?

I proceeded to detune his guitar and the guitars belonging to the two other members of his Trio. All true musicians, the three of them stayed at the bar until the very last second before they were due to perform and then dashed on stage with guitars which they hadn't bothered to check for tuning. As soon as they played their first chords, it sounded bloody awful. A cacophony of three out of tune guitars while they were trying to sing along! What a noise! I was standing at the back laughing. Karl Denver stopped the act and said, trying to make a joke of it, 'I know who did this to us. It's that Freddie Starr!' but he wouldn't say why I'd done it.

The audience couldn't tell he was actually furious with me, because he had one of those faces that made him look permanently pissed-off. He managed to keep talking to the audience as all three of them tuned their guitars and they eventually started the act again.

Even when all the guitars were properly tuned he still sounded crap to me.

That final summer season in Rhyl with The Delmonts was one of the most miserable experiences of my life. Not that there was anything wrong with Rhyl itself. When the weather's good it's still a delightful holiday resort. We were doing the business at the theatre at night and relaxing – separately – during the day. But The Delmonts couldn't resist pulling the odd trick on me, despite what Mike Hughes had told them.

Every Monday morning I used to drive to Blackpool from Liverpool with my clothes all cleaned for the week, including several crisply ironed shirts. I used to hang them up in our dressing room ready for each performance and when I'd worn them, I would put them in my bag to take home on Saturday night. Betty would wash and iron them and I'd start all over again. Well, after a couple of weeks, some of these shirts of mine started to disappear. I'd go out and buy new ones and the odd one of those would mysteriously vanish too. And we didn't have any magicians on the bill. No, I knew exactly what was happening. The Delmonts were up to their old tricks. But I only had a couple of months left with them and decided to swallow my pride and just get on with the work I was paid to do.

Before the season ended, though, Mike Hughes phoned us with some bad news, not necessarily for The Delmonts, but definitely for me. He wanted us to fulfil some club engagements which wouldn't take more than a month. So we were going to have to put up with each other for a while longer. I had no reason to tell them, because we were going our separate ways soon, but I had already been in touch with a club pianist I knew named Brian and asked him if he could write out some arrangements for me as solo performer. I've always liked to be prepared and if Mike had any gigs lined up for as soon as I left The Delmonts, I wanted to appear completely professional and have my own 'dots' – as musical arrangements are referred to in my business.

'What do you want me to do for you exactly?' Brian said.

'I'm going to be doing comedy impressions of Cliff Richard, Elvis, Ray Charles, Adam Faith and other pop stars,' I said. 'Here's a list of the songs I do. Can you write me some arrangements?'

He studied the list and said, 'I could write you out some dots for piano, bass and drums? Would that be enough for cabaret work?'

'That'd be brilliant,' I replied.

He told me how much he wanted and I agreed his fee. In just over a week I owned a folder full of pristine musical arrangements. Enough for an entire act, whenever it was needed.

That last month with The Delmonts seemed endless. The gigs were great and the audiences fabulous, but all the rest was crap. I wasn't the only one preparing in advance of our split. The Delmonts were learning some new songs and wanted to play a couple on stage before I came out to do the impressions. Which I agreed to.

Well, those two songs soon became four. And when they eventually finished, the audience would be getting restless, wondering where I was. They'd announce me without any build-up or enthusiasm and I'd run on to the stage and say, 'Good evening, ladies and gentlemen, my name's Freddie Starr!' (because it is!) and get into the comedy, quick.

By the end of that month, The Delmonts were doing half an hour on their own before they brought me out. Kevin would eventually say in a bored voice, 'Here's Freddie Starr!' and actually spit on the floor as he mentioned my name. He did it so regularly I used to wonder if he was related to Karl Denver. The audience didn't like him spitting, never sure if he was joking or not. I'd walk out and try to lighten the situation by pulling faces at him and saying, 'Thank you for that warm, if wet and sticky, welcome, Kevin!' I'd look him up and down, turn to the crowd and say, 'Just look at him. Multi-talented . . . sophisticated . . . urbane! Just three of the many words he can't spell!'

He hated me having a pop at him, but he'd been behaving like a prat, so what was I going to do in those final weeks we were together? Let him get away with it? No, that's not my style. I'd wind him up by saying to the audience, 'He's not in a good mood tonight. I didn't kiss him good morning when we woke up together. I was so annoyed with him. He kept pulling the sheets off me all night!' The crowd loved me having a go at him. I said, 'Don't worry about Kev treating me so nastily, like that. He's actually suffering from a medical condition that makes him spit whenever he hears my name. I believe it's called "jealousy"!' And the crowd would laugh, Kevin would pretend to be amused and I'd start my act.

Kevin was definitely jealous of me and I really couldn't understand it. He wasn't a comedian. He wasn't even much of a singer. He couldn't have cracked jokes and done impressions. So what was his problem? Jealousy among performers is such a negative emotion. Yes, I can understand how, say, two world-class opera singers with exactly the same range could be jealous of each other if one of them becomes more famous or sells more concert tickets. That's two performers of equal standing and talent. But Kevin being jealous of me makes about as much sense as me being jealous of Elton John. He does what he does on stage and I do what I do. I think Kevin was a frustrated pop singer. He would rather have had solo success than stayed with a band and when he saw how I was developing with my comedy, he must have known that I'd be leaving at some point. But he had no one telling him how talented he was and how he could pursue his own career.

In the final few days of our uneasy relationship, we played a club in Middlesbrough. Kevin and the others were playing their thirty minutes of songs and the crowd started shouting, 'Where's Freddie Starr? Where's Freddie Starr?' and Kevin would try and placate them by saying, 'He'll be out in a minute!', hating the fact that the crowd were waiting for me to appear. Especially when they got tired of just listening to The Delmonts and started booing them. The time came when he had to say, 'Here's Freddie Starr,' which he followed by spitting on the stage.

He really was stupid beyond belief, doing that in front of several hundred people who were waiting to see me! They turned on him instantly, shouting, 'Get off, you bum! Get off!' I walked on and they cheered me, which took the heat off smirk-features Kevin for a while. But this time I wasn't just going to crack a few jokes about him.

I said to the audience, 'You can obviously see the difficulties I've had to put up with during the last year. But they've come to an end tonight!'

I turned to The Delmonts and said, 'You can all go now. Thank you lads!' They didn't understand what was happening. I'd never dismissed them like that before. They weren't sure whether I really wanted them to go. I looked at them as if they were thick as shit and said, 'Boys, are you deaf or what? I just asked you to leave. That means I want you all to go . . . a . . . way!' So they put down their instruments and drumsticks and left the stage.

What they didn't know was, I'd had a meeting that afternoon with the club's resident trio of piano, bass and drums and shown them my 'dots'. I asked if I could go through it with them, we rehearsed for an hour, and I'd asked them if they'd play for me that evening. I saw them standing by the stage and asked them to come up and join me. The audience, while still good-natured, was a little unsettled by what was happening.

'Don't worry,' I said, 'I will be entertaining you tonight, but without The Delmonts. These three gentlemen . . .' I turned around to see the trio standing and sitting by their instruments, '. . . have kindly offered to help me out. Is that all right with you?' The audience gave me another cheer and I saw The Delmonts standing against the wall at the side of the club, arms folded, looking like they'd been slapped by a wet trout.

They were shocked I'd been organised enough to pay for my own arrangements and had the balls to go out on stage and try the act out without their backing. In the afternoon, rehearsing with the trio, one of them said, 'I can't understand how you stuck with those bastards so long.'

'It was bloody difficult,' I said. 'But that's it. After tonight they can do what they want to do and I'll do things my way. I've got a chance to move on, with your help.'

They were a fantastic help to me that night. They played like demons, and knew exactly when they should allow the audience laughter to fade slightly before they moved on to the next musical segment. We'd only had one afternoon's rehearsal but it worked beautifully. I tore through my act and at the end the audience were cheering and whistling and stamping their feet, shouting, 'Freddie! Freddie! Freddie Starr!' like a football crowd. Then they started with 'Freddie Starr! You're a star! Freddie Starr! You're a star!' I filled up with emotion. All those nights doing my impressions with The Delmonts paid off. I'd learned the craft of making an audience laugh. I still had a long way to go, but there was no doubt I could do it. The proof was right in front of me. The crowd didn't want me to go. 'Freddie! Freddie! Freddie Starr!'

What a night! And The Delmonts were there to see it.

I was 29 then and professionally I was in good shape. Mike Hughes, sensibly, didn't give me any of that 'You're going to be bigger than Elvis' bollocks. He knew better than to try that with me. Besides, I had a lifesize cardboard cutout of Elvis in my front room so I knew exactly how tall he was . . . and I would never be bigger than him! Mike started getting me dates in clubs that brought in regular work and every time I got an audience laughing, I had gained a little bit more experience.

But at home, things couldn't have been worse. I was bringing in good money and Betty was at home looking after little Carl, but we began drifting apart. I was out all the time, working and meeting new people and having new experiences and she would be at home all the time. She could have organised a baby sitter occasionally and come to one of my shows, but she didn't seem that interested. We drifted apart, she started seeing someone else and eventually we got divorced after twelve years of marriage.

I've always found it hard to express my emotions, even to the people closest to me. Betty might have thought I was being cool towards her, but I wasn't. I know I wasn't the perfect husband during our twelve years together (not that I think the perfect husband or wife actually exist – and who would want to be married to them? It would drive you bonkers!) but I did love Betty.

If you ever get to read this book, Betty, I would like to thank you for the years we shared together and for our son, Carl. I still think of you both and would love it if we could all get together to talk. I know in my heart why you found someone else. He gave you what I couldn't. Time. I was too wrapped up in my work, trying hard to get my career off and running and I neglected you. It was something I had to do and I achieved it eventually, at the cost of our relationship. What happened was nobody's fault and I even forgive you for the stories you sold to the newspapers. You and I know they were untrue, but I've got no hard feelings about it after thirty years.

I wish you all the happiness in the world.

Marriages suffer in showbusiness. It's hard to find the right balance between work and family when you're offered tours and long seasons and weeks in a television studio, all far away from home. Success in showbusiness can give you a weird, off-kilter outlook on life If you *can* make it to the top, then these terrible personal sacrifices can make you think, 'Well, I have no wife and my children won't speak to me. But I *do* have an eighteen week season in Cromer! So things aren't that bad!'

It's even worse for the people who stay on the lower rungs of the business for their entire career. The support acts who will never be stars. Now most of the summer seasons are gone, I don't even know if there are many support acts any more. But in the 1970s, there'd be two or three summer shows in each big resort, with maybe five or six lesser names supporting the star. Some support acts become very bitter because they realise that they'll never become household names. They don't look at what they do in a positive way. They don't think, 'If I'm good at what I do and don't act like a prick, trying to outshine the star of the show, I'll always make a good living and not have to endure life under a microscope like a celebrity has to.'

They may be talented, but they lack that extra something that makes someone a headliner – including that little bit of luck we all need. Some support acts don't even realise they are support acts. They think they're stars-in-waiting and walk around being complete pricks.

In 1977 I was in summer season in Margate, in Kent, as top of the bill. There was a stage hand called George with the show, a lovely old guy who must have been over seventy and had been at the theatre a few years. George and the other members of the stage crew used to have a quick fag on the side of the stage sometimes. Several weeks into the run of the show a young singer, let's call him Danny Pratt, ran past George, who was standing having a smoke, and accidentally bumped into him. It was Pratt's fault, but he had a real go at George for no reason other than he probably enjoyed frightening an old man. George apologised, though he needn't have, and Pratt ignored him and said 'You shouldn't have been smoking on the side of the stage! It's dangerous!'

So suddenly he's a Health and Safety Officer as well as a not-so-hot singer!

Danny then realised that he'd torn the sleeve of his jacket on something and went ape-shit, blaming the old man for that too! I'd just got to the theatre for the first house and could hear this conversation, although Danny couldn't see me.

George had been a tailor in his younger years and he offered to repair Pratt's sleeve. He tried to examine the tear, but Pratt pulled his arm away and told the old chap to go and fuck himself, running back upstairs to his dressing room in a filthy temper. I gave him a couple of minutes then followed him up. My stomach was churning.

His door wasn't locked and I pushed it open. He looked at me and said, 'Ah! The star of the show! Come to see little old me! I am honoured!'

'Danny,' I said, 'I heard you talking to that old man just now and I think you're a nasty, evil little bully!'

'Fuck off. What's it got to do with you?'

'Don't concern yourself what has and hasn't got to do with me. And by the way, how long have you been in show business? Three minutes? If a support act wants to get on, he does not tell the star of the show to "fuck off". There are only a few basic rules in this game and that's one of them. But you're so stupid you wouldn't be aware of that. What a waste!'

'What . . . what's a waste?'

'You . . . having a head as big as that, with fuck . . . all in it!'

He was a tough guy with old men in their seventies but he didn't look very hard to me. I took out a ten-pence coin, and did what my Dad had done that day on the building site with that other bully, Rowdy. I threw the coin at him and he caught it.

What is it about my family wanting to teach bullies a lesson?

'What's this for?' he said, looking at the coin in his hand.

'It's a gift from me to you. To phone for an ambulance. You'll need one when I've finished with you!'

He threw the coin on the floor. 'I've got four brothers who are real hard cases. Touch me and they'll fucking have you!'

'I'll deal with your brothers when the time comes. Right now, you have to be taught not to push little old men around!'

He threw a punch at me, trying to catch me by surprise. I moved my head to the left and the punch hit the air. I came up with a right that made hard and heavy contact with his jaw. Oh shit! I'd broken it. No one can sing with a broken jaw. He'd be out of the show. What a pity! An ambulance was called and he went off in it to the hospital. I didn't mean to break his jaw. I meant to break his bastard *face!* No, I only wanted to give him a bit of pain. But I didn't know my own strength. I hope something good came out of the episode and he thought twice about bullying old people again.

Margate wasn't a bad season for me, once Danny Pratt was safely tucked up in his hospital bed, but I had many other summer seasons that were much more fun.

In 1970 I had a fantastic time at the Opera House, Blackpool with the Irish vocal trio The Bachelors, made up of brothers Con and Dec Cluskey and John Stokes. They'd had loads of big hits in the 1960s like 'Ramona' and 'I Wouldn't Trade You For The World' and although they no longer had records in the Top Twenty, they were always turning up on television and were still a huge draw as a live act that audiences loved to come out and see.

It was a big show with eight or nine acts on the bill, plus twelve dancers and a sixteen-piece orchestra! Our dressing room doors were always open and depending on what your tipple was, people would wander in and have beer or a cup of tea with you between houses or during the intermissions. It was a very happy atmosphere.

It didn't take us long to start playing harmless little tricks on each other. I used to stand in the wings and watch The

Bachelors every night so I knew exactly how long their act lasted. One night after they'd started their first number, I dashed up to their dressing room and took out every item of furniture, chairs, dressing tables etc., plus their carpet and curtains. I put it all in my dressing room along the corridor. I waited until after we did the big finale with everyone on stage, and walked upstairs with them to their dressing room.

As they opened the door I said, 'See you later' and pretended to go to my room. Instead I hung about outside to hear and see their reaction to a completely bare room.

'Well, I thought it was our dressing room, but it can't be!' I could hear, and 'It looked just like our dressing room door. We must have been too busy talking to Freddie and came into the wrong room' and they came out and saw me standing there.

'Anything wrong?' I asked innocently.

'I know it sounds daft,' Con Clusky said, 'but someone's stolen everything from our dressing room. There's nothing left, look!' and he opened the door and showed me their bare room.

I looked suitably shocked and said, 'Well, I've heard of things being nicked from a dressing room but this takes the biscuit! Let's go and have a word with the manager and see what he has to say about security in this place.'

I took the boys down to the manager, who was in on the joke and while we were talking, I'd arranged for a couple of the stage crew to take all The Bachelors' furniture out of my room, and put it back in theirs, putting everything back as it was. Having got the signal from a member of the crew that the boys' room was back to normal, the manager said, 'Well, let's go and have a look at this mysterious room of yours then.' We all trooped upstairs and Dec opened the door of their room to show the manager what had happened. He peered in, looked at me and the boys still standing in the corridor and said, 'Are you taking the piss or what?'

The Bachelors didn't know what he was talking about. As soon as they walked into their room and saw everything had been returned, they all burst into laughter and turned around and looked at me.

'Freddie! It was you . . . you bastard!'

I suppose I can be sometimes.

The girl dancers in the show used to do a routine that started off with them wearing unflattering boiler suits and, to the music of 'The Stripper', they'd provocatively remove their boiler suits to reveal frilly undies, stockings and suspenders. These girls looked really sexy and knew how to undulate their bodies. They were so sexy in fact, that during the season, at least ten old men sat in the front row had a stroke. Dirty buggers!

Once they'd got rid of the boiler suits, the twelve girls would make their way to the front of the stage where twelve pairs of black high-heeled shoes stood in a row, ready for them to slip their feet into before they resumed their raunchy routine.

I couldn't resist it. After weeks of watching them, I had to do something to trick the girls. They were dancing away one night and swayed seductively down to the front of the stage where their high heeled shoes awaited. They slipped their feet inside them, went to move off . . . and they all fell arse over tit! It was chaos! Before they'd arrived I'd nailed all their shoes to the stage! The audience were in fits at the sight of these lovely showgirls sprawled all over the stage. Suspenders twanged, stockings laddered and the odd little bum was bruised. The girls saw the funny side too. I had a bollocking from the management, but it was worth it.

It was during the early September of that Blackpool season that I got a phone call from Mike Hughes that would totally change my life.

CHAPTER NINE

I was asleep when the phone rang. I had no idea what time it was. The curtains were drawn. But the rest of the furniture was real. Sorry. I just like that daft joke. The curtains *were* drawn and I could see daylight peeking through the gaps. I was so tired from the two shows I'd done the night before I thought, 'Let them phone back. It can't be important,' but it kept on ringing, so still half-asleep, I crawled out from under the sheets and picked up the phone. It was Mike Hughes at his Liverpool office. I looked at my watch. It was half-past eleven. Mike sounded very cheerful.

'You're awake then!'

'Yeah, well I am now.'

'Do you know what time it is?'

'Don't tell me you phoned just to ask me the time!'

'Always with the funny lines! Look, I want you to come over to my office today. I've got some important news for you!'

'If it's important, tell me now.'

'It's more important than that.'

'What do you mean? Christ . . . I need a cup of tea.'

'You can have a cup of tea with me. Get dressed and get over here.'

'What . . . *now?*'

'Yes. You can be here in just over an hour. I'll buy you lunch.'

'This *must* be important.'

'It is, believe me. It could affect both our futures!'

'Shit, you're not pregnant are you? You told me you were on the pill!'

'Just get dressed and be here at one o'clock.' And he put the phone down.

So I got showered and dressed and, still gasping for a cup of tea, drove sixty miles to Liverpool so Mike could tell me whatever this important news of his was, to my face. I walked into his office and he had a smile on his face that could have charmed a traffic warden. He pointed at the chair in front of his desk.

'Sit down Freddie. I've got some great news for you! You're going to be very excited!'

'We're having chocolate biscuits with our tea?'

He shook his head. 'No. Guess what it is I'm going to tell you!'

Was he pulling my leg? I'd driven sixty miles to play guessing games. 'I have no idea.'

'Well have a wild guess!'

'Mike, I haven't got a clue why I'm here. Now, unless you want the headlines in tomorrow's papers to read "Comedian dies of dehydration in his manager's office!", would you *please* ask your secretary to bring us some tea?'

He picked up the phone and called his secretary who worked in the outer office. 'Could you kindly make a pot of tea for Freddie and myself. Thanks very much. Oh . . . and are there any chocolate biscuits? You bought a new packet this morning? Marvellous. Bring two with you, there's a dear!'

He stood up and walked around the desk to where I was stood. He looked like a hyperactive little boy on Christmas morning, waiting to open his presents.

'Freddie . . . are you ready for this?'

'I don't know, Mike. What is it?'

'You . . . Freddie Starr . . . in November . . . will be appearing at the London Palladium . . . on this year's Royal Variety Performance! How about that?' His eyes twinkled and he shook my hand vigorously. You'd have thought he'd just won the pools.

After he'd given me my hand back, I shifted uneasily in my chair. Is that why I was making a round trip of 120 miles, just so he could tell me I was booked for a one-off gig? He looked absolutely delighted. I don't think I smiled or gave any sort of reaction at first. He put a hand on my shoulder.

'Well . . . what have you got to say to your genius of a manager? You're on the Royal . . . Variety . . . Performance . . . 1970!'

'That's good, isn't it?'

He looked crushed. 'Is that all you've got to say?'

'No, of course not,' I said, 'you're a bit mean with your chocolate biscuits, aren't you?'

I was winding him up a little, but truthfully I hadn't found his 'great news' that great. The Royal Variety didn't mean that much to me.

'Freddie, the Royal is the biggest television variety show of the year. It's a show that millions watch, including everybody in the business.'

'And . . .?'

'How can you sit there saying "And . . ."? I know of at least ten British comedians who would give their eyeteeth to be on the show.'

He looked so dejected, I thought I'd better sound a bit more interested. 'So . . . what are they paying me?'

Mike looked at me as if I was a complete idiot. 'They're paying you nothing! Nobody gets paid to appear on a Royal show. It's for charity!'

Now it was worse! He'd made me drive all that way to tell me I'd be doing a show for nothing! 'How am I supposed to be excited about a show that doesn't pay me a fee for chrissake?'

'Freddie, Freddie. You're in showbusiness. You're an entertainer. All entertainers want to do the Royal. I've got it for you and now you're moaning there's no fee!'

The door was pushed open and his secretary walked in with a tea-tray. Mike took it off her and she left. As he poured me a cup he said, 'Seriously, Freddie, if you do well on the night . . . it could open up a lot of doors for you.'

I grabbed one of the two chocolate biscuits on the plate. 'Well, Mike, when those doors open, let's hope there's more than just two scabby chocolate biscuits behind them!'

Mike handed me my cup. 'Oh yes. This is important. They only need five minutes from you!'

Five minutes! What could I do in five minutes? When you're a comedian, it takes a normal audience a couple of minutes to decide whether they like you or not.

The Royal Variety audiences were notoriously frosty to unknown comedians. One or two established comics had died a death in front of them too. And they want me to impress them in five minutes!

I ate my biscuit and washed it down with a mouthful of tea. 'This means a lot to you, doesn't it Mike?'

He nodded. 'Yeah. I've never had one of my acts on a Royal before. You're going to be brilliant. I know it.'

He raised his teacup in a toast. 'Here's to *your* success on the Royal Variety . . . and any that might come *my* way in its wake!'

I liked and trusted Mike. If my appearing on the show was that important to him, I wouldn't give him cause to be disappointed. I raised my cup and we 'chinked' cups together.

'Which members of the Royal Family will be there on the night?' I asked.

'I'm not exactly sure of the complete line-up,' Mike replied. 'But the Queen Mum's going to be there, definitely. Why?' He took a big sip of tea.

'Oh, I was just wondering how many times I could say "fuck" in my act!'

He laughed and sprayed tea all over his white shirt.

The Royal Variety performance, apart from being a big event in the television calendar, produced on alternative years by the BBC and LWT, raises thousands of pounds for the home for retired performers, Brinsworth House in Twickenham, Middlesex. Over the years it has been home to entertainers who are either down on their luck, or because of age or illness are unable to look after themselves 24 hours a day.

The show is normally rehearsed all day Saturday and Sunday, with the dress rehearsal on the Monday the show is recorded. Only three days to rehearse a huge show packed with international stars from every corner of showbusiness. Ballet dancers, acrobats, pop singers, opera singers, Chinese kung-fu monks and comedians. Royals, as I've learned over the years, can be very kind or very cruel to comedians. Anyone remember that Royal Variety Show in which Mel Smith and Griff Rhys Jones dressed as stage hands in brown overalls, struggled through a terrible laugh-free sketch, which they had written? It was so ponderous, it had to be timed with a calendar.

My rehearsal at the Palladium was called for the Sunday morning and because Mike Hughes was terrified I might be late for it, he insisted that I spend the Saturday night at his house in Liverpool. He planned that we'd get up at the crack of dawn to start the four-hour drive to London and arrive at the theatre well before my call time, which I think was 11 a.m. As I went up to bed on the Saturday night, Mike had told me his mother would give me a shout around 6 a.m. and we'd leave at 6.30. 'There's no need for you to set your alarm clock, because *mum* will be your alarm clock after she's got me up!'

You could always trust Mike's mum. If she said she was going to do something, she'd do it. And she did wake me up. At half past seven! She had overslept and had woken in a panic! 'Get up, Freddie! Look at the time. I'm so sorry! I overslept and just woke Mike up. He'll be out of the bathroom in a couple of minutes and you can get ready. I'm so sorry!'

Mike's mother was a lovely lady and I always used to pull her leg about this incident in later years. I have never got washed and dressed so quickly. We threw our bags in the car and headed for the motorway. The original plan was that Mike would drive, while I relaxed in the passenger seat, to think about my act. But if we were two hours late and had to be in central London by 10.30, I knew I would have to drive.

You'll find this hard to believe, but I made the journey from Liverpool to London in under two hours. I drove like a maniac because I was determined that I would not be one minute late for the rehearsal. I put my foot down and headed south, using the hard shoulder of the motorway to overtake when necessary. It was just pure luck that I had a full tank of petrol, otherwise we might have wasted valuable time looking for a garage. Mike was hanging on for grim death. Seat belts weren't compulsory then. But speeding fines and endorsements on your licence were, so I kept an eye out for the boys in blue.

I pulled up outside the Palladium, dashed down the sloping walkway to the stage-door entrance – and Mike Hughes will corroborate this story because I realise it sounds so fantastic – at the precise moment I walked into the theatre, a voice on the tannoy said, 'Mr Freddie Starr to the stage please!' I couldn't have timed it any better. Mike handed my my stage suit, and I walked on to the stage as if I'd been waiting in the wings for my call.

Depending on your view, the Royal is either a theatre show produced for television or a television show produced in a theatre. I planted my feet on the stage where so many showbiz greats had stood and was mesmerised. I was suddenly hit by memories of watching *Sunday Night at the London Palladium* every week on our little black and white telly at home when I was growing up. All the stars whom I'd seen on the show like Bob Hope, Sophie Tucker, Bing Crosby, Norman Wisdom. And all the comedians who'd hosted the show – Jimmy Tarbuck, Bruce Forsyth, Norman Vaughan, Don Arrol.

Looking around the impossibly glamorous, red and gold auditorium, I understood why Mike Hughes had got so excited about me appearing on the show. Butterflies did little jigs inside my stomach and I had to fight to control my nerves. I looked out at the shadowy figures sat in the stalls. Television people, theatre people, performers, agents, representatives of the Brinsworth House charity and the producer, Albert Knight. He leaned forward in his plush red seat and said, 'We're going to have a band call now and we'll watch you run through your act.' The musicians in the pit below me had already been given my dots by the musical director, who had received them from Mike a few days before. These shows aren't just thrown together!

I started my act, the orchestra kicked in at the right times I needed them for the musical impressions and I thought I was doing OK, for a first run-through. When you're used to doing a 20-minute spot in a summer season, whittling it down to five minutes is hard, but I'd managed to do it and with Mike's help had gone over and over it during any spare time I'd had in Blackpool. I got to the part where I do a comedy striptease and end up as a bare-chested Mick Jagger. I was aware of some noise from the stalls and Albert Knight stood up and said, 'No! We can't allow that!' The music stopped and I went cold. This was my act. The one I'd rehearsed for weeks.

I looked down at the producer. 'What is it you can't allow, Mr Knight?'

'You can't show your bare chest to the Royal family,' he said. 'You'll have to do something else there. Carry on!'

Carry on? I felt like finding a corner and crawling into it. He had just criticised something I did in my act every night that no one took offence at. It was always one of my strongest bits of business and got big laughs. I believe it went down so well because I was the only impressionist taking-off pop stars then. All the others were still doing Arthur Askey or Cary Grant.

I did carry on with my act and when I'd finished I went down, with Mike, to have a chat with Albert Knight and his small army of assistants. After a heated discussion during which I was convinced he was going to say, 'Well, if you don't do it the way I want it, you're out of the show!' we compromised. The strip routine was back in, but I'd have to agree to wearing a vest, which would be cut in certain places to reveal small patches of my bare chest. There were also some other points about the act he wasn't happy with and he said he'd give me some notes later. As we made our way back to my dressing room I said to Mike, 'I thought you told me there was no fee for this show! That man just said he's going to give me some notes!'

Mike said, 'He didn't mean fivers or tenners. He wants to give you some "notes" about your act. Recommendations. Ideas. That sort of thing.'

As far as I was concerned, I didn't need any more ideas. I knew what was funny and that was that. This was my first encounter with television people who didn't really understand Freddie Starr and my approach to comedy or why I go down so well with 'live' audiences.

By climbing several flights of stairs, I found my dressing room. Was it high up? The lift attendant was Sherpa Tensing! According to the cardboard sign sellotaped to my dressing-room door, I was sharing with Leslie Crowther and Marty Feldman.

Mike could see I was upset with my act being messed around with, but convinced me that by the time we got to the Monday dress rehearsal everything would be fine.

On most TV shows there's usually more than one producer. There's an executive producer, an associate producer, an assistant producer etc. But on a mammoth show like a Royal Variety, there seem to be dozens of them. Each an absolute 'expert' on comedy. They'd never assume that they knew everything about juggling or singing (excuse me Miss Bassey, but that song you're closing the show with . . . we think it's awful!'), but comedy seems to be something that everyone in television wants to voice their opinions on. From the sad state of today's comedy on the box you can see where this 'comedy by committee' has got us. Stand-up gagmen are all under 35 and relegated to late-night Channel 4 and BBC2 so the jokes are all about masturbation techniques and periods. And if the first year of the twenty-first century is anything to go by, the sitcoms of the next decade will all be about pain-in-the-neck young achievers living in a flat, with drinking and shagging their favourite pastimes. For crissakes bring back Victor Meldrew, Del Boy and Basil Fawlty! And please, Galton and Simpson. Come out of retirement!

Whoops! Did Freddie go off on one again? Stick with me. There's more to come.

Dickie Hurran was another producer of that 1970 Royal Variety Show. Whether he was an executive, an associate or had just written in and said he could do it, I don't know. But I do know he was very kind and helpful to me. He took me under his wing. It sounds pathetic, but at that stage of my career, I didn't know I should have a dressing gown in my room, that I could slip into when I was sitting around, so my stage clothes wouldn't crease, and when he found out, he took me around the shops so I could buy one.

The dress rehearsal went well considering, so I thought that Albert Knight had accepted my slightly revised act. But no, there was a knock on my dressing room door just a couple of hours before the curtain was going up. A couple of Mr Knight's assistant 'comedy experts' came in to tell me that Mr Knight now wanted me to cut this line and that impression and that bit and . . . they basically cut me down to three minutes! Fuck! Why invite me on the show if they were going to undermine my act and my performance? They had me tearing my hair out! I hadn't been that nervous up until then, although Marty Feldman and Leslie Crowther were pacing around the room. Another comedy original, Marty was more established than me – he'd been a writer on that classic comedy radio series *Round the Horne* before working on TV. He went to Hollywood in the 1970s and made a lot of money and several bad films. Someone once said of him, 'Success went to his cock!'

Watching these two stars being so nervous helped me in a way. I just sat there quietly, in my new dressing gown, my stage suit hanging neatly on a hanger, as if that's what I was always used to! I calmed myself down. I knew I could be funny. I knew if luck was on my side I'd do OK. That's as much as I could hope for, that the audience would laugh a bit and that Mike Hughes, Betty and all the people supporting me in Liverpool wouldn't feel I'd let them down. I was going to ignore all the 'experts' and just go out and be myself.

There was a speaker on the wall of the dressing room that relayed the sound from the stage. I could hear the buzz of the audience during the arrival of the Queen Mother, Princess Margaret and rest of the Royal Party. Bernard Delfont would also have accompanied them into the Royal Box. I heard the National Anthem, the opening music . . . it was soon going to be me out there. Someone knocked on the door and told me to get into my suit. I'd already been to make-up. I was taken down to the wings. Peter Noone and Herman's Hermits were on before me and they were halfway through their final song. I took a deep breath. Peter finished, bowed and took his applause and came off. Max Bygraves appeared from out of the darkness (it's always pitch black, backstage at these shows – I think it's to prevent everyone seeing the fear in each others' eyes) and walked onto the stage. I took an even deeper breath. 'It's only a couple of minutes out of your life,' I thought, 'but don't waste them.'

Max might have cracked a few gags, I can't be sure. But when I heard him say, 'Ladies and gentlemen. Please welcome Freddie Starr!', the hairs on the back of my neck stood up and my stomach flipped. One more deep breath and I walked out on to the Palladium stage. There were 2,500 people sitting there waiting for me, out of which maybe ten people at the most knew who I was and what I did. I couldn't even think about the TV cameras placed around the auditorium. I was going to make at least 2,499 people laugh.

I tore into my act and the gods of comedy must have been in the theatre that night, because within thirty seconds I had the audience helpless with laughter. I ran through the gags and my impressions of Billy Fury and Adam Faith and all the others I did, finishing with the comedy striptease and my Mick Jagger take-off. Then it was all over. They'd laughed all the way through my act and when I took my bow and looked down at the audience . . . *they were on their feet applauding. I was getting a standing ovation!*

Never in my wildest dreams could I have hoped to get that sort of reaction. I had only done a few minutes of my act, and they'd loved it! My legs were shaking.

I had no idea what I was supposed to do if this happened. Dickie Hurran had mentioned to me on our shopping trip that no one had ever taken an encore at a Royal show. It wasn't allowed. The show was always so full of acts, if they all took an encore the Royal family wouldn't get home until breakfast time. I came off stage and Dickie was waiting in the wings with my dressing gown and I was just going to put it on when I heard the audience shouting, 'More! More! More!'

Max went on and said, 'That was Freddie Starr, ladies and gentlemen. Freddie Starr!' and the audience kept shouting 'More! More!' It was Max's job as compère to keep the show moving along, but the audience wouldn't listen to him. I had one arm in my dressing gown when Max looked into the wings where I was standing and said, 'Come on back, Freddie!' and I looked at Dickie Hurran who smiled, took the dressing gown from me and said, 'Go on. Take your encore!'

I felt so confused. I wanted to go out there and bask in the audience's approval, but I had been told what the protocol was and didn't want to get on the wrong side of Albert Knight. Dickie Hurran gently pushed me towards the stage and I could see Max smiling and waiting to bring me on. I walked back out there and I almost drowned in a warm, friendly sea of cheers and laughter and whistles and cries of 'More! More!'

I couldn't have planned for a reaction like that. That sort of thing only happened to unknown performers in old Hollywood films. I smiled at the audience, I even glanced discreetly at the Royal Box. Did I hear a genteel cry of 'More!' from up there too?

I knew I had to get off, otherwise the show would start over-running, so I took another polite bow, smiled and walked ... no, make that *floated* back to the wings, where Dickie Hurran said, 'Freddie. You're the first artiste in 47 years who has ever taken been allowed to take an encore!'

Bloody hell! Now I had something to talk to the Queen Mother about later, when we all lined up to meet her.

Of course when I did meet the Queen Mother afterwards, I couldn't say very much at all. The after-show party was a mad blur of faces and interviews and photographs. I felt like saying to the press boys, 'There's Andy Williams over there. And Dionne Warwick. They were on the show too!' That was my first taste of press attention. They were all over me like flies around a dung-heap. The only dung heap to have had an encore at a Royal Variety! My photo was in all the papers the next day and they called me 'an overnight sensation'. *Overnight?* Yeah, I'd gone to bed in 1960 and only come down to breakfast in November 1970.

Everyone at the party wanted to meet me and various excited-looking agents and producers and impresarios, none of whom I'd ever seen before and whose names I didn't know, put pieces of paper and business cards in my hand, asking me to phone them, saying things like 'We need to talk!' I was never very ambitious, but even I could see that all sorts of wonderful possibilities lay ahead of me. I would need Mike Hughes's assistance and advice more than ever. I might be able to earn enough money to buy his mother a new alarm clock.

Betty was thrilled for me, although she had been a bit off with me in the weeks before the show, as she wanted to be in the audience and I bluntly told her I didn't want her there. In fact I didn't want any of my family to be there, because I didn't want to have to worry about how they were or if they had a good seat or anything other than how funny I could be.

I'm a bit more relaxed about it now, but I just couldn't cope with having family members around when I was recording a TV show or had a big opening night in a theatre. A comedian has enough on his plate without having to worry about what his wife may be thinking about his performance as she sits in the stalls. Some wives and girlfriends don't understand this at first and mistake it for selfishness.

My first meeting with Mike Hughes after the Royal brought me down to earth with a hell of a bump. My earnings wouldn't be going up immediately, he told me, despite the fuss the newspapers were making about me, with headlines like 'a starr is born¼' and other obvious play on words that journalists slap themselves on the back for inventing, but be honest, if the papers were raving about you, I think *you'd* feel pretty good about it.

Mike admitted to me that despite all the confidence injections he'd been administering to me in the weeks leading up to the Royal, he had no idea how well I would go. He was right. No one could have predicted it. So to ensure I'd keep working, he'd already booked me into nightclubs for the rest of that year and the whole of 1971 at the same money I'd been on before. The contracts were all done and dusted and there was no way he could go back to them and ask for a higher fee. The 'overnight sensation' of the Royal Show was going to have to work in clubs all over Britain for the next twelve months for bugger-all money. My potential earnings would have been sky-high and I would have gone into television a lot sooner than I did. In view of my love–hate relationship with television companies and executives over the past thirty years, maybe it was fate that stopped me going into a series of my own straight away. I might have screwed things up or, more likely, been screwed. There'd be plenty of time for that to happen.

CHAPTER TEN

The first time I appeared on television regularly was in *Who Do You Do?*, a series made by London Weekend Television. It started in 1972 and ran to for five series and three specials up until the time it finished in 1976. I say 'finished', but it just won't go away. It was being repeated yet again every weekday night at seven on the Granada Plus digital channel earlier this year. I'll look forward to receiving your cheque very soon, Granada! The idea behind the show was to put together a group of impressionists who'd never worked together before and put them in a frantic collection of sketches, some only lasting twenty seconds. Here comes Tommy Cooper as a cowboy! Bang! Here comes Max Wall as a milkman. Bam! And here's John Wayne and Stanley Unwin discussing the merits of flock wallpaper. It was fast, fresh and furious and the viewers lapped it up. Although LWT kept moving it around the schedules, from Saturday night to Sunday night and even Fridays occasionally, the public stuck with us to give us some pretty impressive ratings.

I was on the first four series and that constant exposure made my name. It also gave me the opportunity to dress up in a variety of outlandish costumes. Once I was in my Tarzan loincloth or my Max Wall wig and tights ('Good . . . evening'), we'd record as many sketches as we could based around that character. The more surreal his surroundings the funnier it seemed, like Tarzan looking for work down the Job Centre or the Labour Exchange as it was then. Actually that sounds quite funny! If they didn't ever use that idea I might use it myself some day.

We had a small team of experienced comedy writers beavering away (when they weren't writing!) including Dick Vosburgh, Wally Malston and Garry Chambers and we taped an incredible number of sketches. The third series had thirteen shows. That meant a lot of material was needed. So all the impressionists would be encouraged to throw in ideas too. Barry Cryer wrote for us and also appeared as Groucho Marx from time to time, either in sketches with us or just doing the Groucho walk, waggling his cigar in unison with his eyebrows and delivering the odd one-liner.

By that time, 1972, I was able to capitalise on my TV appearances and my fees for cabaret and summer season work went up. One of the best things about being in this business is that you often find yourself on the same bill as a performer you've always admired. That can sometimes be a disappointment, but it can also be a rewarding experience. When I found out I would be appearing in summer season with the jovial piano player Mrs Mills and that topping the bill was my comedy hero Norman Wisdom, I was thrilled. Not about meeting Mrs Mills, although Glad was a lovely lady. It was Norman I was a huge fan of. I've already told you how massive he was at the cinema box office in the 1950s and 1960s. I'd go and see his films like *A Stitch in Time* and *The Bulldog Breed* at the local fleapit and be doubled-up laughing at his stunts.

So what was he going to be like? On the first day of rehearsals I expected him to burst through the door in his 'gump' suit and cap and fall over, shouting "Ere! Mr Grimsdale! *Mister Grimsdale!*' Perhaps I'd spent *too* much time at the pictures.

In breezed a dapper little man, in a beautiful suit, his hair immaculate, his manner very much that of a confident, established star. 'Hello!' he said in a very upper-class, actorish voice. 'I'm Norman Wisdom!'

I nervously shook his hand and said something like, 'It's great to meet you, Mr Wisdom. You've seen all my films!' which made him smile. He turned to his straight man, Tony Fayne and said, 'Tony! I think Freddie and I are going to get along fine!' Norman is a gentleman of the old school who has appeared in many summer seasons and long-running West End revues. If you get a chance to see Norman 'live' on one of his occasional UK tours, then grab it! His comedy timing is superb. He was, and still is, an inspiration to me and my generation of comedians. If I was a TV executive I'd give him two series a year and a Christmas special!

That was a fantastic season for me. I watched Norman rehearse and perform, rehearse and perform over and over. Norman was a perfectionist and really worked at his comedy, which impressed me. His international success in films hadn't made him big-headed and we had some wonderful dressing-room chats about comedy.

When it came to what would or wouldn't make an audience laugh, he'd approach it in an almost scientific way. He knew that if a chair was placed on stage at one particular point, whatever happened on or near that chair would get much bigger laughs than if the chair had been placed one foot over to the left or the right. How the hell do you learn these things?

It's interesting that the King of Knotty Ash, Ken Dodd, who like Norman, is another national treasure, has a different approach to comedy. You may well be aware that his 'live' shows can over-run sometimes. That isn't an exaggeration. He has been known to start a show at 8.30 in the evening and still be on stage, getting roars of laughter, at one o' clock in the morning. But what you may not know is that he often times his arrival at the theatre he's playing to coincide with the time he is due on stage. His car pulls up outside the stage door, he walks into the theatre already made-up and in his stage suit and walks straight out onto the stage. Which is not to say that Ken treats his art lightly. Doddie is an encycla ... encyclep ... eclypto ... Ken is *very* knowledgeable about comedy. He knows that what works in one area of the country may not work in another. He once famously said that he could tell a very funny joke in Birmingham and it wouldn't get a laugh in Newcastle. Why? Because they couldn't *hear* it in Newcastle!

Norman and I got on so well, we did two more summer seasons together and they were equally as much fun. Thanks Norman!

In 1974, in between series of *Who Do You Do?*, LWT gave me the chance to make my own series produced by David Bell who went on to become Controller of Entertainment at London Weekend. During the rehearsals, I had to be Controller of My Temper, because hardly any of the ideas I was given to do were funny. I wasn't at all happy about things and sensed that David didn't like me very much. The whole thing was a disaster and after two shows the series was scrapped.

Bits of both shows were stitched together like Frankenstein's monster and lumbered on to the screens as a 45 minute special entitled *Ready Freddie Starr* which they put out at 5.15 on a Saturday afternoon. That's how much faith they had in it . . . and me. But I took solace in the fact that it might not necessarily be the end of my TV career. I remembered reading somewhere that the day after Morecambe and Wise made their television debut in a now-forgotten series called *Running Wild* in 1954, one newspaper critic wrote: 'Definition of "Television": The box they buried Morecambe and Wise in!'. Less than ten years later they became Britain's favourite comedians.

Two years later, the BBC approached me to do a couple of specials for them. The producer was a man named Terry Hughes, who later became the BBC's Head of Comedy, before moving to Hollywood where he worked on the long-running sitcom *The Golden Girls* and now *The Third Rock from the Sun*. An undoubtedly talented man, but we definitely weren't on the same wavelength on what I thought was funny. At our very first production meeting I mentioned to Terry that I thought it would be funny if for a couple of sketches I dressed up as Hitler, with the cap and the moustache, but wearing shorts and wellies to make him look ridiculous. I assumed he would pass on my ideas to the writers and, in turn, to wardrobe and make-up.

I turned up for the first day's rehearsal, sat at the table next to Terry and said to the two scriptwriters (who shall remain shameless), 'So, what have you got for me to look at boys?'

They looked at me as if I were talking Japanese. 'We haven't written you anything yet. We were about to ask you what sort of stuff you wanted us to write for you.'

Did I hear them correctly? They had nothing for me to read? What the fuck were they thinking? Why had we battled through the London traffic to get to the rehearsal room at that early hour if we had no material to read through, discuss, argue about, change, tear up and rewrite?

It would have been courteous, I thought, to come along to the first day's rehearsal with a performer you hadn't written for before with *something! Anything!* Even if they'd just rewritten one of Dan Leno's old routines, it would have shown they were a bit interested at least!

One of them asked, 'What have you written that we can take a look at?' Was he taking the piss or what? Did I have a thick pile of Freddie Starr sketches, all neatly typed, laid out on the table in front of me?

'I wasn't asked to write anything,' I said. 'You are professional comedy writers, aren't you?'

They nodded.

'Yeah, well, I'll be the judge of that when I see what you've written!' I said. We obviously weren't going to be the closest of chums. 'Didn't Terry tell you about my Hitler idea?'

From the baffled looks on their faces it was obvious he hadn't.

I turned to Terry and said, 'You and me talked about ideas a week ago and you knew what I wanted the writers to do for me. But you didn't bother to tell them. What was the point of me explaining to you exactly what I was looking for, if you were going to ignore me?'

Terry shrugged and looked embarrassed. Why hadn't he spoken to the writers? If he hadn't liked my ideas, why hadn't he said so? I could have given him loads more.

I stood up and said to the writers: 'We're all wasting our time here. I am going home now and will not be back until Terry phones me and tells me you have written at least twenty sketches.' I picked up my coat and said to the producer, 'Terry, as you've got nothing to do, and this room is available all day, why don't you speak to these boys and give them the ideas I gave you seven days ago. I'll await your phone call. Goodbye!' and I walked out.

We did manage to make two 45-minute shows eventually and with the same bizarre logic when it comes to scheduling that the BBC still possesses today, one show went out in February 1976 on BBC2 and the second show went out on New Year's Eve of that same year on BBC1!

I suppose that made me a cross-channel Freddie!

I don't mind admitting that, with one or two exceptions, all through my television career I've suffered from being given inferior material. I know I'm very different from a lot of comedians because I don't just tell gags and a lot of the stuff I do is visual, but you really should see some of the crap that's been handed to me in the name of comedy over the years. Writers have jotted down a basic idea, sometimes half an idea, and handed it to me to finish off! I've always tried to do my best with the ideas they gave me, but you can't make a silk purse out of a sow's ear. However, a sow's ear can make a useful little container for crisps, cashew nuts and tortilla chips, which is ideal for those social evenings when your friends come around.

I've been in some dire comedy sketches on TV, because I wouldn't question the producers who assured me they were funny. The problem was, I never played the 'But who's the star of this show?' card, which maybe I should have. Other performers, seeing a show crumbling around them, would have demanded better material, better writers, more jokes, more sight gags. But my TV shows hardly ever captured me as I am on stage. 'Live and dangerous!'

I had loads of ideas. My head was full of so many surreal sketch ideas and gags it would have taken me months to write them all down. As the BBC didn't seem over-eager to throw more programmes in my direction, I arranged a meeting with Michael Grade, who was then the Controller of Entertainment at London Weekend Television – where I'd worked on *Ready Freddie Starr* five years before. Michael knew a lot about variety performers because he'd once been a theatrical agent and with such illustrious relatives as Leslie and Lew Grade and Bernard Delfont, I felt he would be the man to talk to. I had known him in his earlier career as a very young but enthusiastic agent and the two of us had sat around talking showbusiness many times over a coffee, so although he was now a high-powered TV executive, I wasn't intimidated by him. He eventually left LWT to run Channel 4 and during his time there the *Daily Mail* referred to him as 'The Pornographer In-Chief'.

What a load of bollocks! He must have got tired of being in charge of all that pornography, because he left Channel 4 to become Head of Pinewood Studios. What's wrong with the man? He can't settle down for five minutes!

I knew Michael was looking for Saturday night entertainment show formats and I pitched him my idea, which had as its basis a sitcom storyline about a run-down theatre, barely making a profit and run by two people who were totally useless at managing the place. In between the comedy dialogue, there'd be segments of the show supposedly on at the theatre, featuring guest spots by comedians and singers.

My title was 'Freddie Starr's Variety Madhouse'. I had no qualms putting the word 'Variety' in the title. In 1979 it was a word that TV executives still embraced and did not despise.

I had actually written out the idea in a first draft form, but when I arrived at his office high above the River Thames at the London Weekend Television building on the South Bank, he preferred me to act it all out for him. Michael waited for me to finish explaining everything and then said, 'Who do you have in mind to be on the show with you?'

'Russ Abbot, Norman Collier . . . a few others with the same sense of the absurd as me.'

'By "sense of the absurd" you mean, daft, crazy, silly, whacky, zany, maybe a little childish at times? The sort of comedy that all the family can have a good belly laugh at?'

'That's the only comedy I know.'

He sat back and said, 'I like the idea, Freddie. But it'll need a lot of work. I'll think about it and give Mike Hughes a ring in a week or two.'

True to his word, Michael began planning a brand new television series. I used to be amazed at the number of people involved in taking an idea and turning it into a TV series. Set designers, sound and lighting experts, wardrobe, make-up, cameras . . . and all that's before there's anything to point a camera at! Having set the wheels in motion, had Michael Grade also invested in a shit-hot writing team too?

Three or four months later, while the final touches were being applied to the sets and costumes at the LWT studios, I went to the first script read-through at a rehearsal room somewhere in South London. Mike Hughes had already told me I would be working with David Bell again, who was the executive producer, which annoyed me a little, but I thought, 'Five years have gone by since our last show together. Maybe he's mellowed a bit towards me.' I'll say he had. He couldn't keep his wandering hands off my arse! I knew David was gay, as were several other producers and directors at the studios.

David Bell, a tall, distinguished-looking man who had started out as a television cameraman in his native Scotland, would have been in his early forties around that time, I would have guessed. He looked like a laid-back geography teacher, his usual mode of dress being an open-necked shirt, grey flannel trousers and a green sports jacket and he'd wander the corridors of LWT with his hands deep in his pockets. Outwardly he wasn't anyone's idea of a camp TV producer. He was very well respected in the business for creating popular entertainment shows like *Blind Date* and *Live From Her Majesty's* and *The Palladium* when he was the Controller in the 1980s.

But I couldn't take to him at all. And when I repelled his advances he took a terrible revenge on me. He tried to destroy my television career .

As Michael Grade planned the series, he began to see it more as a fast-paced sketch show than a sitcom with the odd guest performer. He asked me if I minded these changes and I said 'As long as we have the comics I asked for and lots of great material, let's get on with it.' He was happy to keep my original title.

The first morning at the South London rehearsal rooms reminded me of my traumatic experience at the BBC. The material just wasn't up to scratch. The small army of writers LWT had hired gave me their stuff to read and as I went through it sheet by sheet, I just didn't find any of it funny. I mean, it's possible a Latvian stand-up yak-herder might have found it all hysterical. But sadly, we didn't have a Latvian stand-up yak-herder on the show. The only way the scripts would have made an audience laugh would be for the writers to have rolled them up, shoved them right up their arses and then set light to them. It would made me laugh anyway!

It was happening again. I wasn't being served properly by writers. This was very frightening to me because we had six

45-minute shows planned, the publicity machine was ready to roll, telling the world how funny and 'different' this new series was going to be, and I'd just discovered that the writers had given me crap material.

I looked around at Russ Abbot and Bella Emberg and the other performers around the table. They weren't too pleased either. We decided to work on the material ourselves for a couple of hours and told the writers to go and have a cup of tea. I found out quite early in my TV career that's what most comedy writers do best – drink gallons of tea in rehearsal rooms and television studios. Some of the more talented ones will reach into their battered leather hold-alls (they always seem to carry giant hold-alls packed with Christ knows what) and bring out their own biscuits. They don't think it's at all shameful to sit around drinking tea all day, muttering to each other 'What a twat that comedian is. He keeps fucking-up my best lines', because, so they tell me, they've done all the hard work at home at the typewriter or word processor.

That night and every night I sat up writing new material – lines, gags, ideas, mad ways of getting performers on and off the stage. I'd work right through the night and get to bed around 4 a.m. I'd get up at 7 a.m. and drive to the rehearsal room, hand the material to the writers and let them put it all together. I think it might well have been the first day of rehearsals that David touched my bum and smiled at me. I didn't take very much notice because people in showbiz do things like that to each other sometimes. Just like schoolkids larking about pinching each others' backsides.

But when he began touching my arse three or four times a day, it got on my nerves.

I started off being polite with him, asking him not to do it, but that didn't work. If I had gone around touching-up a girl dancer or a production secretary or, heaven forbid, Bella Emberg, I might have been accused of sexual harassment. But David would make a grab for my buttocks whenever he felt like it. I can't remember seeing him molest any of the other male performers' arses during the making of that series, so I have to assume he found me stunningly attractive. Which is understandable, I know.

When my polite but firm approach failed to work, I showed David I *really* didn't like him arsing about by turning around and saying straight to his face, 'David! Get off!' When that didn't work, 'Get off!' became 'Sod off!' which in turn became 'Piss off!', before I let rip with the usually effective 'Fuck off!' When that didn't put him off, I wrapped them all up into one big angry 'David! Pissing sod off, for fuck's sake!' but he was enjoying himself too much, playing the role he loved: the all-powerful TV boss who could do what he liked with young performers hungry for success. Having gone through my entire library of naughty words and several that Russ Abbot kindly let me borrow off him, it was obvious that the only way I could get 'Ding Dong' Bell off my back(side) would be to frighten him physically. A big confrontation was on the cards and one day when the two of us were alone in the lift, he went to grab my arse again and I punched him hard in the stomach. He clutched his middle and gasped in pain. He looked pathetic, hurt, crushed. What the hell had I done? I'd just punched the executive producer! But fuck him. He had to learn he couldn't go around touching-up young performers. When rehearsals finished that day, one of David's assistants was sent to tell me that the next day I wouldn't be needed until one o'clock, which was fine by me because it would give me more time to write new material. I didn't mention the lift incident to anyone and I'm sure David wouldn't have.

I will state that although I found Ding-Dong a nightmare to work with, there are many comedians (including some straight ones) who are grateful to him for establishing their television careers. He even resurrected Jimmy Tarbuck's TV career after seeing him reduce Michael Parkinson and his audience to tears of laughter on Parkie's chat show, giving Tarby the plum job of host of the big Sunday evening show *Live From Her Majesty's*.

The day after I'd thumped David Bell, I turned up at rehearsals at one o'clock as asked, and as I walked into the room, I could see that people were just breaking for lunch. What the hell was going on? I asked Russ Abbot what time he'd arrived and he said, 'We were all here at nine o'clock as usual. Where were you? We've got loads of stuff to rehearse!'

He looked a bit pissed-off, just as I would have been if I'd thought that a fellow performer was four hours late for no reason.

David had stitched me up. He had got his assistant to tell me to come in late. Now I looked like a lazy bugger who turned up when he felt like it. I soon put Russ and the others straight about what David had done and I was in at 9 a.m. sharp every morning after that. But David still hadn't finished with me. He was really on the warpath. Once he had been after my arse. Now he was after my career.

By now Russ, Bella, Bella Emberg and Toni Palmer were happy with the lines that the writers were giving them, but I'd still be up half the night writing down ideas.

I'd come in first thing, hand my notes to the writers and hope that they could turn them into sketches for me as Adolf, Max Wall, whoever. But what would happen was this. I'd be sat there watching Russ and Bella rehearse a sketch that I wasn't involved in and *they'd be speaking the lines I'd been up all night scribbling!* This happened every day for almost a week. I'd come in and hear my lines being delivered by the other performers. It wasn't their fault. Neither David nor the writers had told them where these new lines and sight gags were coming from. I was furious! That's . . . *fucking furious!*

I felt betrayed by television and the shits who ran it. We moved from the rehearsal room to the studio and started making the shows and I wasn't happy with any of them.

David Bell became ruder and ruder to me and apart from distributing lines I'd written for myself among the other performers, the writers had little to do with me. It became obvious to me that David was eager to feature Russ and the others much more than me – even though the show had been my idea and it was my name in the title!

My TV career was on the verge of being flushed down the lav because *one* man, whose homosexual advances I'd firmly repelled, had made that decision!

Whether you're straight, gay, a 'don't know' or a 'can't be bothered any more', you have to admit that what he was doing to me was very unfair.

One afternoon when I was rehearsing yet another poxy sketch on the studio floor, I stopped for a minute and looked right into camera 3. I'd had enough. I knew David and the director were sat in the gallery, watching me on all the TV monitors on the wall in front of them. I said, 'David Bell. I know you can hear me. I'm walking out of the studio and away from this show because for the past couple of weeks you've treated me with utter contempt and we both know why. So as far as I'm concerned, you can stick this show, this set and this fucking awful script right up your arsehole!'

As I walked off the set, I passed Russ Abbot who was standing there with his jaw still hanging down on his chest in shock at my outburst. I said, 'Russ, this is your show now,' and I left the building. The six *Freddie Starr's Variety Madhouse* shows went out in the autumn of 1979. When the show returned the following spring it was retitled *Russ Abbot's Madhouse* and ran for another five series.

David Bell died of AIDS in 1990 and as a tribute to him, LWT produced a special *Night Of One Hundred Stars* show at the London Palladium, which featured many of the performers who had worked with him. I wasn't invited to appear.

What you should bear in mind is that, by this stage in my career, the late 1970s and early 80s, when I wasn't getting stressed-out in television studios and rehearsal rooms, I was continuously working all over the country in cabaret or on theatre tours. There was a kind of stability being locked into a summer season in one resort for several months, but that still meant I was away from home almost the whole year round.

At the beginning of 1974 Betty and I started divorce proceedings. As far as I was concerned, I would never get married again, because I knew my crazy workload had ruined my first marriage. I was booked to headline a five-month summer season at the North Pier, Blackpool, from early June to the end of October. A summer season running until late autumn? Yes, and some of them still run that long in Blackpool, some until early November. Of course by then the topless sunbathers on the beach have swapped their Factor 15s for Vic Chest-rub and Deep Heat, but the place is still packed, especially at weekends.

Before a summer show opens at a resort, there's usually a couple of weeks' rehearsal in London. The principals, the dancers and the band all go through their routines in another one of those rehearsal halls scattered around London. It's the first chance that everyone gets to meet each other. That year I had a wonderful selection of support acts like Janet Brown and Paul Melba. I had a driver called John at the time and he drove me down to London from Liverpool where I was still based. I was quite excited at the prospect of a long summer season, because there was always the prospect of romance in the air with the female dancers and, after all, I was almost a totally free man again.

John dropped me off and as I walked up the steps to the rehearsal room I could hear the rehearsal pianist playing something bright and poppy and the sound of dancers bouncing up and down on the sprung floor. How was I to know as I walked into the room that I was about to meet the woman I would be spending the next eighteen years with?

CHAPTER ELEVEN

The sight that greeted me as I opened the double-doors to the rehearsal room was very familiar. It was almost June and everyone, apart from the girl dancers who wore their usual rehearsal costume of leotards and baggy sweatshirts, was dressed in jeans and T-shirts. The male choreographer stood, arms folded, watching every move the young female dancers were making, purely in a professional capacity. The producer, director, their various assistants and some of the supporting company sat around a knackered old table on uncomfortable wooden chairs that were probably bought in a job lot when the workhouses closed down. They spoke loudly to each other, trying to be heard over the combined sound of the piano and 24 pounding feet and when they spotted me they all waved and smiled. So far so good. Would we still be waving and smiling at each other at the end of the season?

The producer called a tea break and for fifteen minutes he explained how well the dance routines were coming along, (they'd already been rehearsing for a week before my presence was requested) and how funny the support acts were. As I listened to him, I took a sneaky look at the dancers who were stood around the room, chatting to each other and I could see they were all very attractive. One of them in particular stood out, a beautiful girl with dark hair, so when I went over to introduce myself to the dancers, when I came to the one I'd noticed, I couldn't help myself.

She said 'Hello! I'm Sandy Morgan,' and I went into straight into my 'cheeky bastard' mode and said, 'Hello Sandy. Can I play with your fur purse?'

For those of you who have led a sheltered life, a 'fur purse' is another word for 'pussy', which of course is another word for . . . oh don't pretend you don't know!

Instead of blushing and behaving all coy and girly at my outrageous opening line, she snapped back, 'No. I've got a boyfriend who does that!' and walked away. I thought, 'Well, that's one you won't be getting off with in Blackpool, but there's eleven more to chose from!' Because dance rehearsals are so strenuous, the girls don't usually wear make-up because, frankly, they sweat a lot and any carefully applied make-up would be ruined after seven or eight hours. But the next day when I turned up for rehearsals, I could see that Sandy had her full make-up on. I wondered if she was trying to catch my attention, but remembered she'd said she had a boyfriend, so although I couldn't help watching her (she was a fantastic dancer) I tried not to make eye contact. At the end of two weeks' bloody hard rehearsals in London, the whole team went out for a meal, except for Sandy, which I found disappointing. Why it should have bothered me I couldn't understand, because we'd hardly spoken a dozen words ('fur' and 'purse' being my poetic contributions), and the other dancers were all very pretty and bright and attentive. In particular one named Laura, who I could tell was beginning to take a fancy to me.

One of the first things I learned when I started doing long summer seasons was how to get off with a dancer. Any feminists reading this should move on a page or two.

Once the show was up and running, I'd stand in the wings every night and watch the dancers and decide which one I'd move in on first. There'd usually be three or four real stunners among them, and no really ugly ones, so it could be a tough job sometimes!

During the first week of my very first summer season without the Delmonts, I noticed the dancers would hardly speak to me on the Monday or Tuesday, but on the Wednesday night they were suddenly very interested in me and extremely friendly. I thought it was because one of the stage crew had seen me naked and had reported back to the girls that I was hung like a stallion. But another, more experienced comic on the same bill told me it was because dancers' wages were very low and by the Wednesday they were always broke. Because she wouldn't get paid until Friday, it was a mid-week ritual for a dancer to get friendly with anyone in the company she thought had a few quid in his wallet and who would be prepared to take her out to dinner. Men being men, they were always flattered by a leggy dancer's attention and would be more than happy to oblige. The question of whether the pretty girl sat across the dinner table, knocking back a bottle or two of wine, would be dropping her knickers at the end of the meal was uppermost in the performer's mind.

In one memorable season (no, I'm not going to tell you where or what year!) there were twenty dancers in the company. All of them stunners. Now, I'm not boasting. I've never been a shagger-bragger. I chose the three most attractive girls and started a rogering rota. I would take one of the dancers, I'll call her Jane, back to my digs on a Monday and Tuesday night and bonk her brains out. Another dancer, whom I'll call Wendy, would come back to my place on the Wednesday and Thursday night. And the third girl, let's call her Suzy, on the Friday and Saturday. There were some nights when one of them might not be in the mood or wasn't able to indulge in sex. They'd still come back to my place and we'd just talk or listen to music. We didn't have all-night television then. On average I was enjoying six nights of passion with three different girls. On Sundays I gave myself the day off. It was grateful for the rest and enjoyed relaxing on the sofa watching old black and white films on television. Then Monday night, I'd start all over again. My bill for condoms that summer would have paid off the national debt of a small African country.

I'd have been happy to carry on all the way through to the end of October, but it was inevitable that one of the girls, Jane, would open her mouth to two of the other girls (who had already kindly opened their mouths for me) and told them she'd been given a good seeing-to by Freddie Starr. When all three of them realised they'd opened their hearts and legs to yours truly, they were all pissed off. I wasn't married, engaged or even 'going out' with any of them. We just enjoyed having sex. But with a bizarre logic born out of jealousy, they considered I'd been unfaithful to . . . well . . . all of them and decided to have it out with me.

Wendy, Suzy and Jane came storming into my dressing room one night between shows and as they walked in, it was like one of my fantasies come to life. Three gorgeous girls, in various stages of undress, all cramped together in one small room with me! They weren't happy with they way I'd behaved and told me so. They felt used. They thought I was a male chauvinist pig.

Can a vegetarian male be a chauvinist pig? Just a thought.

They demanded an explanation. 'What the hell are you playing at? You've been taking the piss out of the three of us!' They wanted 'this'. They wanted 'that'. Let's be frank, they'd already had 'the other'!

'Girls! Please!' I said. 'Now sit down and let me explain!' I took Jane's hand and said, 'Do you or do you not enjoy my company on Monday and Tuesday nights?' She nodded. I said, 'Do you enjoy the meals and bottles of champagne I buy you?' She smiled and nodded again. 'And when you come back to my place, if you're in the mood, do you or do you not enjoy a beautiful night of passion?' She looked at Suzy and Wendy and then at me. 'Yes!' she said. I let go of her hand.

'Wendy. Suzy. Does exactly the same apply to you two?' They both nodded.

'So you all admit I look after you all? I treat you like ladies. I've never forced you into sleeping with me. If you're not in the mood you either go back to your place or we just have a cuddle in bed.'

They all had to admit that what I'd said was true. They were having a wonderful time, there was no real reason for them to be jealous of each other and if they didn't rock the boat, they'd have meals, champagne and as much sex as they could take for a few more months. I said, 'Let's meet after the show and we'll all go for a meal? What do you say?' They were all smiles by now and could see I was talking sense.

They also knew that if one of them dropped off my rogering rota, it wouldn't take me long to find a replacement. And they didn't want any 'outsider' into our exclusive little circle. As they went off to get ready for the second house, I thought, 'You got out of that one alright!' I did better than just get out of it. The girls must have had a very interesting chat after they left my room, because when they all met me after the show they were all dressed up to the nines. Each of them looked like she'd stepped off the cover of *Playboy*. I'd never seen them looking so horny.

We all went to my favourite Blackpool restaurant for a meal and while I stuck to water and Coca Cola, they knocked back the champagne. I paid the bill and as we left the restaurant I thought we'd be going our separate ways, but the girls had planned a little surprise for me. Jane and Wendy each grabbed one of my arms and with a giggling Suzy leading the way, we went back to my place, where we had a fantastic time wallpapering the back bedroom until dawn.

That's not what you wanted to read, is it?

What actually happened was, as soon as we got in my hallway, we were so hot and horny we started tearing each others clothes off and went through as many different permutations of the sex act that three females and one male could think of. We used every surface in my flat. Sofa. Armchair. Table. Floor. Ironing board. No. I made that up. But one of the girls was so perverted, she actually suggested we all tried doing it on the bed! The *bed* for crissake! What was she thinking? Even *I* have my standards!

What a night! Me and three amazingly flexible dancers. Having sex. Together.

Oh! You've never experienced anything like that? I am so sorry!

I'm telling you all this so you'll understand that by the time I started that 1974 season in Blackpool I was more than familiar with what went on between girl dancers and comedians. And singers. And ventriloquists. And acrobats. And sometimes, if he was lucky, the man operating the lights. It was Sandy to whom I was most attracted out of all the dancers but I kept my distance because she had a boyfriend. After the first couple of weeks we would see each other backstage and make small talk and out of the blue she told me that if she turned up at the theatre before a show and I wasn't in the building, she felt disappointed, but if she saw me in the wings or chatting to someone by the stage door, she felt happy. Only a short time before she had warned me off because she had a boyfriend and now she was hinting that she liked seeing me around. I found out later that she liked playing mind games.

It turned out that the house where she was staying with three other dancers was only a few miles from the place I was renting and as we got to know each other, and we were all part of the same company, I'd pop in to see her when the other girls were at home. Sandy and I were never left alone. But I often caught her glancing across the room at me when I was talking with the other girls and there was definitely something in the way she looked that made me think she might fancy me. Other times she would totally ignore me. I put this down to one thing. She'd mention that she was going to marry her boyfriend, Roger, who lived in Plymouth, the following September, which at first I took to mean that she was spoken for and wasn't interested in having a summer-season romance with me. She'd tell me what a wonderful man he was and how happy they were going to be together. Then she'd flash me one of her devastating little smiles.

Was she as confused in her feeling as I was? Why couldn't she talk to me about it? When Sandy smiled she rarely revealed her teeth. She didn't like them, because there were little gaps between them which she was very self-conscious about. They hadn't stopped her from being a photographic model and she'd proudly shown me her portfolio of photos in which she advertised various products. I didn't even notice her teeth. To me she was beautiful and I felt more and more attracted to her. Whenever she mentioned her boyfriend I didn't know what to say. I certainly felt little pangs of jealousy, but with her 'one-day hot, one-day cold' attitude to me, I didn't know what to make of her. If she hadn't mentioned Roger, then I wouldn't have hesitated to ask her out. I hadn't been that confused about a girl since I'd been a tongue-tied teenager. I was falling in love with someone who was engaged to a man she seemed to be crazy about and it was killing me inside.

One night, about a month into the run, I couldn't hold on to my feelings any more and took the risk of telling Sandy how I felt about her and how upset I was because, although my divorce from Betty would soon be through and technically I was no longer a married man, I knew it was impossible for Sandy and me to be together. She started crying and confessed she felt the same way about me. She kissed me tenderly and we held each other tight. From that moment we were inseparable.

I started buying her presents and can even remember the very first thing I bought her. Three purple table mats! Why three and not four I have no idea. I then bought her a suede trouser suit which she looked absolutely beautiful in. Because I knew she wasn't earning great money and because she was always delighted when I treated her to nice things, I bought her lots of clothes and jewellery during that season. I must have spent anywhere between seven and ten thousand pounds on her. That was in 1974 when the average national wage wasn't much more. I didn't mind. I was crazy about her and loved spending money on her. We knew that we would have to tell Roger what was going on soon, before he found out from some 'kind soul' in the company.

We had speakers on our dressing room walls through which we could hear the stage manager telling us how long we had before we were due on stage. It was also used by the stage-door keeper to let us know if there were any phone calls for us. Every day I'd hear on my speaker, 'Telephone call for Sandy Morgan! Telephone call for Sandy Morgan!' and these calls, which I assumed were from her boyfriend, seemed to be more and more frequent. Did he suspect that Sandy was being unfaithful to him?

After we'd finished work one warm August night, we left the theatre and walked along the pier together, holding hands, towards the promenade. The illuminations weren't yet switched on, but in the distance the prom was aglow with lights from bars and nightclubs and amusement arcades, and the Irish Sea lapped against the piers wooden struts beneath us. Halfway down the pier, Sandy slowly pulled me towards a bench and we sat down. She said, 'Freddie. I'm scared. What are we going to do? I love you but I still like Roger. I don't want to hurt him. I'm sure he suspects something's going on.'

'You'll have to tell him the truth,' I said. 'There's no other way.'

A day or so later, Roger phoned her and said, 'You're going out with Freddie Starr, aren't you?' How could he have suspected? He was hundreds of miles away in Plymouth. It seemed some 'kind soul' *had* snitched on us. At first, Sandy denied it but in the days and phone calls that followed, he kept the pressure up until she admitted it. Sandy came to my dressing room straight after she'd put the phone down on Roger and told me he was going to drive up to sort things out. He probably wanted to sort *me* out at the same time. What man wouldn't if he thought his wife-to-be had been seduced away from him? But our affair wasn't a case of an innocent girl falling into the lecherous clutches of an older man. Sandy and I had deep feelings for each other and if it had just been a fling, I knew she would have treated it as such and gone back to Roger.

Even though I loved Sandy, there were certain facets of her personality that concerned me. She could blow hot and cold. She could look bored or disinterested in me, then change into someone loving and attentive. Her behaviour sometimes baffled me. One morning I drove around to her rented house in my Rolls Royce, which she hadn't seen before because it had been in the garage for a service, although I had told her about it. She came to the front door, saw my car parked outside and said, 'I didn't know you owned a Rolls Royce! Why didn't you tell me?' But I had, several times! What was she talking about?

Unfortunately I was at Sandy's rented house the day that Roger arrived from Plymouth to find out answers to all the questions that must have been tearing at his guts. That's when I saw yet another side of Sandy – her temper and how quickly she could lose it. As soon as Roger walked into the house he didn't waste any time and asked Sandy to explain what the hell was going on. I thought it best to be in the room to support Sandy but didn't want to make what was already a complicated matter even more complicated by interrupting their conversation, so I sat back on the sofa and kept my mouth shut. I can't remember exactly what they said, but after a while, tears were streaming from Rogers eyes. He knew he'd lost her and it was breaking his heart. How he didn't take a knife from the kitchen and stab me I don't know. The tears had no affect on Sandy, other than to make her very annoyed with him. I do remember her saying quite bluntly, 'There's no point us talking any more. Go away and leave me alone. It's over. I don't want to see you any more!'

It was at that point I stepped in and said, 'Be a bit more gentle with Roger. You can see how upset he is.'

She suddenly turned on me in a way I'd never experienced before and almost snarled at me, 'I'm sick of telling him! Why can't he get the message?'

She was being incredibly cold towards Roger and it shocked me. By now Roger was sobbing. It was a terrible sight. He still loved her and would have done anything to have her back. The atmosphere in the room was deadly. I stood up and said, 'Look, Roger. Would you mind coming outside to my car. I think Sandy should be left alone for a minute.'

Roger, still sobbing, followed me to the car and sat in the front passenger seat next to me. We drove down to the prom and parked up. We talked for a while, well he talked and I listened while he got everything off his chest. One thing I did manage to say was, 'We both love Sandy but we can't cut her in half. One of us is going to have to say goodbye to her and move on.'

It was then that Roger started saying things about Sandy that were detrimental towards her.

I told him firmly not to speak about her that way. What had happened between Sandy and other men before I'd met her was none of my business. Roger suddenly started crying again and he looked such a defeated, broken man, I put my arm around him for a few seconds.

'I can't believe how cold she was towards me,' he said, and by now his eyes were so bloodshot I didn't think he had any tears left to shed.

I drove back to Sandy's place and dropped him off. He had planned on staying there overnight if she'd still let him. At the very least he wanted to talk to her without me being around. It must have been a Sunday because we weren't working that night. I went back to my house and tried to sleep. I wondered if the two of them would get back together and I would be the one elbowed out of the relationship. I paced the floor. I tried watching TV. My head was buzzing with pictures of the two of them embracing and forgiving each other and making plans for their wedding. Knowing Sandy's sudden change of moods from hot to freezing, anything was possible. She could have decided that Roger really was the only man she loved, that our relationship was nothing more than a short episode in her life and she was going to leave the show.

I became more and more convinced I'd never see her again. If you've ever fallen in love or been infatuated with someone, in the first stages of that relationship, when you have incredibly strong feelings for that person, a certain type of insanity takes you over. You become obsessed with them and hope your obsession is reciprocated. The more time you spend with that person, the less time you want to spend apart. There may be a scientific, biological explanation for it, but the plain fact is, love can drive you fucking nuts! Why hasn't anyone been brave enough to write a song with that title?

And that night I went through hell. Sandy had become the most important part of my life in a matter of weeks and I wanted to be with her all the time. I couldn't live without her.

What could I do to take my mind off Sandy? Who can you talk to at four o'clock in the morning when you're at your lowest? The Samaritans? They do a fantastic job. But I didn't want to tie up their lines when there might be a potential suicide trying to get through. I had some friends who were pilots at Blackpool airport, just a short car ride away. They'd be turning up for work about now, ready for the first flights of the day. I decided there was no point pacing the floor any more and that I'd drive over to the airport and have a coffee and a chat with them. When I got there I saw a pilot friend of mine called Brian who was a little surprised to see me. I didn't give him the whole story, just telling him I couldn't sleep.

'How would you like to go to Spain?' he said.

'I haven't planned where I'm going on holiday yet,' I replied. 'I'll have a break when the season's over.'

'No. How would you like to go to Spain *now*?' Brian explained he was going to fly his private jet to Madrid to pick someone up and had to bring him back to Blackpool that same day! He assured me I'd be walking down the North Pier in plenty of time for my first show at 6.10 p.m. This was perfect! Something to take my mind off my complicated love life. He didn't have to ask me twice. I jumped on board his jet and took off for Madrid.

The flight went by very quickly as we were chatting and laughing all the way. With the coffee I'd been drinking and my lack of sleep I must have been pretty hyper by then. Less than two hours later we landed in Madrid. I remember getting off the jet and having to remove my shirt because it was so hot. It was September and back home the early mornings would have been a little cool. But in Spain, wow! I wandered around for an hour, trying to forget Sandy for a little while and eventually Brian's passenger turned up, we all got on board and flew back to Blighty! I think we landed just after two o'clock in the afternoon. I thanked Brian for the unique experience and made my way back to my car. I suddenly felt tired. I'd been up 36 hours. I sat behind the steering wheel, deciding whether to drive back to my place or Sandy's. I really should have gone home and got my head down for an hour. I had two shows to do that night. What if I drove to Sandy's and Roger's car was still parked outside? Would that mean they were back together?

I had to know what was happening with Sandy and drove to her place. As I turned the corner into her road, my heart was pounding. I couldn't see Roger's car anywhere, so I pulled up outside Sandy's house. I knocked on her front door. No answer. I put two and two together. Roger's car had gone. Sandy wasn't home. Therefore the two of them must have made up, spent the night together and cleared off back to Plymouth where they were going to live happy ever after. Is it possible to live happy ever after in Plymouth? Perhaps you'd let me know.

On the other hand, it's dangerous putting two and two together when you're as crap at maths as I was. What's the expression, 'A fair heart never wins a fainting lady' or something like that? After knocking the door a couple more times and peering in through the front window, I decided I'd have one final look around the back of the house. I walked around to the back garden and there, sunbathing on the grass, in a tiny bikini, was Sandy! She must have heard me approaching because she sat up and looked in my direction. With her sunglasses on I couldn't see her eyes. Was she glad to see me or annoyed? For fuck's sake! What is it about love that screws you up so much?

She stood up and walked towards me, quickening her pace. Then she threw her arms around me and we held each other tight. A wonderful feeling of love, like a warm cloak draped around my shoulders, came over me and I prayed that she felt the same about me.

After a long, long time, still holding on tight as if we didn't want each other to be anywhere else than *there*, she whispered, 'I was so worried about you. Where have you been?'

Not thinking how weird it might sound, I told her the truth. 'I couldn't sleep so I flew over to Madrid!'

I won't tell you what her reply was.

The rest of the season went by in a blur. I woke up every morning and the first thing I thought of was Sandy and what time we'd be meeting. I felt like I'd be born again. I didn't have the slightest inclination to look at any other girl. Sandy was perfect. Well . . . she was *most* of the time, but there was something in her personality that worried me sometimes. We'd have three or four perfect days together and then she'd turn around and do something thoughtless or hurtful. One day I told her I'd booked a table at our favourite restaurant, Greensleeves, for an after-show supper and I was really looking forward to it. After the second house I showered and changed into a smart outfit and ran down the stairs to the stage door to wait for her. I know women take longer to get ready than men, but after waiting twenty minutes for her I began to wonder what the hell she was doing up there in her dressing room.

She eventually clattered down the stone stairs in her high heels, accompanied by one of the other dancers, Jane (no, not the four-in-a-bed Jane of legend) and they both looked beautiful. Sandy started to explain that she couldn't come to supper with me because she had made previous arrangements and she was going to a party with Jane. I offered to come along, but she immediately snapped at me in the same tone of voice she'd used on Roger. 'No, you can't come. You weren't invited!'

I stood back against the wall and let them both pass by without saying a word. I was disappointed with her attitude, but I wasn't going to start an argument.

I lay awake on my bed until the early hours, wondering what she was getting up to at the party and whether there was a chance I was making a fool of myself.

We didn't speak or even look at each other for another five days. Then one night I saw her standing in the wings watching another act and I stood next to her, pretending to be interested in what was happening on stage. I took a chance and touched her hand which she gently held and, feeling her positive response I slipped my arm around her waist. She turned towards me and held me tight. We had made up without a word being said. Marcel Marceau couldn't have done it any better.

But still, those strange moods of hers would come and go. We were sat on the floor at her place one night, drinking tea in front of a little gas fire – very showbiz – and she suddenly accused me of fancying another dancer in the show named Laura. I had liked the look of her right back at the beginning of the season, but since I'd been going out with Sandy, the only things I'd said to Laura were normal everyday exchanges 'Hello!' and 'Wow! Nice tits!' You thought I was being serious then, didn't you?

I denied fancying Laura but Sandy was off and running and wouldn't listen to me. She stood up and while I was still sat on the floor she kicked me in the back of the head and ran out of the house. Is that normal behaviour? Am I the right person to ask that question?

I found her hours later sat in one of the shelters along the promenade. She wouldn't come back home. She could be *really* stubborn when she wanted to. I'd almost got to the point where I was prepared to get down on my knees to beg her to come home, when she relented and we started walking back to her place, Sandy making it plain she was *not* going to hold my hand. As we walked along the deserted prom I kept asking her what the problem was.

She wasn't prepared to discuss why she'd kicked me in the head. She wasn't going to tell me whether she did or didn't love me. She had no idea what she wanted to do at the end of the season. She was doing my head in! I made sure she was safely home and as I knew there was no point in me staying with her that night, I went back to my rented house. I was a man in turmoil. My first marriage was almost over. I'd found a beautiful girl I was sure I was in love with, but I couldn't be 100 per cent sure how she felt about me. And twice nightly, I had to go out on stage and make 2,000 people laugh their socks off, six nights a week.

If you were one of the holidaymakers in Blackpool in 1974 who came up to me in the street and asked me for my autograph and I said, 'Why don't you piss off and stick that effing pen up your jacksy, prick features!', perhaps you can now understand why I was in such a crappy mood and forgive me? If you can't, I quite understand. Now why don't you piss off, prick features, and let me get on with this heartbreaking story?

We kissed and made up the next day and went out shopping together so I could buy her something new to cheer her up. But it was an uneasy relationship. Sandy's moods were as cold and unpredictable as the October winds off the Irish Sea that whipped up the sand on Blackpool beach.

A few weeks before the end of the season, I took Sandy to the cafe opposite the theatre and presented her with a jewellery box. Her face lit up and she kissed me, before opening the lid.

'I didn't just buy you a box,' I said. 'Take a look inside.'

She opened it and quickly slammed the lid shut. She looked at me with a little smile on her lips and opened the box again, this time taking out the engagement ring it contained. I took the ring from her and, placing it on her finger, I said, 'Will you marry me, Sandy?'

She leant across the table, kissed me and said, 'Yes. I love you and want to marry you.' I was overjoyed and instantly forgave her all her previous mood swings. But quite accidentally I did get my revenge on her for kicking me in the head.

That night we went to Greensleeves for a meal. We'd been going there a lot during the season and we always had a great time. I'd make her laugh by messing around with the waiters and doing daft things with the cutlery and the cork tablemats (look, it was very funny in 1974, OK?) and that particular night I picked up one of the table mats and slapped it on her head, pretending it was a hat (it *really* was hysterically funny in 1974!). Sandy screamed in pain and had tears in her eyes. As the tablemat clattered on to the floor, I realised why. Since the last time we'd eaten there they'd changed the cork mats for wooden ones! I'd whacked her on the head with a quarter-inch thick piece of wood! This was supposed to be a romantic celebration of our engagement and she was crying and rubbing her head and I was apologising and the waiters were running around looking for plasters and cold compresses and the other diners were all chattering away: 'Did you see that? Freddie Starr just whacked his girlfriend!' It was absolute chaos for ten minutes!

Sandy eventually saw the funny side of it – possibly the moment the paramedics arrived and insisted on giving her oxygen and putting her head in a splint! – and we got married in Coventry the following spring.

We moved into a flat in West Ealing, in the same block as my manager Mike Hughes, where we stayed for eighteen months. During that time Sandy became pregnant which delighted us both and when it was time for her to have the baby, I was present, as I was at the birth of all our children. Sandy and I had been told she would have to have a Caesarian and before I joined her in the operating theatre I had to put on the regulation green cap, mask, gown and wellies. They'd given Sandy an injection in her hand that put her to sleep and I watched as they cut open her stomach and the surgeon put his hand inside and pulled out our first baby, a girl! Watching our baby appearing from inside Sandy's tummy was an incredible emotional experience, but it was nowhere near as emotional as the moment our baby was first handed to me to hold.

I looked down at this little bundle of life, our daughter, with her tiny fingers and that beautiful little squashed face and I burst into tears. Holding your child moments after it's been born is an indescribable experience. I defy any man, however macho, not to be reduced to tears by it. You have no defence against the huge emotional force that hits you.

After a couple of minutes a nurse took my baby daughter from me and placed her in an incubator. A little while later, still unconscious, Sandy was taken up to a private ward. The birth had really weakened her and when they let me into the ward, I could see that she had drips in her arm. I sat next to the bed and stroked her hair but she just slept and slept. The nurses were excellent and told me it was best for her to sleep as long as she could after the operation. She was asleep for more than ten hours and when she awoke she was still very drowsy. I told her we had a baby girl but she was so out of it I wasn't sure if it registered. Later, after they'd finished all their tests on our baby to make sure she was healthy, a nurse brought her to the ward to show Sandy. The nurse handed the tiny bundle to me, then I passed her over to Sandy who was sat up in bed, still with drips in her arms. Sandy started crying tears of happiness and I wiped them away for her and kissed her and the baby, whom we named Donna.

A cot was placed at the end of the bed, I put little Donna inside it, and Sandy and I watched as our baby yawned and fell asleep.

Once we knew the baby was fine and Sandy was on the mend, my sense of humour, which I'd kept a firm reign on, started bubbling to the surface again. Despite having drips in both arms and clamps on her stomach, Sandy wanted to use the toilet rather than suffer the embarrassment of using a bedpan. She got out of bed and very slowly and very painfully made her way to the toilet. A few minutes later I heard the toilet flushing and she came out looking pale and tired. She made her way slowly back to the bed and, taking my time, I helped her to get back into bed. As she lay back against the pillows she let out a moan, closed her eyes and grabbed my arm. The poor girl was in agony. All I could do to comfort her was to hold her hand and whisper in her ear, 'Sandy!'

She opened her eyes and, wincing with pain, said 'What?'

'I suppose a fuck's out of the question?'

She started laughing and then she'd stop because it hurt so much, then she'd start laughing again. Three days later we took our baby home.

Now we were a family of three, the flat was too small for us so we started looking for houses around the outskirts of London. We saw loads of places, finally settling on a large house in St Leonard's Hill, Berkshire, that had previously belonged to Britain's most famous circus boss, Billy Smart. You would never have guessed it had belonged to a circus owner, apart from the fact that instead of carpets on the floor, there was sawdust. And when you pressed the front door bell it played 'Send In The Clowns'. Billy Smart had named his house My Way and I saw no reason to change it.

Sandy thought a place as special as that couldn't be filled with ordinary, chain-store tables, chairs and beds etc., so I went straight out and spent thousands of pounds on furniture from Harrods. Whatever Sandy wanted, Sandy got.

We were very happy there. Sandy recovered from the operation and little Donna was a wonderful baby. I hated having to leave them and our beautiful new house to go on tour, but a house that size didn't come cheap and the mortgage and the amount of its upkeep was enormous. I'd be sat in a dressing room 300 miles from home, with the 'House Full' signs up outside the theatre and I'd be thinking of Sandy and Donna and how much I'd rather be at home with them.

Not that we lived on a little pink fluffy cloud of love and affection all the time. Like any married couple, we had arguments. When Sandy had a temper on her, she had bigger bollocks than Mike Tyson. She had no fear at all. She'd start raising her voice. I'd raise mine to make myself heard over her voice and so it would go on until we were screaming at each other until she'd fly at me with her fists clenched, ready to give me a good hiding! You can talk some people out of a filthy temper, by being reasonable and quiet and good-humoured with them. Not with Sandy. When I tried to calm her down it was like someone throwing petrol on a coal fire. It blazed twice as high and twice as hot!

As the years went by, we had two more children, Jody and Stacey and eventually moved from My Way to Viners, a mansion set in sixteen acres of the Berkshire countryside that set me back well over half a million pounds in 1983.

Talking of Berkshire, just as I started to get famous, I called round at John Lennon's house at Tittenhurst Park, Ascot. I hadn't spoken to him for years, but I was 99 per cent sure he'd remember me. I knocked on his front door, mentally rehearsing what I was going to say to his butler or house-keeper, or whoever it was a multi-millionaire ex-Beatle employed to answer his door. 'Good morning. My name is Freddie Starr and I'm an old acquaintance of Mr Lennon. Is he receiving visitors today?'

The door opened and I was staring at the unmistakable face of John Lennon.

I said, 'Alright, John?'

'Alright, Freddie?' he said. 'Come on in.'

He took me into a huge stainless-steel kitchen and said, 'Do you want some dinner?'

I said, 'OK.'

He opened a cupboard and took out two large tins of baked beans. He opened them both with a can opener and handed one to me, with a fork. We both sat in his kitchen eating cold beans just as we used to do in 1961, except the seedy Hamburg hotel had been replaced by a mansion. We talked about everything under the sun and all our mutual friends . . . and enemies. He remembered we'd both been in the audience with Billy J. Kramer to see Jerry Lee Lewis at the New Brighton Ballroom in 1960 and the fantastic reaction Jerry had got when he came on stage. A fight had broken out. Five fellahs giving another one a good hiding. Betty was also with me that night and she asked me to help the poor sod on the ground, so I waded in. Luckily the bouncers saw what was going on and threw the five troublemakers out.

When we finished our 'bean feast', John showed me into a room with a white piano and shutters on the windows where we talked for a short while. Then I thanked him for his hospitality and left. Because I had such a busy schedule and John was always flying back and forth to the States, I only went around his house once more. I'd heard he was selling it and wanted to have a chat with him before it actually went on the market, to find out how much he wanted for it. I had every intention of making him an offer. We had another informal chat and he told me how much he wanted for the house, which was not unreasonable for such a wonderful property. As we talked, Yoko Ono wandered in, looked at us and, without saying a word, went out again. I shook John's hand and, telling him I'd genuinely think about purchasing his house, I left him standing at his front door. I never saw him again.

Whenever a newspaper reporter has asked me how someone can be successful in show business I've always told them this. The only way to succeed is to work hard and be prepared to be away from home for most of your life. Which means your private, family life will suffer because you're never there. I honestly felt that any performer trying to make a name for him- or herself should stay single. Well, it's worked for Cliff Richard!

But performers *do* fall in love and get married and try to make their relationship work even when they're on tour or in panto or summer season at the other end of the country. It's a difficult, almost impossible situation. What's a performers top priority? Work or family? But he has to work to provide for his family.

If he's a TV personality whose face is recognised everywhere he goes, he can't move into a little semi-detached or terraced house surrounded by people who are understandably going to be curious about him, his lifestyle, his family and any other famous faces who might call round to see him. His neighbours would be knocking on his front door for autographs day and night and if he just once said, 'No, I'm busy,' they could easily spread malicious gossip about 'that miserable, stuck-up, big-headed bastard at Number 7!' because some people are like that.

That's why famous people *have* to buy big houses with a high wall around them, because otherwise they won't get any privacy. The other thing to remember, especially for any performer in the pop music business (which chews people up and spits them out with the same callousness that television did with mainstream comedians a couple of years back), is that you may well have a very short shelf life at the top. At least if you've bought a big house with your royalties you come away with something.

During my years with Sandy I worked my bollocks off for her and the family. I was always away from home. On the road. In a theatre or television studio. I missed so much: seeing my children grow up; reading them bedtime stories every night and tucking them in; letting them know I'd see them at breakfast when we'd plan where we were going that day; just snuggling up on the sofa with Sandy in front of the TV. The little things that people who finish work at five o'clock take for granted.

I loved Sandy and the children with all my heart. She was more than just a wife to me. She was my soulmate. I truly believe that. We should have been together all our lives. But I let work fuck up my marriage. Yes, it was mostly my fault. I could have said 'No' to another fifty-date tour or a long season in Scarborough or Margate. But there was always that niggling thought, 'What if they don't ask me next year? Where will I earn that sort of money?'

I must lay some of the blame on my management, who worked me into the ground as if they thought I was going to be out of favour in twelve months' time. I've no doubt about that. They were trying to earn every penny they could from me while I could still put bums on seats. It got to a point where, in February 1980, Sandy insisted that I took some time off before I ended up in hospital. She could see my workload was killing me and our marriage. I told my manager at the time I had to get away. As he was being paid handsomely for looking after me, I made it plain he had to sort out any problems my taking a holiday at such short notice might cause.

The venues where I had been due to appear had to be informed that I was taking a break on medical grounds. I even obtained a doctor's note explaining that I was suffering with exhaustion. My immediate bookings, including the Lakeside Club, in Surrey, would have to be re-arranged (I was being paid £21,000 for a week's cabaret and didn't want to lose it completely – just have it put back a few months) and other artistes would have to be brought in to replace me. I was relaxed – we'd covered any possible problems.

I'd been in Barbados just 24 hours when someone handed me a British newspaper. I was on the cover, being made out to be an unprofessional prick because, according to the paper, I'd been kidnapped. The club owners where I'd been booked were screaming blue murder and threatening legal action. What a disaster! I made arrangements to fly back home the following day. Of course, Sandy was furious. Another little nail was being hammered in the coffin of our marriage. But this wasn't me just putting work before my family. My professional reputation was at stake. Other newspapers would start picking up the story and I could end up being blacklisted from every nightclub in Britain. In 1980 the club scene was still very healthy and if you were a big draw for customers, you got paid well; and I couldn't risk losing that.

Of course the press lapped it all up and for a couple of days I was all over the papers. This has happened all through my career. I get blamed for things that are totally beyond my control and I always carry the can. Bob Potter said that he didn't care whose fault the cock-up had been, he felt so badly let down he would never allow Freddie Starr to perform at the Lakeside club again. Ever!

A couple of years later I was asked to attend the Variety Club Awards, where I was honoured to receive the Entertainer of the Year award. Where did they hold the ceremony? Bob Potter's Lakeside Club.

Isn't it funny how things work out sometimes?

My stay in Barbados was very brief that time, but I've holidayed there many times since and have often met up with other stars having a break from the spotlight and cameras. On one holiday I met Bruce Springsteen. He'd been a frequent visitor to Britain and recognised me from TV. He and I got on well and often went for long walks along the beach.

No, not hand in hand in the moonlight. I liked Bruce, but not *that* much.

Christ knows what we talked about. Music . . . comedy . . . life . . . everything. I used to wear a gold pendant around my neck in the shape of a guitar, and he mentioned a couple of times how great he thought it looked. So before the end of my holiday I took it off and gave it to him. Why not? Of course I knew he was a wealthy man. He could have bought a hundred solid gold pendants, paid cash and not even asked for the change back. But he was friendly, down-to-earth guy and I'd enjoyed his company during my holiday, so I gave it to him. The pendant was worth a couple of bob and when he went back to the States he took it to a pawn shop and got 500 dollars for it. He wrote a song about it – 'Pawned In The USA'. I made this bit up.

Another time in Barbados, the phone rang in my room and a voice said, 'Is that Mr Starr?'

'Yes,' I said. 'Ringo here!'

'This is Oliver Reed here, Freddie. Now stop pissing about and get down to the bar so you can buy me a drink!'

'Who the fuck is this?' I said.

A throaty laugh exploded from the phone. 'It's Oliver Reed. Don't you recognise my voice, you little bastard? Get your arse down here!'

Whoever it was speaking to me did the best Oliver Reed impression I'd ever heard and as I walked down to the bar I expected to see Bobby Davro or Paul Melba standing there pissing himself. But there he was! The great Oliver Reed, putting his hand out to shake mine. 'Freddie! I hear you don't drink!'

'That's right, Oliver. And . . .' I added straight-faced '. . . I don't go out with women either. But I *do* make all my own frocks!'

He roared laughing and I asked the barman for a Coca Cola and whatever Oliver wanted. Oliver had heard we both staying in the same hotel and as he preferred the company of comedians and musicians to his fellow actors, he wanted to meet me.

Despite the fact I didn't touch alcohol and I'd heard he had no time for teetotallers, we got on like a house on fire and traded rude jokes and unprintable, libellous stories about well-known showbusiness personalities. A couple of hours went by and then he realised he had to be somewhere else to meet his wife or girlfriend or both. He stood up to go, bent forward to shake my hand and let rip an enormous fart that rattled the glasses on the bar. He tapped the side of his nose and winked, 'I hear thunder! They said we'd have some before night fall! Good day young man!' Then he staggered off and I didn't see him for three days.

Oliver and I were friends for years and apart from the fact that I admired him as an actor, right through his career from *Curse of the Werewolf* in 1961 to his final role in *Gladiator*, I also liked him as a man. He was barely into his sixties when he died filming *Gladiator* in Malta in 1999.

Oliver played the media at their own game, which is brilliant if you can do it. Yes, he enjoyed a drink or ten, but he wasn't permanently pissed. You don't get to work with some of the world's greatest directors if you're a pisshead. He only pretended to be drunk half the time he turned up on television. After he'd caused an uproar because he really had been 'a little under the weather' on a couple of chat shows, he thought it was expected of him. He was great company, pissed or sober. Wherever you are tonight Oliver, cheers!

The fact that I'd had come back to Britain to resolve a massive problem with the Lakeside Club didn't concern Sandy. She thought I was being selfish putting my career first. Maybe I was right to do that, maybe I wasn't. But you look around and see how many other 'mainstream' comedians who broke through in the 1970s and 1980s are still touring theatres and packing them out in the twenty-first century. It's just me and Chubby Brown. And that's it. I think one of the reasons I'm still in demand is that I've never stopped working. I kept learning my craft.

Once I was back in the country, it didn't take me long to climb on that treadmill again. A fifty-date tour. A summer season. Another tour. And in between, numerous cabaret dates from Land's End to John O'Groats. That's bollocks really because as far as I know there's no nightclub in John O'Groats and there *definitely* isn't one at Land's End. But you know what I mean. It was non-stop work. I'll explain about the little capsules of calm that got me through this period in a later chapter. But as I was becoming more and more in demand, I became a commodity that had to be sold. Every theatre, concert hall, nightclub, leisure centre and village hall wanted to put Freddie Starr on their stage because *they knew it was impossible for them to lose money!* I was even working Christmas Eve and New Year's Eve. You can imagine what sort of state my marriage was in.

On my many tours around the UK, up and down the motorways, staying in some khazi of a hotel at the opposite end of the country from my home, I was always thinking of Sandy and the children. When you're on stage for only two hours out of 24, that gives you lots of time to brood about your family.

Perhaps it would have been better if we'd sat down and seriously discussed selling the big house and cutting my workload in half. If we had maybe we'd still be together.

CHAPTER TWELVE

To try to ease the situation with Sandy, sometimes I'd drive through the night from a gig at the other end of the country so I could see her and the children the next morning. But even if I got in at the relatively early time of one or two o'clock in the morning, she hardly ever waited up for me. I know she went to bed during the week at 10.30 because she had to get up early to take the kids to school, but she wouldn't even wait up for me on a Friday or Saturday night. There wasn't any need for her to take the kids to school because that was one of the live-in housekeeper's duties.

For years, this was the pattern for me. I'd drive a hundred miles to get home, pull up outside the house and it would be in darkness. I'd let myself in and go to the kitchen where I'd be greeted by the cheering sight of a sandwich on a plate, covered in clingfilm. Next to that was a cup with a teabag in it. I'd fill the kettle and while I waited for it to boil, I'd sit at the kitchen table and glance at a day-old newspaper. A couple of hours before, I'd been entertaining several hundred, maybe a couple of thousand people who'd laughed and cheered me. But my wife couldn't be bothered to wait up for a couple of hours to ask how the show had gone and to kiss me goodnight.

After a few years of this you become a bit despondent and you start to question your wife's loyalty and what the point is of you tearing around the country to misbehave on stage for a couple of hours. The money you may have earned from the gig that night doesn't seem that important.

I knew that Sandy had fallen out of love with me, if she'd ever really loved me at all. I wondered if she'd married 'Freddie Starr', the wealthy comedian with the exciting lifestyle. She had the life of Riley. From the day of our wedding until the day we divorced, she didn't put one penny on our table. I was the breadwinner and, as much as she moaned at me for being away, she didn't attempt to earn a living, even when the children were older. I even offered to set her up in business by buying her a shop. But she wasn't interested.

My mother had remarried and her new husband Jack was a smashing fellah. But I don't think Sandy invited them to visit us from Liverpool more than once during our marriage. But . . . *Sandy's* parents, now they were a different matter. They came to stay with us every Christmas without fail. In the run-up to the festive season, I'd say, 'Any chance of my parents staying with us this year?' and Sandy would snap at me and say, 'I've already told my parents they could come this year!' and change the subject. She could easily have invited my mother and Jack as well, because we had loads of spare bedrooms and plenty of room around the dining table. But I knew if I persisted in asking her, it would lead to arguments and long sulking sessions. I didn't need any more of those.

Christmas in our house, especially the first years when we were happy, was bloody marvellous. Sandy would have loads of Christmas trees all over the house. I counted *eighteen* trees one year, all of them fully decorated, with twinkling lights.

'Sandy,' I said. 'Why have we got eighteen Christmas trees?'

'I really like Christmas trees!' she said.

I made a joke of it and said something like 'But Sting's just been on the phone complaining! He thinks you've cut down a bloody rain forest!' and instead of ignoring me or . . . heaven forbid . . . having a giggle at what I'd said, she snapped at me, 'What's the matter with you? It's Christmas time!'

There was always that undercurrent of tenseness between us. God knows I wasn't easy to live with. I don't think any performers are. We all suffer from neuroses and insecurities and the occasional boil on our arse. All the more reason to be with someone who can give you tender loving care, try and convince you there's no need to be wracked by self-doubt and is always willing to help you through the bad days, no matter how frequently they come along. I don't think Sandy had it in her to be that understanding, certainly not after the first five or six years of our marriage.

Whenever I think about Christmas I vividly remember being on stage at some nightclub miles from home one

Christmas Eve. The cabaret didn't start until eleven o'clock and after forty minutes or so, I looked at the audience and, although I obviously didn't show how I felt, I was thinking, what are you people doing here on Christmas Eve? Why aren't you home wrapping presents for your loved ones?

They were a friendly audience, not too pissed, but I still hated being there, entertaining them, when they and I should have been at home.

While I was married to Sandy from 1975 to 1994, throughout all my tours, summer seasons and television series, I was only ever unfaithful to her once. I got close several times. I was surrounded by beautiful, sexy women all day and night. Sandy was always questioning me about the dancers I was in summer season with, because that's how we had got together and she knew what comedians and dancers got up to.

One autumn, after I'd finished a long summer season, I went back home to Viners. By now my children were in their teens. Donna was a lovely girl – at six, she'd dress as Wonder Woman, and twirl around, which always made me laugh. It seems just like yesterday!

I drove home with butterflies in my stomach. How would Sandy react when I got home? When I pulled up outside my house, after three months away, Sandy didn't rush out to hug me and welcome me back. She was there with the children in our home, the one I went out to work for to pay for and there was no 'Hello love. Give us a kiss' or 'I've missed you so much.' Just a polite welcome. For all the warmth and affection in her welcome I might as well have been an insurance salesman or the man who's come to mend the leaky taps. Not for the first time, she made me feel like an outsider. I wasn't part of *her* family. Her attitude gradually got worse and worse over the years as Sandy and the children made a life for themselves that didn't include the man who financed them all. She had her own lifestyle and friends I didn't know and they went to places I'd never heard of. I wasn't a husband, I was just a bank account in a suit.

I had a couple of weeks off before my next UK tour started (my manager must have slipped up badly there – letting fourteen days go by when I didn't earn him any money!) and during that time I tried to spend time with my family and build bridges between us. Not easy when you're planning to be away again, or thinking up new comedy routines.

Touring. I never looked forward to it. Performing is fantastic – I love that. But when you're on tour it soon becomes repetitive. You drive all day to get to the theatre. You have a band call about four o'clock, hoping that all the musicians have found the place. Because you've been sat in a car for hours, you're sweaty and feel like shit, so you take a shower. You don't want a heavy meal before you go on stage so you have a cup of tea and a ham roll or something similar, before getting into your stage gear. You entertain a packed theatre for two hours. Then you come off stage, take another shower because you're sweaty and feel like shit.

You get dressed, sign a few autographs for the fans waiting at the stage door (only the dedicated ones hang around if it's raining) and then, depending where the venue is, you either head for home or the hotel. Next day you get up and it starts all over again. But you forget all about the constant travelling and motorway food and the 101 problems that get thrown at you every day, as soon as you walk out on stage and the audience look pleased to see you.

So, without a hug and a kiss from Sandy, I set out on the road again, travelling from venue to venue. Sometimes I wouldn't even know what town I was in. That's not me being arrogant, saying all British towns look the same. Let me explain. Once you're in a theatre, they all look very much the same backstage. I'd be in the building from about two o'clock in the afternoon until the show finished at eleven, losing all track of where I was. I couldn't really go sightseeing because I might get spotted. Besides there were always things to rehearse, new songs to learn, gags to work out, phone calls to make and receive. The afternoon would be a blur of activity sometimes followed, if I was lucky, by a half-hour nap to recharge my batteries. So there have been times when I've been on tour, walked out on stage and said, 'Good evening, ladies and gentlemen. It's wonderful to be here in . . .' and had to turn to the band and ask, 'Quick! Tell me! What fucking town are we in?' and the audience would all start laughing, thinking I was joking.

It was during that autumn tour that I was unfaithful to Sandy for the one and only time in our marriage. Foolishly, I ended up in bed with a young lady but it could hardly be described as an 'affair'. We slept together a few times – that's all. Not a deep obsessive passion. Nevertheless, I felt so guilty about it, that when I got home it didn't take me long to confess to Sandy what had happened.

Sandy was devastated by the news and I felt ashamed.

'I've done wrong,' I said. 'I'm very, very sorry. If you want me to go I will.'

I had screwed-up big time and I took the responsibility. Amazingly, though, once she knew I wasn't in love, Sandy forgave me and said I could stay. But she never fully trusted me again.

I continued living at Viners with Sandy and the tours and the summer seasons were as hectic as ever. I was working myself into the ground again and everything started getting on top of me. I was getting closed in. Demands were being made of me day and night. I was tempted to say, 'Oh, fuck it! I'm packing in the business and I'm going to spend more time with my family. I'll sell the huge mansion and buy a smaller mansion.' At least me and Sandy would have had a chance to get to know each other again. Maybe she would have rekindled her original feelings for me. There were times when I was constantly wound-up mentally and physically, bad-tempered, short-fused, a real pain to be with.

As my marriage was crumbling I kept thinking, 'What a price to pay for being able to make an audience laugh!' I had no life other than the couple of hours I spent on stage every night. Even so, sometimes I'd find I was performing on automatic pilot and I'd suddenly be in the middle of a routine in front of 1,000 people and snap out of it! 'Whoa! Where was I up to?' I'd been thinking about being at home or on holiday in Barbados with Sandy and have to pull myself back in.

I found it a very sad time when I look back. I should have been more sociable. I should have spent more time with the children and attended their sports days and school concerts. Sandy would make me feel like a lousy father when she'd say 'How is it that Billy Connolly could find time to watch his children in the school play last night and you were too busy?' I felt really shitty and started resenting the business that took me away from home so much. Maybe Billy was better at dividing his time between work and family. With me it was always work, work, work.

Why? Because I didn't want my children to go short of anything. When I was a kid, and I'll quote Chubby Brown again, I had 'fook all!' and I worked hard to make sure my children and my wife wanted for nothing. I always made sure their Christmases were fabulous times. I spent thousand on gifts for them. This is going to sound very glib now, but it's true and straight from my heart. I realise now that what Donna, Jody and Stacey needed most wasn't my presents. *It was my presence*.

Despite all the problems we were having, Sandy didn't mention a divorce. It was me who brought it up. I was an idiot to mention it. And it's something I regret to this day. I truly believe that if I hadn't said, 'Do you think we should get divorced?' (which, really, I only said to see what her reaction would be), if only I'd let things carry on, I would have eventually slowed down my career and spent more time at home anyway. I was getting older and I didn't want or even need to go out on a spring tour and an autumn tour every bloody year. We had loads of money and a big house. As it turned out, I did eventually cut down and then cut out my summer seasons. The children would have left home and Sandy and me would still be together. Living in Spain most of the year, possibly, as I do now. I put my hand up and say loud and clear that I ruined a marriage that, with more care on my part, could have been saved.

It sounds a bit complicated but after I first talked to Sandy about getting a divorce, we didn't actually get divorced for another three years. I went back home on three occasions, each time hoping we could make a go of it. But we'd only end up arguing. On one occasion in 1994 we went on a family holiday to Florida in the hope it might bring us together and while we were away, our gardener was having a wild time drinking champagne in our swimming pool and our bedroom with his gay friends – which I'll be telling you about later.

I'm not sure if Sandy did things deliberately to wind me up, to see how far she could push me, but on one of the occasions I went back with her we were having an argument and she said, 'I bought you that watch on your wrist!'

'What do you mean you bought it?' I said. 'You haven't done a day's work since we got married. If you look around this house you won't see a single thing that you paid for!' Then there was the time, during our divorce, when I asked her if I could buy our house Viners from her and she said that I could. I got the money together and two days later I phoned her up and said, 'I've got the money to buy the house from you,' and she said, 'Over my dead body! Do you think I'd let you bring another woman into this house?'

'But two days ago you were willing to sell it to me.'

'I've changed my mind,' she said. That was it. She wasn't selling it to me.

After our divorce (described by the newspapers as one of the most acrimonious in showbusiness) we met on the steps of the court and I said, 'Sandy, we were together for twenty years. Isn't there anything good you can say about me?'

'Yes,' she said. 'You were always a good provider' and walked away.

So that's all I was to her. A good provider.

I had hoped to grow old with Sandy. I'm not the same person I was then. The man who always put work first. The elusive father and husband. I've had six or seven years to think about what happened and while I know that we shouldn't have regrets in life, I can't help but regret losing the beautiful person I first saw in that London rehearsal room in 1974.

My little collector of Christmas trees.

My wife of twenty years.

My soulmate.

CHAPTER THIRTEEN

Now we're divorced, Sandy and the children are free of the pressure we were all under because, make no mistake about it, every time my picture was in the paper, it affected my children. It didn't matter whether they'd seen the paper themselves. Their school friends would always make sure they knew what their dad was up to. I have little time for reporters but I know that anyone in the public eye is a legitimate target for the press. What I hated was the way it affected my children. Every time I saw my name in the paper next to a sensational headline, I didn't care about what it did to me. I used to worry about my children being tormented in school that morning.

I used to look at Jody when he was a lad, riding his pony across the paddocks and think, 'Poor little sod. He hasn't got any friends to play with,' which may have been true but I thought he should have been content to live in the lap of luxury. He was very clever with mechanical things and became an instructor, teaching people how to sail boats. He was like me at school, not academically minded. So I knew exactly how he felt when his test marks were low. I didn't mind that, I just wanted my children to be happy and healthy. Stacey and Donna were brilliant swimmers. I always thought that if Stacey had wanted to, she could have earned herself a couple of gold medals.

The children are grown up now and have all formed their own opinions of me. Living with their mother during the years when I was hardly ever home, they would naturally tend to side with Sandy if we had an argument or slight disagreement. My children probably see me as an out and out bastard, their view of me affected by things Sandy told them about me when they were growing up. After the divorce I sent Donna and Jody a letter, in which I apologised to them for causing them and their mother so much pain and heartache.

Some years later, I bought a house just 200 yards from where Sandy was living at the time. The press (bless 'em) got wind of this and reporters turned up on my doorstep to ask why I'd chosen to live so close to my ex-wife. It must have been a very quiet news day for them to get excited about such a non-story. I told them, 'What does it matter where she lives? Two hundred yards away or 200 miles. We've both accepted the marriage is over. But if Sandy needs my help or advice at any time, she's always welcome to ask me.'

A strange thing happened about two years after the divorce, when I was living in a house in Winter Hill, the umpteenth place I'd moved into after our split. (I found it hard to settle anywhere for very long. I'll give you an idea how often I moved, I had the removal men on a retainer.) Around quarter to ten one evening, Sandy phoned me. She sounded upset and asked me to go around to her place straight away. I thought she might be in some kind of trouble and as I only lived a short distance from her, I was there in five minutes. Her front door was open and she was pacing up and down, as if she had something troubling her. She calmed down a little and made me a cup of tea.

What she did next caught me by surprise. She leaned forward and kissed me on the lips. It was only for an instant, then she pulled away saying, 'No . . . no,' as if she was fighting against her feelings. Then she said, 'Don't you think I haven't had sex for the last two years!' Which seemed an odd thing to come out with, bearing in mind I hadn't mentioned anything about her sex life. She was in a very weird mood.

'Sandy, it's none of my business if you've made love to the entire American Army,' I said. 'I really couldn't care!'

I could see from the way she was dressed that she'd been out for the evening, but as it was barely ten o'clock, I took a guess that something had happened to make her come back home early.

'Have you had boyfriend trouble?' I asked.

'Men!' she said. 'They're all the same!' What the hell was she talking about? If something had happened while she was out, why didn't she just come out and tell me? And what was that kiss all about?

She fell silent for a while. I wasn't sure if it was the right moment to tell her that my latest news, but as I didn't see Sandy very often, I thought I may as well.

'By the way,' I said, 'my girfriend's pregnant.'

When she heard this she jumped up and said, 'Right! *That's* it! That *is it!*'

She was actually jealous! It was alright to tell me she'd had plenty of sex since our divorce, but I wasn't allowed to have a girlfriend!

I thought it best to leave her in her strange mood. I've no real idea why she wanted to see me that night. Maybe she had plans for us to get back together and I fucked them up again by giving her some bad news. All I know is she's never phoned me since, although she's known me long enough to know I'll always be there for her whenever she wants any help or advice. I say that despite all the terrible things she said about me in the papers like 'My Twenty Years Of Hell Living With Freddie Starr' in which she and the children said they slept with knives under their pillows because I was so unpredictable. That was complete bollocks. Can you imagine the scene at bedtime in my house? With Sandy kissing the children goodnight, saying 'Off to bed now Jody, Donna, Stacey! Don't forget to brush your teeth, put on your clean pyjamas and . . . oh yes . . . I want each of you to take a sharp knife from the kitchen drawer! What was that, little Jody? No, you can't take the long carving knife. *Mummy's* taking that one to bed with her!'

There was a period after we'd discussed having a divorce when we went through a period of reconciliation and I thought it would be a good idea to take the family away on holiday to Florida. It was a second honeymoon, except we took our three children with us! While we were away, Viners and its extensive grounds were left in the hands of our housekeeper Sue and our two gardeners. One of the gardeners was a man named George and the other was a gay man named Robin, full name Robin Coxhead. We all knew he was gay, and it didn't worry us. I was surrounded by gay men and women in showbusiness and as long as they kept themselves to themselves it made no difference to me, although it was strange to see Robin Coxhead weeding the lawn wearing pillar-box red nail-varnish sometimes. I mean for a start, red doesn't really go with green fingers! When he started work for us, he asked me if the fact he was gay worried me. I joked, 'Of course not. But I must warn you that I do like to exercise completely nude in the grounds sometimes, so if you ever see me bending over when you're gardening, just keep your dibber to yourself!'

The other gardener, George, was a bit old-fashioned in his outlook and wasn't keen on working alongside a man who wore nail varnish. I rarely heard George call Robin by his first name. He'd usually attract his attention by shouting 'Oi! Poofter!'

Robin was with us for nine years. We paid him a decent wage and provided him with a rent-free cottage in the grounds. Of course that all came to an end when we found out the truth about him and the shit hit the fan.

By the way, did you know that a couple of years back, David Baddiel was on stage at a comedy club and a member of the audience walked on stage and belted him right in his annoying face. It was the first-ever recorded case of *the fan hitting the shit!*

When we returned from Florida, everything seemed fine at the house and within a few days I was off on another tour. One of the venues was only an hour from Viners so I came home that night. Sandy mentioned that some of her jewellery was missing, including a £12,000 engagement ring I'd recently bought Sandy. Yes, we'd been married for years and I had bought her an engagement ring in Blackpool, but she wanted another one and I wanted to keep her happy.

The next day Sandy asked Sue, our housekeeper if she knew anything about the missing ring. It wasn't that she mistrusted her, it was more because she had no idea what had happened to the ring and was clutching at straws. Sue became upset and said, 'Oh, Mrs Starr. I didn't know how to tell you this, but when you were on holiday, Robin Coxhead invited some of gay friends into the house and they were drinking your champagne and eating food from your fridge. I caught them having sex in your swimming pool . . . and your bedroom. I tried to stop them, I really did, but there were so many of them. Robin just laughed at me and said I shouldn't worry, because you and Mr Starr wouldn't miss a few bottle of champagne and I should keep my mouth shut.' And she went on in great detail about the mess that Robin and his friends had made in our bedroom ... our private room for crissake ... that she had to clean up afterwards and change the sheets. How could Coxhead do a thing like that after all we'd done? We treated him as a friend. He'd once told me he'd been mugged and had all his saving taken. I had no reason to disbelieve him, so I gave him £5,000 in cash. In retrospect, which one of us had really been mugged?

I went straight outside to find Coxhead but he'd pissed off. He wasn't at his cottage, his car was gone and he wasn't answering his mobile phone. I had a long drive ahead of me as that night's tour venue was some distance away so I had to leave Sandy to sort things out, asking her to keep me updated by phoning my mobile. She called the police who tracked Coxhead down in Reading at four o'clock in the morning and arrested him. Apparently the first thing he said wasn't, 'What the fucking hell are you arresting me for? I'm just a humble gardener!' as most people would. He said, 'I want my lawyer here!'

The papers wanted to know what had happened, so I explained in a *News of the World* article in April 1994 that while we'd been away, thousands of pounds worth of jewellery had gone missing and the police suspected Coxhead. On top of that, our housekeeper had seen Coxhead having sex with a boyfriend in our bed. In the same article Coxhead denied everything and said he couldn't possibly have sex because he'd had a hernia operation.

What follows is a series of events that may or may not be in the correct order they happened. From March 1994 to the court case a year later, I had lots of things to deal with. I was touring or in summer season or cabaret. My marriage was falling apart and I was having problems with my manager. However I remember very well the court case that all this led up to and will give you a full account of it. It's just some of the things leading up to it that I'm a bit shaky on. But it'll all make sense.

Obviously we fired Coxhead but we couldn't do very much about the missing jewellery because we had no evidence.

Then a jeweller in Reading recognised Coxhead's picture from the article in the *News of the World*. The jeweller contacted the police and they were round to his shop in five minutes. He had records of all the transactions that had gone on between him and Coxhead who had sold various items of jewellery to him. The police brought the list around to me and Sandy and as we looked through it we recognised items of jewellery we'd forgotten we owned. Two rings and two watches, one Sandy's, the other mine. He's also been stealing from sixteen or seventeen other people. How he'd found the time to mow our lawns I have no idea.

The police arrested Coxhead and he admitted he was in debt to the amount of £38,000! He confessed that he'd stolen our jewellery but that he hadn't profited from the thefts because he'd thrown it all in the River Thames. The police asked him on what stretch of the Thames he'd thrown it in and he showed them. Frogmen were sent down to look for the jewels but they couldn't find anything.

While he was still being questioned at the station, I got a visit from two detectives who told me they wanted a word with me in private. Both Sandy and I were surprised by such a request but she went into the kitchen and I was left with the two CID fellahs.

'Robin Coxhead has changed his story again,' said one of the detectives. 'He's told us that you gave him the jewellery.'

'Why would I give a gardener jewels worth more than £40,000?'

'He says you gave him the jewels in exchange for . . . oral sex!' said the other detective.

'What? Do you really think I would hand over valuables worth £40,000 for oral sex with another man? He's talking through his arsehole!'

'All Coxhead has told us,' said the second detective, 'is that he gave you oral sex, on and off over a period of five years and every time he did it, you gave him items of jewellery in payment.'

'For fuck's sake,' I said. 'Over five years? The man is off his fucking head! If I was ever that horny and that desperate for a blowjob, there are half a dozen places that *you boys* know in Reading, where I could get a good-looking blonde with big tits to suck my cock for fifty quid or less. Why the fuck would a heterosexual like myself want a man to suck me off and then present him with my wife's engagement ring worth twelve and a half thousand quid? I can't believe he thinks he can get away with it!'

The detectives were very sympathetic and we chatted some more about Coxhead and what a slippery so and so he was and a thought struck me. I said, 'Hang on one moment. If Coxhead has been blowing me for five years, like he says he has, he must know my old boy quite well. Will you do me a favour while you've still got the bastard in custody? Ask him if Freddie Starr is circumcised or uncircumcised.'

So the police went back to the station and half an hour later they were back.

'Coxhead gave us a reply to your question. Would you like to come down to the station with us so that a police doctor can take a look at your . . . so that you can . . .'

'Just a minute,' I said. 'Tell me. Did he say I was circumcised or uncircumcised?'

One of the detectives told me Coxhead's description of my willie.

'Right boys,' I said. 'There's no need for me to come down to the station,' I unzipped my trousers, 'because I can prove here and now he was lying,' and I took my knob out and slapped it on the table. The two detectives looked at it and it didn't take them very long to realise that Coxhead had given the wrong answer. What a prick!

No, that's *not* what the detectives said as I whipped mine out.

Fast forward to March 1995. I was divorced from Sandy by then and had to attend the first day of Robin Coxhead's trial for theft at Reading Crown Court. As soon as I walked into the court I saw a large TV screen and I knew that at some point they would be showing a video. And it wasn't going to be *Naked Gun*.

Coxhead's barrister handed me the list of jewels that Coxhead had sold to the Reading jeweller. The writing was quite small and spidery and I found it impossible to read because I hadn't brought my glasses. The clerk of the court, a woman, was standing close to me and I could see she was wearing a pair of ornate 'Dame Edna' spectacles, with pointy frames and I asked her if I could borrow them. They were a perfect fit and as I put them and peered at the court through them, I heard laughter. However the glasses did help me to read the list and I confirmed which items on it belonged to Sandy. I returned the glasses to the Clerk and thanked her.

Then they showed the court a videotape of Robin Coxhead and some of his friends 'Doing The Time Warp' from *The Rocky Horror Show* all in drag. When it was finished the barrister said, 'Having watched that short piece of video tape, would you like to comment on what you saw?'

I said, 'Yes. As a matter of fact I would. The lighting was awful. The camerawork was atrocious and the choreography was the worse I've ever seen!'

'No, no, no!' the barrister shouted at me, 'did you see what Mr Coxhead had on the end of his wrist?'

I said, 'Yes. His hand!'

Judge Crocker said, 'This is a serious matter, Mr Starr. A man might go to prison!'

I said, 'Well I do hope it's not me. I've got a booking in Skegness on Saturday night!'

By now the court wasn't quite in uproar, but it was on the brink. The barrister said, 'Let's watch the video again, shall we?'

I said, 'Oh, yes let's!'

'And,' he continued, 'please pay close attention this time!'

The video started again. The barrister said, 'Now . . . what do you see?'

I said, 'Six fellahs in drag, dancing.'

He said, 'No! Look at Mr Coxhead's wrists!'

I said, 'Excuse me, your wigness. I know you're supposed to be the professional here and I do know I'm way out of my depth. But aren't you leading me?'

He got all huffy and said, 'Just do as you're told!' Which is something I hadn't heard since I was eleven!

'Now . . . what is that on his wrist . . . there!' he went on.

'It's hard to tell. It looks like a watch or a bracelet. But I can't make it out.'

'Ah! You are saying it's a bracelet?'

'No . . . I said it *could* be a bracelet.' Without my glasses the amateur videotape looked fuzzy, slightly out of focus.

The barrister obtained a photo of the bracelet and showed it to me. 'Tell me, Mr Starr. Is that the bracelet you just saw on the video?'

I looked at the photo for a couple of seconds. Then I turned it upside down and looked at it again. I turned to the judge, who was peering at me through a pair of small gold spectacles perched on the end of his nose, and said, 'May I borrow your glasses, your worship?' By now the court was in total uproar. The jury were in danger of wetting themselves. Court was adjourned for the day.

The following morning, Coxhead's barrister's opening line was 'I want you to understand, Mr Starr, that I am not here to humiliate you!'

And I said, 'I want *you* to understand that I'm not here to be humiliated.'

He puffed himself up and said, 'I put it to you that the items of jewellery you allege were stolen were in fact gifts that you presented to Mr Coxhead in payment for his having oral sex with you!'

I said, 'And I put it to you, that you are talking complete bollocks!' I hadn't finished. 'I am a heterosexual . . . you *are* familiar with the word? . . . I am a heterosexual from my head to my toes and that includes everything in between. I'm not even one per cent of a half of a third bisexual either. I am a pussy man. I assume you are familiar with *that* word too? And I don't know any man on this earth who has a pussy. Only women have pussies. I love pussies. Ergo . . . I am not homosexual.'

The press were falling about at this. The jury were trying to keep their faces straight. But I hadn't even got into first gear yet.

'I'll be perfectly honest with you. I have nothing against gays . . . provided they don't try and put something against me! But I do take exception to someone, who is accused of a crime, telling bare-faced lies about my sexuality in order to get off the hook! I heard suppressed giggles and stifled laughter among the jury.

'That's all well and goo . . .!' the barrister started to say but I wasn't going to let him break in. I was on a roll.

'I'm sorry!' I said. 'Did you think I'd finished? No, I have something to say which the court needs to hear. When Mr Coxhead was arrested the second time, I was visited by the arresting detectives. They told me he alleged I gave him jewels in exchange for oral sex over a period of five years. In view of something he'd said, I found it necessary to show them my porridge-gun right there and then, and . . .'

The judge interrupted. 'Err . . . porridge-gun? What are you referring to, Mr Starr?'

I said, 'Isn't it obvious? The one-eyed, blue-veined trouser snake! My chopper!'

'Ah! I see!' said the judge. 'You are referring to *your cock!*'

'Precisely, your worshipfulness! And Mr Coxhead told the police that he had been gobbling mine for five years, which is ridiculous! M'lud, if you'd had your cock sucked for five years, don't you think you'd know about it?'

The judge removed his spectacles and said, 'Well . . . if you put it that way . . . I suppose I . . . !' he put his glasses back on and said, 'Mr Starr! If you must refer to your male member . . . or indeed anybody else's in future, would you please restrict yourself to referring to it by its far less offensive name . . . the penis? Thank you!'

I nodded and said, 'If you want penis in future, penis you will have, your honour! Now, let me go back to what I was saying because this is a very important point. In fact, as you will learn, *my* point is a very important point in this case!'

I paused for a drink of water. I was coming up to my big finish. I was only going to have one chance to prove my manhood in court, because if I couldn't, the press would start all sorts of crap rumours about me. Despite the fact they'd know it was untrue, the reporters would lap it up. Imagine the headlines – 'FREDDIE'S GARDENER TENDED HIS HARDY PERENNIAL!' and all that shite.

I put my glass down and continued, 'Mr Penis says he sucked my Coxhead . . . sorry! Mr Coxhead says he sucked my penis for five years. The police came around to tell me what he'd said and asked me if I'd mind being examined by a police doctor. If Coxhead had been sucking my . . . er . . . giving me oral sex for five years he should know it inside out, don't you agree M'lud?'

'It's "your honour"!' said the judge, 'but do continue, Mr Starr.'

'Well, he described my penis to the detectives, and when I whipped it out in front of them, almost knocking over a priceless Chinese vase as I swung it out on to the table, they could see he had mis-described my penis!'

'Mis-described?' the judge said.

'Sir,' I continued, 'not to put too fine a point on it, generally speaking a man's penis is usually in one of two conditions. Circumcised or uncircumcised. Coxhead was asked whether mine was or wasn't. And he gave the wrong answer. That being the case, how likely is it that he has, as he was only too eager to tell the police, been giving me oral sex for five years? We couldn't have done it in the dark every time. I must have left the light on once or twice. So he must have had a good look at it.'

The barrister stuck his oar in. 'Well, will you share your secret with us, Mr Starr? Is your penis circumcised or uncircumcised?'

I said, 'That's none of your business. Your client, who said he knew me very intimately, failed to describe a penis correctly he says he'd been gobbling regularly over a number of years. Frankly, I've been very honest and up front with the court today and given them and you quite enough details about my private parts. I don't want to discuss or describe my penis any longer. Your honour, ladies and gentlemen of the jury . . . I rest my cock . . . case!'

Robin Coxhead was found guilty by the jury and was sent to prison for fifteen months.

The detectives on that case were very fair with me, once they knew that Coxhead was not just a liar but a thief. But I haven't always been treated fairly by the police. In particular, motorway police have been right bastards to me at times. During one short season at the Circus Tavern, I was driving to the gig, listening to a tape I had of some songs I recorded. I was doing 65 miles per hour in the middle lane. I saw a police car coming up behind me, lights flashing and as he drew alongside he indicated that he wanted me to pull over, so I did. I got out of my car and I could see he knew who I was. He had a real go at me, telling me what a terrible driver I was and he really got on my nerves.

'I clocked you travelling at 110 miles per hour just then!'

'A hundred and five? You horrible bastard! If that's the best you can do, make it 150 if you like. It's all bollocks anyway. I was doing 65 mph and you know it!'

He wasn't going to back down now. 'No, sir, I saw exactly what you did. You started off at 50 . . . slowing the traffic down . . . with all the cars overtaking you . . . and that's when I started following you. By the time I caught up with you, you were doing 110.' He walked around the car. 'A Mercedes car, eh? I suppose you think you're a big shot!' He had a shite attitude and the right hump with me!'

'No,' I said. 'I don't think I'm a big shot.'

We went all around the houses, arguing and it was all a waste of time because he did me for travelling at 110. I got back in the car and headed off for the Circus Tavern. I had left home in plenty of time but I was a little bit late now. I'd only driven ten miles down the road and another policeman, parked on the side of the road, held up his hand and made me pull over. For fuck's sake! Were they taking the piss or what?'

The copper said, 'I saw you. You were doing 110!' What was wrong with these coppers' equipment? Did they only ever register 110 miles per hour?

I wasn't going to put up with any more crap from the boys in blue so I said, 'You know full well I've just been stopped down the road by one of your mates. He's been on the radio to you and don't bother to deny it. I could easily lose my rag with you and I'd end up in the papers. So just tell me, will you. How did you work out that I was travelling at 110 miles per hour?'

He pointed at a marker on the side of the road. 'That's the speed you were travelling between post A192 to post A167. Now let's have all your documents please.'

But I hired a road expert who examined the stretch of road where I'd been stopped that second time and in his report he stated that 'Because of the position of the police car, parked-up just after a bend in the road, the only way that police officer could have seen you driving between those posts was if he was standing on the roof of his car, which he patently was not. If he could not have seen those posts, that means he cannot prove what speed you were travelling.' It cost me a lot of money to pay for that report but I'd rather have paid for that than handed over money to the police for something I hadn't done.

During one fortnight when I played the Circus Tavern, I got stopped by the police twelve times. For no reason. 'Just a routine check, sir!' They were waiting for me along various points of the M25, like it was a game they were playing with a celebrity just to piss him off. Every time they stopped me they asked me the same questions.

'Are you the owner of this car?' 'Where are you going?' 'Where have you been?' Always taking their time, checking my documents ve-ry slow-ly. They checked my lights, tyres and windscreen wipers. At one point I thought they were going to check my tapes to see if they approved of the music I played in my car. Then, when they decided they'd annoyed me for long enough, they sent me on my way.

My solicitor sent the police a letter accusing them of harassing me, which of course they denied. But isn't it strange. Not long after, I changed the name of the registered owner of all my cars from my own name to a company name. And the police didn't stop me after that, even though I used that stretch of the M25 time and time again.

What's your opinion on the likelihood of a coincidence like that occurring?

CHAPTER FOURTEEN

It's a sad fact but the glorious days of the Great British Summer Show are numbered.

Journalists and TV trendies who have never spent more that 24 hours in a seaside town, if they've ever visited one at all, like to look down their noses at middle-of-the-road entertainment and disdainfully refer to them as 'end of the pier shows' when they haven't got a clue what they're talking about.

Most seaside shows are put on in theatres or concert halls. It's just lazy journalism. They've heard the expression before, have never seen a summer show in a theatre so continue to perpetuate their ignorance. Yes, there are a few theatres that happen to be situated at the end of a Victorian pier, which will still be there long after the journalists who take the piss out of them are sacked from their bitchy columns in their meaninglessly trendy publications and replaced by someone even trendier and bitchier.

'End of the pier' to previous generations conjured up delightful images of song and dance and comedy at a pierrot show, enjoyed with a jolly, friendly audience. Why is it so 'cool' to look down on our British heritage? If someone took the mickey out of 'Muslim music hall acts' or Indian 'end of the pyre shows' they'd have a right bollocking from every quarter.

Summer shows that feature a couple of big star names and several support acts and run six days a week are still popular in a handful of British seaside resorts, like Blackpool and Bournemouth, but increasingly performers will restrict themselves to two nights in each resort from Monday to Saturday and then go on to do a Sunday concert somewhere else. An example would be two nights in Scarborough, two in Bournemouth, two in Torquay and every Sunday night a show in Skegness. Quite some mileage over an eight-week season. The days when Britain's twelve biggest resorts can all have three or four shows all headlined by a TV performer, running from June to September or beyond, have long gone. Part of the reason is that more people go abroad for their two-week summer holidays and people tend only to spend a day or a couple of days at a British resort before moving on to another one further down the coast. So it's a social change in one way, although I would add that Blackpool still gets an average sixteen million visitors every year. Which is why the theatres and cabaret rooms in that town usually do excellent business.

The other reason is even simpler. There just aren't enough mainstream entertainers around, capable of topping a bill and pulling the crowds in any more. The majority of young comics coming through would rather play to a hundred young people (all dressed in black T-shirts and jeans just like him) in a London comedy cellar than put on a suit and try to entertain an audience of 1,000 people made up of all ages.

Now that's hard! You have to be clean and clever or just the right 'naughty but nice' side of blue to make a twelve-year-old laugh at the same joke as his grandfather.

But you'll always get a laugh with a young audience if you come on stage with 'an attitude' and talk about periods and wanking. Well that's what Barbara Cartland once told me when we bumped into each other in a Soho massage parlour ten years ago. The massage had done her the world of good. She looked in the pink.

I realised how quickly changes and trends can happen in showbusiness when about eight years ago I had a summer season lined up at the enormous Bournemouth International Centre, a barn of a place, with a capacity of 3,500. I'd been there the previous year and I'd sold out both houses every night. That's 7,000 people through the doors every night. Six nights a week! The town had really been buzzing that season, with hotels and B&Bs jam-packed. So the BIC asked me to come back the following year, hoping for a repeat of the sensational business they'd done.

Christ! What a difference in just twelve months! Bournemouth was a ghost town. It wasn't just that the weather was a bit iffy. There were some lovely days. The town just felt emptier. And this was reflected in the business the theatres did. My engagement at the BIC started later than the previous year. They only wanted one performance per evening. And some nights I was lucky to have 800 to 1,000 people in. The business just wasn't there. Eight hundred to a thousand bums on seats is quite a healthy number if it's the Grand at Blackpool, but in the cavernous BIC it ain't good!

Summer seasons can definitely bring out the best and the worst in performers. By far the worst were ordinary 'pit' musicians. Now I've employed hundreds of musicians and heard from other performers what they've had to put up with and with very few exceptions they have absolutely no loyalty to a performer. They'll agree to do a tour for you for a certain weekly or daily wage and after a couple of days on the road they might be approached by someone who needs, say, a drummer and can offer them a couple of hundred quid for a gig and without telling the star who employed him for the tour, he'll take the better paid gig and put in a deputy drummer that night. He might be a brilliant dep drummer, but he doesn't know my act. The guy I employed to do the entire tour with me doesn't care, because he's fifty miles away playing for someone else.

Musicians are a breed apart. They turn up, read their dots, play their instruments and then head for the bar.

They generally have little empathy with the performers they play for. I know there are major exceptions like Tony Bennett who has been touring with the Ralph Sharon Trio for donkeys' years but mostly, performers have to look for new musicians every time they tour. There's simply no loyalty on the muso's behalf.

Here's a story that helps to illustrate just how offhand musicians can be with performers, even thought we're supposed to be in the same business.

One year I was headlining a summer show in Scarborough which had some great support acts, including comedian Mike Lancaster and a twenty-piece orchestra actually on the stage, conducted by the musical director Maurice Merry. Until they needed to be seen, the orchestra were hidden behind a gauze curtain and one night, early on in the run, Mike Lancaster was in the middle of his act and the orchestra started tuning up behind the curtain. The noise was so loud it started putting Mike off his stride and his act suffered because of it. He was in a terrible state when he came off stage.

After the show I said to Maurice Merry, 'Would you please tell your musicians not to tune up when Mike or anyone else is on stage! It's very unprofessional!'

He was a bit huffy with me and said, 'But they've got to tune up!'

'I realise that Maurice,' I said. 'I have worked with orchestras before. Your boys had plenty of opportunity to tune up in the band room. That's why we have a band room. So the musicians can tune up in there.'

He wasn't listening to me. 'Freddie, they have to tune up!'

'Maurice,' I said. 'I'm telling you straight. Your musicians are not to tune up while the acts are on. Have you any idea what it's like trying to get laughs out there with a fucking fiddle player practising his scales twenty feet away?'

He gave me a blank stare. He had no idea what I was talking about.

'Maurice. In future, if they need to retune their instruments, they can do it in the intermission. If you can tear them away from the bar!'

Did he listen to me? Fuck no.

The same thing happened the following night. Mike Lancaster's doing well, getting big laughs, then all of a sudden behind him, the drummer starts testing his bass drum and cymbals at the same time the bass player runs up and down the strings. Mike hesitated and couldn't focus on his act. He was getting bits of his act jumbled up, his timing went, he was sweating and worst of all . . . his mouth went dry with nerves.

Once again he came off almost in tears, saying, 'Those fucking bastards in the orchestra were tuning up again!'

'Mike,' I said, 'I know what they're doing and you did great to get through your act like you did. Don't worry about it.'

The next night, he went on and exactly the same thing happened. They were doing it deliberately now, just to get up Mike's nose. Well, they were getting right up mine too.

Mike came off, purple with rage, angry and crying and fucking furious. My dander was up (no jokes here please) and

I thought, 'How dare those arseholes treat a performer like this!' and I grabbed a fire extinguisher from the wall and walked over to the orchestra. I hit the top of the extinguisher and pointed it at Maurice Merry. White powder, not foam, exploded out of the nozzle with such force it knocked him arse over tit. He and the entire orchestra were covered with the stuff.

I went on stage and all the orchestra walked off with the exception of the pianist.

Maybe I was a bit naughty, but they could have wiped themselves down and come back on stage. But they fucked off. After that their attitude got even worse.

A couple of nights later, about half an hour before a show, B*****, my old mentor from Liverpool, came to see me with five other lads I knew from the early days and during our conversation he mentioned he'd heard about what the orchestra had been up to (not from me!). He also knew where the 'gentlemen of the orchestra' would be before the show.

'Let's got over the pub for a drink,' said B*****.

'But you know I don't drink,' I said.

'Come on,' he said. 'The lads fancy a pint.'

So we walk into the pub that everyone connected with the show used regularly and when we'd sat down with our drinks, B***** looked at the crowd around the bar and said, 'Which one is Maurice Merry?'

I pointed at the MD and said, 'Him over there. Why?'

'Relax,' said B*****, and he stood up and shouted over to Maurice, 'Oi! You! Fucking come here!'

Maurice went pale. He saw B***** was surrounded by five very heaving looking fellahs and didn't need asking twice. 'Can I help you?' Maurice said, his eyes glancing between B***** and me.

B***** nodded. 'Yes, you can help me and you can fucking help yourself too. Do you want to play the piano again? Do you?'

Maurice looked puzzled, until he saw the knife that B***** had brought out of his pocket so quickly he thought it had suddenly materialised in his hand. 'Yes . . . of course I d . . . d . . . do!'

'If you and your musician friends walk off stage again when Freddie's on,' said B*****, 'I'll cut your fucking fingers off one . . . by . . . one! Understood?' He placed the end of the blade under Maurice's sweaty chin. He nodded and his right eye suddenly developed a nervous twitch.

B***** hadn't finished. 'When Freddie's on stage, you and the orchestra stay put. Otherwise I'll take you down to the beach and hold your head under water for a couple of hours! Now go and tell your friends what I said,' and he had the knife back in his pocket before anyone else could see it.

For the rest of the run the orchestra behaved themselves impeccably every night for me and Mike Lancaster. And after getting the B***** treatment, Maurice Merry changed his name to Maurice-Not-So-Bleeding-Merry!

I did a few summer seasons and tours with Lennie Bennett, the comedian who hosted several TV series in the 70s like *Punchlines* and *Lucky Ladders* but who is more at home 'live' on stage. He's very busy today on the after-dinner and corporate function circuits. He won't mind me saying that there was a time when he was a bit of a ladies' man and I loved winding him up about his womanising.

Once, when we were in summer season, he pulled a beautiful young girl and, purely to get on his nerves, I kept hinting how much I fancied her and how much I'd love to get her into my bed. Whenever Lennie pulled, he hated any other comic getting too close to the female in question and he told me in no uncertain terms that I was to stay away from this one. 'Fuck off spells *no!*'

'But . . . can't I just ask her if she'd like ten minutes in my bed after you've finished?'

'No, you can't!' Lennie said. 'At least I think that's what he said! He pointed his finger at me and said, 'I know you, you little swine! You'll be sniffing around her when we get back to the digs, but you can fuck off! I haven't pulled a girl as beautiful as this for at least a month! So stay away from her!'

She did look amazing. Tall, blonde and very athletic. She also turned out to have a great sense of humour.

Lennie and I went back to our theatrical digs and he went back to his room with the young lady and I went back to mine with a meat pie and a small portion of chips.

Lennie's room was right next to mine and just as I was about to unwrap my chips, I heard Lennie's door open and the sound of his footsteps running downstairs. Our rooms weren't en suite, so if we needed to use the bathroom we had to go downstairs.

I crept on to the landing and knocked on his door and when the girl opened it I said, 'I want to wind Lennie up. But it'll need your help. Are you game?'

God bless her, she was! I followed her into the room and locked the door. 'Lennie will blow a fuse if he thinks I've got off with you,' I said, 'so we have to make it sound convincing! Just follow what I do!'

So I started jumping up and down on the bed and moaning as if I was giving her a good seeing to and she jumped up and down on the bed moaning as if she was getting a good seeing to. Lennie must have heard it from the bottom of the stairs because I could hear him galloping up to his room. He then started pounding on the door, shouting, 'Starr! I'll have you, you little bastard! Get off her! She's mine!'

But we kept it up for a couple more minutes, until we both gave out a great big gigantic orgasmic moan and collapsed on the bed. Ten seconds later I unlocked the door and walked out, pretending to do my zip up. As I passed Lennie, who wasn't entirely sure if it was a wind-up, I said, 'She's ready for you now!' and ran into my room, locking my door in case he came after me. Ah! Such larks, Pip!

After all that fun and games, my meat pie and chips were still warm.

Lennie and I are still pals, but we fell out for a few years. I can't even remember why or how or where we fell out. But we met up again in 1986 when we both attended a party thrown by Lester Piggott at Silks restaurant in London. Without me knowing, Lennie had arranged for the chef to create a special dish, which he delivered to my table himself. He held out a silver tray, covered with a white cloth which I pulled back to see what was hidden underneath. When I saw what it was I roared laughing and Lennie and I became friends again.

What had he persuaded the chef to make me? A chocolate hamster!

Which brings me to *that* story!

CHAPTER FIFTEEN

British tabloid newspapers. I've always had a love–hate relationship with them. They love reporting stories based on hearsay and rumour about me and then *hate* it when my solicitors point out they've printed lies about me and they have to print a retraction. Here's one example. On 23 December 1992, one paper ran an article in which they claimed I'd sold the story of my divorce to Sandy to another for £25,000. This was not true, but a lot of people actually believe every word that's written in their paper and wouldn't think to question the logic of why I would want to tell a paper that I'm getting divorced and get paid for it. Why would they hand over £25,000 to me when they had plenty of other means of finding out whether it was true or not which would cost them a lot less?

So my solicitors contacted the tabloid in question and asked them to set the record straight and admit they had printed an untruth. This is where the newspapers are at their craftiest. The original article had taken a prominent place on page 3 or 4; the retraction they printed was about an inch square and hidden away between the crossword and an advert for fertiliser.

Not only did they hate having to say they were wrong, they waited until 12 March 1993 to do it! By which time the Great British Public had already made their mind up what sort of person Freddie Starr was!

FREDDIE STARR ATE MY HAMSTER!

That was the bizarre front-page headline in the *Sun* newspaper. Have a guess how long ago that was. Eight years ago? Ten, possibly? No. The date of that headline was Thursday, 13 March *1986*! I've been quoted as saying that story will follow me to the grave and it's true.

According to the *Sun*, the newspaper that prides itself in seeking out the truth, even if it sometimes has to fabricate stories in order to achieve that honourable aim, 23-year-old 'model girl' Lea La Salle (real name 'Doris Slapper'?) and described as a 'former Miss UK runner-up' (wow! with such a high profile, *she* didn't need any additional publicity, obviously!) met me when she was living with her boyfriend Vince McCaffrey at his home in Birchwood, Cheshire. Doris . . . sorry . . . Lea . . . said I was staying with them while I was in cabaret at a Manchester nightclub and when I returned in the early hours after finishing work, I 'demanded' that she made me a sandwich. She refused so I went into the kitchen and came back with her pet hamster 'Supersonic' between two slices of bread.

I then proceeded to *eat a 'live' hamster!* Well, that's Doris's . . . err . . . Lea's account of the story. But Vince McCaffrey was quoted as saying, 'It's hard to believe the guy actually did this!'

You said it, Vince!

The only time I've ever stayed at Vince McCaffrey's house was in 1979. Seven years before the alleged 'hamster incident', which would mean that Doris . . . sorry . . . Lea, would only have been sixteen and wouldn't even have met Mr McCaffrey.

Let me put this story to rest once and for all. I have *never* eaten or even nibbled a live hamster, gerbil, guinea pig, mouse, shrew, vole or any other small mammal. However I will happily admit to eating several pussies in my time, but they all lived to tell the tale. Usually to the *News of the World* for £10,000.

The man behind the Hamster story is publicist Max Clifford, who only this year was asked on the *Esther* chat show on BBC2 if Freddie Starr had actually eaten a hamster. His answer was a terse 'Of course not!' But he followed that up by admitting, 'When Freddie's UK tour started, a few weeks after the *Sun* printed that story, it was a complete sell-out!' The press can be right bastards to people in the public eye, so it's only fair that, once in a while, we get a chance to get our own back on them.

Max Clifford and I were good friends and when I started to make a name for myself in the business he arranged for me to be interviewed by a wide range of publications. One day he rang me up and said, 'Freddie. I've got you three pages in (he named a high profile women's magazine) and they want to interview you in my office at eleven o'clock tomorrow morning.'

'What am I going to talk to a woman's magazine about?' I said.

'They want the usual "Gags To Riches" story,' he said. 'Your early days with the Liverpool groups and your struggle to the top. The usual bollocks. See you in the morning!'

The reporter the magazine sent to interview me was a charming man who obviously knew very little about me or any aspect of showbusiness. I suspect he normally covered stories about someone who was digging his garden and found a potato that looked like Jesus, or about a pet goldfish who could speak eight languages.

Max sat in on the interview, just behind me to the right, just in case I needed to consult with him about anything. Or to butt in if I started going off at a tangent! The reporter asked me a few boring questions, and I could tell he didn't have much of a clue about me, so rather than waste an hour of my time, I thought I'd have a bit of fun with him. Here's a shortened account of the only part of the interview that stuck in my memory. Most of this is true.

'Now, Freddie, we all know you as a comedian and impressionist, but didn't you start off as singer in the Liverpool clubs?'

'That's right. I was in several groups, like The Seniors, The Delmonts and probably the one that I'll always be remembered for . . . Deep Minge!'

'Deep Minge?' He started to write it down.

'Make sure you spell it right. We have different ways of spelling it in the north of England. I was in Deep Minge with a "g" and not minje with a "j". It's quite interesting that the Liverpool "minge" is different from the Manchester "minje". I've nothing against Manchester's "minje", but even if I say so myself, in Liverpool the Deep Minge that I spent so much time in was legendary.'

I didn't dare turn around and look at Max because we would both have broken up and given the game away. I was gripping on to the chair to stop myself from laughing.

'Yes, when I set out as a singer in the clubs at the tender age of sixteen, I had no idea that within a couple of years I'd be in something as big as Deep Minge.'

The reporter was busy scribbling all this down, so I waited for him to catch up and continued, 'Here's an exclusive for your magazine. There was a lot of rivalry between the groups then. Once we heard that someone was leaving a successful group, we all tried to get in it. Before the group picked me to be their lead singer, Paul McCartney and Gerry Marsden both desperately wanted to be in Deep Minge.'

The reporter said, 'Really! So how did you get into Deep Minge?'

'That's an interesting story,' I said. 'The lad who'd been singing with them for a year got fed up and decided to pull out of Deep Minge. He told me it was a painful moment for him, but he'd got fed up of singing in Deep Minge seven nights a week So he left to form his own group.'

'Do you remember what they were called?'

'Yes. Harry Quim And The Beavers!'

'Right . . . right . . .' he was writing nineteen to the dozen and I hoped that he'd spelt Harry correctly. He seemed much more interested in my musical career than my comedy. 'So . . . Freddie . . . how long were you in Deep Minge?'

'I was very lucky to be in Deep Minge for two wonderful years. But it got to the point when I had to leave to pursue a solo career. Frankly I was up to here with Deep Minge, and I left.'

'Would you say that your leaving left a big hole in Deep Minge?'

'Yes, I'd agree with you. Because just after I left, Deep Minge split. But they still get together once a year for a charity gig and if I'm available I join them on stage. I'd never turn down the chance to play with Deep Minge for free.'

'You must let me know the next time you get invited to play with Deep Minge. We'll send a photographer along.'

'Yes, I'm sure the ladies who read your magazine would find it fascinating. By the way, I've heard there's a Deep Minge tribute band in Liverpool now.'

'What are they called?'

'Imitation Minge!'

And so it went on for another 45 minutes, with me inventing outrageous things about the mythical group that he was so fascinated with. I felt sure he'd twig at some point that I was taking the piss, but no, he just kept on asking questions and after he'd left, I said to Max, 'For fuck's sake! That was a waste of time. They'll never print that. Once the editor sees what he's written it'll just be thrown in the bin!'

But two weeks later I looked through my morning post and saw a large brown envelope with the women's magazine title on the front. I tore the envelope open and took out the magazine. There inside, nestled between the knitting patterns and the recipes was my interview. And every reference I'd made about *that* group was intact! It was hilarious! I nearly wet myself as I read it over and over. I must have re-read it twenty times, because I couldn't believe they would print it! I almost choked when I saw what title they'd given to the article.

FREDDIE STARR STILL MISSES HIS DAYS IN 'DEEP MINGE'

I led that reporter up the garden path, but it didn't matter. He got more than just a straightforward showbiz interview. He was thrilled because he thought he'd got an exclusive. He got his money, no one wrote in to complain about the name of the group and the magazine wasn't closed down. So what harm was done?

I used to worry about the lies the papers told about me regularly. There have been so many untrue articles about me in the tabloids since my 'overnight success' in 1970 that they all blur into one. My managers and publicists over the years kept all my press cuttings, from the hamster headline to the tiniest reference to me being fined for speeding. Some of the cuttings were helpful to me in writing this book, but if it was up to me I wouldn't keep press cuttings. They're mostly a load of cobblers.

It got to a point in the early 80s when I'd read so many lies in the papers about myself that I couldn't go out of my front door. On the day a paper carried a made-up story about me, I'd hide in the house, maybe even staying in for two or three days, worried what people might think about me. That couldn't go on of course. I had to get over that feeling of wanting to hide myself away, and I did manage to do it, although it took a couple of years and that's when I started deliberately being 'madcap' (how I hate that meaningless word) Freddie Starr. I decided I couldn't beat them so I'd give them something to write about – like the ludicrous 'Deep Minge' story.

Tabloid journalists. What a bunch of sneaky, sleazy, creepy, mischievous, lying, shit-stirring bastards! Would you like to spend your days hounding people just because there was a rumour going around that their marriage was splitting up or they had a bit on the side? What a way to make a living. The press hounded Princess Diana from the day she made her first appearance, looking scared to death and incredibly shy, with Prince Charles. I used to see her on TV or on the papers almost every day. Everywhere she went she had the paparazzi in her face. It must have driven her to despair. I used to feel so sorry for her, I actually felt like driving down to Kensington Palace and saying, 'Come on, Diana. Get in the car and we'll go somewhere for a chat where the press can't find you,' just to take the pressure off her. But of course, if I had, the papers would have written about *that!*

The press know that certain members of the public like to see photos of the Royals in the papers and there are times when the Royals will help them to get the family pictures they're after. When Charles and Diana went on their skiing holidays with the children they'd pose for dozens of photos on the first day, which the press and the public should have been satisfied with. But no. A few days after the official pictures were seen in the papers, the freelance photographers would sneak around trying to get informal pictures of the family. Which was blatant intrusion. The Royals couldn't do much about it, but I could and did on one memorable occasion.

When I was living at Viners with Sandy, I looked out of the window one evening and saw a man creeping around the back of the house, so I grabbed my licensed double-barrelled shotgun and confronted him.

'I don't know who you are or what you're after,' I said, 'but if you don't move your arse off my private property right this minute I will pull this trigger and blow your fucking head off!'

And although the fellah was shitting himself and started backing away, he had the cheek to say to me, 'It's alright Freddie. I'm a reporter, not a burglar!'

Just how did he think that was 'alright'? Whether he was a reporter, a burglar or an astronaut who'd dropped from the sky, he was still an intruder on my land.

'Just fuck off,' I said, 'and think yourself lucky you're able to walk away from this situation.'

I've no idea how he got over my wall or what story he was after, but he should have gone through the official channels and arranged an interview via my manager at some neutral place. The gun wasn't loaded by the way, but it had the right effect on the obnoxious little shit.

The most annoying aspect of the press is that, whereas their job should be just to report on news stories, they seem to spend a lot of their time creating stories themselves or even non-stories. If they're so keen on fiction, why don't they fuck off and write novels instead? I can give you a recent example of how a tabloid reporter can actually create a news story that wouldn't have existed if he'd had something better to occupy his time.

I was all over the *Sun* on 12 April 2000. On the front cover and on pages 4 and 5. With that much coverage, you'd think it was a huge story of interest to the public! Was it hell! It was all about 'Freddie Starr being so badly off he's reduced to living in a caravan in Hitchin, Hertfordshire! It's a far cry from the £2 million Berkshire mansion he shared with his second wife Sandy.' But the next paragraph revealed quite clearly that the whole thing was a non-story because in it the reporter says, 'Starr owns a £350,000 villa in Spain.' Hang on a minute, Mr Sun Reporter. Was I on my arse-end or living in luxury? It was just bad journalism and didn't make any sense. But reporters don't often make a lot of sense. By the way, the villa in Spain is worth a lot more than the figure mentioned in the article.

The reporter in question was Jamie Pyatt, a man I've known for years. One of the few journalists I used to have any time for. I once told him, 'If you ever want to do a story on me, Jamie, phone me and I'll tell you whatever you want. But don't go sneaking around the back of my house or through my dustbins. Come to me direct and you'll get your story.'

He said in his article that I was living in a £10,000 caravan in Fosman Caravan Park and that when I saw him, I attacked him with the help of an 'Irish minder pal' and that afterwards he'd sat in his car, bleeding from a gash on his face. To illustrate the extent of the attack he posed for a photo that revealed the 'terrible injury' he'd received. It looked like he'd taken a red felt tip pen and drawn a one-inch horizontal line on his cheek, with a four-inch vertical line 'bleeding' from it.

Let me tell you my side of the story and when you've read it, you can decide who was telling the truth.

The caravan in Hitchin was a place I used to store my stage gear for my tours. It was also somewhere to crash out occasionally after a gig. But I don't live there!

As the article stated, I actually live in Spain. The *Sun* knew that, so why the fuck did they try and make out my permanent home was a caravan? I was just starting a tour of Britain and when I tour, I normally stay in hotels. But the caravan came in very handy whenever I was performing at a venue less than an hour's drive from Hitchin. Look, if I can save £150 by driving for just 45 minutes I will!

The 'Irish minder pal' who Pyatt described was Johnny Laff, the comedian supporting me on the tour, who is actually a Londoner! 'Top of the morning to you, Johnny! How's your shillelagh?' Mr Laff wouldn't hurt a fly. He'd eat a hamster, yes, but he wouldn't hurt a fly! Can you see a pattern emerging here now?

I was certainly angry when I saw Pyatt hovering outside my caravan, peering in like a perverted Peeping Tom and I chased after him just like anyone would if they thought someone was nosing around their private property. And I did swear at him and grab his tie and tighten it. When I want to scare somebody off my private property I've found that saying, 'Excuse me! I'm awfully sorry I have to ask you this, but would you mind awfully ... er .. going away ... please?' isn't very effective.

But buried in the article is one sentence which Pyatt tries to use as a smokescreen for his underhanded activity: 'When photographer Peter Simpson and I drove into the caravan park in Hitchin, Herts, we expected the usual Starr-style banter.'

Really? Why would he expect that? What the hell he was doing at the caravan park? He hadn't been invited by me. He wasn't my very best friend in all the world who could call around to see me on spec. So why would I want to 'banter' with a reporter who turns up unannounced?

You and I know why he was there. The *Sun* had been tipped off by someone who'd seen me at the caravan. But he was hardly likely to admit to his readers that he'd driven from Wapping to Hitchin just to sniff around looking for a story. What was he moaning about anyway? He got his story. He just didn't expect that he'd be the star of it, complete with red felt tip 'wound'.

Press photographers are even worse. They're sometimes referred to as 'paparazzi' which is Italian for 'a ruthless, desperate, horrible turd holding a camera'. If you're a celebrity or even a wannabe star and would like your picture to appear in the newspapers, don't put on your best clothes and go to a West End premiere. Go on holiday to Barbados, change into your swimming costume on the beach, accidentally drop your towel to reveal some flesh and you'll be in the Sunday papers the following weekend. It's what they call the 'belly shot'. Getting a shot of someone's big belly on a beach, taken from a distance of ten miles so that all you can see is a fuzzy pink lump. They've done it with me countless times. They even took one of me getting undressed next to the pool in my own house! I was half-hidden by a fence and bushes, but they printed the picture anyway! So I put a bit of weight on? You do when you hit 29!

Sometimes the papers get approached by ex-members of your family or ex-friends who have a story to tell. They're never stories like 'Freddie Starr Is A Normal Fellow And I Like Him!' or 'Freddie Turned Down A Passionate Night With Ten

Dancing Girls'. They're always kiss and tell tales or about what a sod I was to be married to, live with, work with etc. I think it's good to remember what someone once said about newspapers: 'They have three uses. They bring you the news of the day. They help to interpret complicated issues to the common man. But their most vital role in society is and always has been, to protect your living room carpet on those occasions when your puppy suddenly needs to take a poop!'

I couldn't have put it better myself.

CHAPTER SIXTEEN

There are times when I wonder if I made the right career choice. I honestly mean that. We all come to points in our lives when we have to decide which route to take. It might be in respect of a relationship (whether to begin one or end one), moving to a different house, job or even a different continent. And because we're human and full of doubts, after we've finally decided on a direction to take, months or years later, we might turn around, look back and wonder about the 'road not travelled'. It's pointless, but we all do it.

I've been married three times. If I'd stayed at Leadco, or Cammell Laird I might still be married to Betty, earning a decent wage and wouldn't be troubled by reporters and photographers with ten-inch zoom lenses following me around.

But I would have missed out on some wonderful times, from my magical night at the 1970 Royal Variety Performance; the fun and mayhem that can be had with a great company during a summer season; acting in the tough TV series *Supply and Demand* and the 1977 feature film *The Squeeze* with Stacey Keach, David Hemmings and Stephen Boyd; and meeting some of the world's greatest stars, including Dean Martin, Jerry Lewis, Muhammed Ali and Elvis Presley. I wouldn't have met and married Sandy or my lovely new wife Donna.

I wouldn't have heard the incredible sound of 3,500 people roaring with laughter, doubled up at my live stage act. I wouldn't have been invited to The Shadows' 25th Anniversary Party, where I met that comedy powerhouse Billy Connolly. We were like two dogs sizing each other up, not knowing whether to make friends or have a fight. We went on stage together and kept the audience laughing for two hours, making up whatever it was we did as we went along. What a pity that wasn't filmed – as far as I know! If anyone had a secret camera on them that day and captured our performance on film or videotape, please write to me care of the publishers!

On the other hand, I doubt very much that if I'd stayed in a 'proper job' I would have got hooked on the tranquilliser Valium, an addiction I revealed to the papers in December 1981 after seven years of relying on the drug to keep me sane and get me through every day. The word 'tranquilliser' is very seductive. It conjures up a picture of tranquillity. Peace. A respite from the problems and aggravations that tug and pull at a performer every day when he's at the top and in demand everywhere. And I got suckered in by the prospect of finding some help in those 'capsules of calm'.

The way it started was so simple. I'd been overwrought, stressed, working myself to a standstill and was hell to live with for a long time, so Sandy arranged for me to see a psychiatrist. At the time (1974) doctors were dishing out Valium and Librium like sweets. They were the cure-all for anyone who was depressed. When I started taking them, the effect was almost immediate. Everything seemed rosy and I calmed down considerably. But when the effect of the tablets start wearing off you feel worse than before. Your hands shake and you *have* to take more. People don't understand how addictive Valium is.

In my case they gave me amazing confidence when I was on stage, but terrible lows afterwards. I had no trouble convincing doctors that I needed the next supply. 'Yes of course. Have some more. They'll sort you out!' Valium was to blame for a lot of things during those years. I was prescribed 16 milligrams a day, but if something happened to me during the day to upset me, I'd take more.

Some people need a few drinks to get them through certain situations. I've worked with television directors who couldn't stop drinking. They'd nip off for a swift one from their hip flask and five minutes later they're back ready to work. But a couple of hours later you could see their hands shake when they needed the next drink. Alcohol, drugs, chocolate . . . people get addicted to all sorts of things. There was a man I worked with at Leadco who was addicted to aspirins. He'd come up to me, shaking and sweating and say, 'Freddie, go and get me a packet of aspirins, quick!'

He was craving aspirins! He still got headaches, *but he never knew when!*

I managed to get off Valium, but it was bloody tough and it took me a year. I had tried just quitting cold turkey before, but that never worked. It was murder and within a couple of days I had to have a couple of tablets just to function. Once I'd decided I *had* to stop taking them, I found a doctor who put me on a sensible long-term course of treatment. I started off by taking my normal intake of tablets and although the tablets I was subsequently given every day appeared outwardly to be the same as the ones I'd taken the day before, week by week and month by month their strength was reduced by such small amounts, I didn't notice. And because I didn't notice, I didn't start to get panicky. Agreeing to undergo that treatment was one of the most sensible things I've ever done.

When I confessed to the papers about my addiction it had a twofold effect. I felt much better for doing it, because some people thought my slurred voice and unfocused appearance meant I was permanently drunk. You'll already know if you've read this far that I'm a teetotaller, so rumours of me being an 'artiste de pis' really got to me. On the other hand, my honesty in confessing my weakness made TV producers throw up their hands and say 'We can't use Freddie Starr any more!', without bothering to find out that I was weening myself off the tranquillisers.

While I was going through my treatment, Des O'Connor took a big chance, for which I will always be grateful, and asked me to guest on his BBC2 chat show. He'd heard the rumours sweeping through the corridors and dressing rooms of our wonderful world of showbusiness that 'Freddie Starr's finished in television!', but he insisted that I appeared on the show. Des and I seemed to have the right comedy chemistry and my appearance was a big success. Suddenly people who hadn't spoken to me or phoned me in years got in touch with me again. For me and Des it was the beginning of a twelve-year working relationship. After five or six years at the BBC, Des took the show's basic format of music and chat with major stars to Thames Television, now Pearsons, and relocated from Television Centre to the Teddington Studios, where it achieved even greater success, with consistently high audience figures. The series ran until quite recently and there may well be more series and specials planned.

I thought it would be a great idea for me and Des to make a one-hour special together, clowning around, chatting and singing and I have mentioned it to his producers. Up until now, because the dates when we're both available have never worked out, it hasn't happened – but anything's possible. Sixty minutes of comedy performed by just two people on TV would take a lot of planning and writing, but I think between us we could make it an entertaining 'event' show, which would be talked about for some times afterwards. And there aren't many of those on the box any more.

You could always rely on Des's production team to book the biggest stars from the worlds of film, stage and television, from Barbra Streisand to Hugh Grant to me! When you watch the show at home, it seems that one continuous stream of guests comes on and off, performing and/or talking to Des. But these sequences may have been filmed on two or three different days, depending when the performers are available. If, for example, The Bee Gees could only turn up on a Tuesday afternoon, that's when they'd be filmed and their sequence would be edited into the finished show. Some of the music acts are filmed at 10.30 in the morning – without an audience, obviously.

If you were invited to talk to Des on the sofa, you'd never know who the other guests might be that night. I once walked into the green room, and who should be sat there, talking to his driver/minder but Hannibal Lecter himself, Sir Anthony Hopkins, who is a big comedy fan. We shook hands and made small talk at first, but when the conversation turned to comedy and who our all-time favourite comedian was, Tommy Cooper's name came up. We were both in the middle of telling old jokes using Tommy's voice and mannerisms when Anthony got the call that he was due on the studio floor.

He was on the show to plug his film *Surviving Picasso*, which he didn't seem very interested in discussing. In fact, after Des showed a clip of the film, he started to ask his guest a question about the part he played, but Anthony made it quite clear, in his easy-going, charming way, that he wasn't thrilled with the picture and suddenly went into his excellent Tommy Cooper impression, cracking gags for the rest of his spot, which took Des and the audience by surprise. Everyone in the studio was reduced to helpless laughter, delighted with the theatrical knight's unactorish behaviour and sharp sense of humour. Even when the chat was over, Anthony behaved like a comedian who was 'on a roll', not wanting to conclude his 'act' and while the cameras were being rearranged for the next item, he borrowed the mic from Des's warm-up man Ted Robbins and delivered another barrage of great gags as Tommy. As he didn't want to plug his latest film, I wonder what he would have talked to Des about for fifteen minutes if we hadn't met up in the green room!

Every time I appeared on *Des O'Connor Tonight* we jelled and had lots of laughs. He would always know the basic idea of what I was going to do, but he also liked to be surprised too. Some of those surprises turned out to be more like shocks! I would always tell the producer what I intended doing to wrongfoot Des, so he'd know where to place the cameras. It was controlled chaos 75 per cent of the time and completely uncontrolled the rest of the time.

Des takes his singing very seriously and people tend to forget or possibly aren't even aware that he had seven Top Thirty hits in three years, including the very moving tear-jerking love song that's now one of late-night radio's most requested tunes, especially by heartbroken lovers who can't be together. I'm talking about the immortal 'Dick A Dum Dum'.

For one of his shows they'd built him a beautiful fountain, complete with spouting water, which he was going to sing a romantic song in front of (possibly 'Dick Another Dum Dum'?) and I asked the producer if, after Des had been singing the song for a minute, he could arrange for the fountain to start making loud gurgling noises as if there were something blocked inside. But it was vital that Des wasn't informed about it. I said, 'You see to the fountain and I'll give you five minutes of comedy!' The producer agreed, took half a dozen indigestion tablets and phoned Thames Television's insurers to see if the show was covered for flood damage.

On the night, the audience unaware of what was about to happen, Des started the song, with the fountain working beautifully behind him. He'd got through about a minute of the song when the fountain started making horrible gurgling noises that ruined the mood of the song. But I was about to ruin it even more. Des kept on singing, hoping the sound in the control room (which was what the viewers would hear at home) was different to the sound in the studio. Of course the audience started giggling and their giggles turned to laughs when I walked on behind Des, dressed as a plumber and holding a tool box. Des still thought the audience were laughing at the gurgles, which were getting louder and louder and sounding funnier and funnier, and gamely went on singing. He knew he shouldn't stop unless he was told to by the 'boss of the studio floor' the floor manager, who, being in on the joke, was just standing there at the side, looking unconcerned. The floor manager would have heard from the director in the control room via his earpiece if the number had to be stopped It was only when Des heard me bashing the fountain with the mallet I'd taken out of my box that he turned around. He laughed, but kept on warbling.

I then started wrestling with a rubber octopus the props men had planted on top of the fountain. Des kept singing and glancing across at the floor manager, who let the number continue. There was an almighty 'splash' as the octopus 'pulled' me into three feet of water! My eight-legged friend (the octopus, not Des) continued to wrestle me and within a few seconds I was soaking wet, occasionally coming up for air before a tentacle would 'drag me' back in the water. Still singing, Des came over to see if I was alright. Bad mistake for Des. Great moment for me! Des, as always, was dressed beautifully in a dark suit, white shirt and smart tie. Thirty quid the lot at Tesco's! More like £1,000 from Armani! I was lying there with water in my eyes, my body covered by a rubber octopus and, as I looked up, all I could see was Des's smiling face and his tie a couple of inches from me. His expensive tie. Dangling there. Well . . . what else could I do?

I grabbed his tie, he lost his balance, went base over apex into the water alongside me with an enormous 'splash' (slightly different to a 'splash' in comedy terms) and ruined his suit. We ended the show with the two of us sat in the fountain, throwing water at each other. Two grown men behaving like kids on prime time television, and getting very well paid for it.

That was great fun, but the Des show I was a guest on that most people probably remember was when, bravely, ITV decided it would be a good idea to broadcast the series live on Wednesday nights. Up in the control room, director Brian Penders was recovering from a broken leg, in fact he still had the plaster on up to his hip and had manoeuvred himself into his seat with the aid of his crutches. He wanted a fast, funny and uneventful show if at all possible.

First guest on was Liverpool comedian Stan ('I hate dose Germans. They bombed our chip shops!') Boardman. I was watching the show on the big screen TV set in the green room and as soon as he went into the gag about German aeroplanes called Fokkers, I sensed that Des was in trouble, because I knew the joke and what the tag (punchline) was. I don't know what had got into Stan that night, because he was well aware the show was going out live at eight o'clock in the evening. There was no doubt about it. As he told the joke, Stan wasn't saying 'Fokkers', he was pronouncing the word, clear as a bell as 'Fuckers'. I have no idea how many times he said it but I could see the perspiration forming on Des's face and imagined the state of his armpits – he must have been sweating for England!

Stan ignored the viewers and worked to the studio audience, who of course were in stitches at the 'fuckers' in the gag and also at Des's panic-stricken face. Upstairs in the control room, Brian Penders was having a blue fit. He was screaming down the floor manager's earpiece, but what could *he* do? Suddenly step in and tell Stan to stop the gag? No . . . the show was going out live.

Stan got to the end of the joke and delivered the punchline. Surrounded by a handful of researchers and assistants and two or three performers, I watched the TV screen in disbelief. There was no mistaking what he said. Twelve million television viewers clearly heard a mainstream comedian say at 8.15 in the evening '. . . that fucker's a Messerschmidt!'

Des 'thanked' Stan and announced a commercial break. Stan left the set and a make-up girl began to wipe Des down. I think she had to send out for more towels.

If his presence is ever needed, a director will sometimes run down to the studio floor during a show to iron out any problems, but with his injured leg and crutches, Brian Penders was in no position to 'run'. He looked at the running order. The big name in Part 2 was going to be actor, hellraiser and world-champion farter Oliver Reed! Brian prayed that Ollie would be a good boy.

I think there was a musical item at the beginning of Part 2 and then Des brought Oliver Reed on. He'd had a drink or three but he wasn't falling-down drunk and didn't pretend to be either, but I could see from the twinkle in his eyes that he had the devilment in him and was going to make the most of his time on live television. Des was supposed to ask him about the tattoo which he had on his bum and steered the conversation in that direction a few times, but Ollie talked about anything and everything that had nothing to do with tattoos. Brian Penders watched the interview, counting the minutes on the control room clock, knowing that another commercial break was due soon and it looked like the Oliver Reed chat would be free of any embarrassing moments. After all, if he did finally answer the question about his tattoo, the viewers couldn't possibly get upset by the word 'bum'!

During the closing moments of the interview, Des said, 'So, Oliver, before you go, are you going to tell us where you have this famous tattoo of yours?'

'Yes,' said Oliver. 'It's on my cock!'

The audience exploded into shocked laughter as soon as they heard that rude word. Des nearly fainted and Brian Penders was so outraged he almost fell out of his chair and broke his other leg.

Des said, but didn't really mean, 'My thanks to Oliver Reed' and another commercial break brought a two-minute respite from the chaos in the studio.

All around the country, parents watching the show with the rest of their family were trying to avoid answering questions from inquisitive children – 'What did the man say, Mummy?'

and 'Why is your face so red, Daddy?' Back at Teddington, the phones started ringing in the control room. The ITV bosses wanted to know what the hell was going on down there! Brian had been concentrating on the Oliver Reed chat so much, he forgot who was on next. After he'd taken a call from one of the powerful ITV men in suits and explained to him that everything that had happened had been beyond his control, but that the rest of the show would definitely, positively be squeaky clean, Brian looked at the clock. Twenty seconds to go until Part 3.

'Right!' he said to his PA. 'Who's on after the break?'

She didn't want him upset any more than he already was, so she whispered the name of the next guest. Brian said, 'Speak up! I can't hear you! Who's on next? Who's on next?'

When she said, 'Freddie Starr!', Brian threw his crutches across the room, put his head in his hands in despair and moaned, 'Oh God no! No!' As far as he was concerned I was yet another mischief maker who was going to make it a television treble. Three guests, three X-rated conversations. But I'd been watching the show in the green room and knew there'd be lots of complaints from viewers and from the Network bosses. As this was my seventh or eighth appearance on the sofa and I considered myself a friend of the series, I wasn't going to add fuel to what was rapidly becoming a bloody big bonfire! I walked on with a naughty look in my eye that worried Des at first, and I was at my most intimidating worst at first, but I kept everything bubbling along and we both got lots of laughs. The thing is, once a studio audience, and the TV viewers, have heard 'fucker' and 'cock' you can't take it any further in that direction at that time of night. You have to pull back and take it in a different direction, which is what Des and I did. Live on stage, with an audience who have paid to see you and *expect* to hear rude words, entirely different rules apply, especially if the posters clearly state 'For Adults Only'.

When the show was over, Des had sweated so much he was carried off on a stretcher and given an emergency perspiration transfusion. It didn't make him feel any better because the donor was Brian Penders.

The trouble with appearing on any series regularly is, you can sometimes be taken for granted by the production team. Maybe by the star too. I think it got to a point where I'd done so many *Des O'Connor Tonights* that they took me for granted.

But it only happened once.

It was after Brian Penders had left and I was asked to turn up at Teddington at three o'clock in the afternoon on the day of recording, which seemed very early to me for a 7.30 start. There was a whole new team on board and I sensed the previously happy atmosphere had gone. The pressure was being put on everyone from the men in suits to crank out as many items as possible and it was around that time that Des was sometimes recording interviews in the afternoon and the evening with two different audiences. I went into see Des and his writers in his dressing room and we all sat around chatting over coffee. I knew his writers were doing their usual trick of picking my brain for material but I wanted Des and myself to have another memorably funny encounter on the sofa, so I threw in ideas with the rest of them.

I was then taken up to my dressing room and given three tapes of previous shows to watch. There was large plate of sandwiches under cellophane on a table. I wouldn't say they'd been there a long time, but there was a note attached that read 'Please accept these with our compliments, Mr Chaplin'. They'd also supplied bottled water and jugs of tea and coffee. All very nice. But I was left in that room from four o'clock until they called me at 9.30! Only one person came and knocked on my door in all that time – a researcher who asked, 'Is there anything you need?' with the blank look of someone who doesn't really want to do anything for anyone. I was really pissed off. No one said, 'Come and have a cup of coffee with us, Freddie!' just to break the boredom. They left me stuck in that room all that time, then, when they say, 'We'll need you in fifteen minutes' they expect you to go out and be hysterically funny. Yeah, I know that's what I get paid for, but they'd taken me for granted and whether you're a comedian or a coalman, it doesn't matter. You still feel slighted. By the time I went on, all the fun had drained out of me and it wasn't one of my better chats with Des. But

Thames must have been happy with it because they asked me back on the show and they showed me much more respect the next time.

There were occasions when I had to be interviewed very early on in the show because as soon as it was over I had to drive to the Circus Tavern for a ten o'clock cabaret.

When I was making a series for Carlton Television in 1987, I asked Des if he'd like to make a guest appearance on one of the shows. But his manager said, 'I'm sorry, he's busy.' He didn't even ask if there were any alternative dates that might have suited Des better. I couldn't believe that he'd turned me down, after all the times I'd been on his show. But I still think a show with just the two of us (and a twenty-piece orchestra) would pull in the viewers.

I made a series and two specials for Carlton in 1993 and 1884, with the man who had produced and directed Benny Hill's shows for Thames Television, Dennis Kirkland. Dennis is a talented man, but he made the mistake of trying to recreate Benny's sketches just a year or two after Benny died, which was a bit of a non-starter. Now might be a good time to try it, almost ten years after Benny's sad death, but Dennis attempted it far too soon. We even had Benny's old co-star Bob Todd on the show. Some of the sketches were so similar to Benny's they could have played 'Yakety Sax' over them and called it *The Freddie Hill Show*! I felt the whole concept was wrong . To me Benny was one of the great British comedians, with a TV career that stretched from his first appearance in 1949 on *Music Hall* until the time Thames Television, shockingly, terminated his contract in 1989. By that time his shows were being repackaged and sold all over the world, earning him and Thames a fortune. So why did Thames drop him? Because in some people's opinion he was . . . here it comes . . . 'politically incorrect'.

He was getting flack from some of the younger comedians, particularly a certain Mr Ben Elton, for being sexist. This accusation was solely based on the 'chase' sketch that ended all his shows, when Benny would run after (in speeded-up fashion) but never catch up with, a bevy of scantily clad nurses or policewomen. The hypocrisy of the alternative comedians as they were just finding their feet in the business was and still is astounding. They would have a go at Benny for his so-called sexism, in an interview to publicise their new TV series, or book or tour, which would be printed in a newspaper that had young girls showing their breasts on Page 3. But they were too busy being pleased with themselves to see the irony.

They ignored the fact that Benny was a brilliant wordsmith and a master of the double entendre. He was a prolific writer of comic poems, monologues and song lyrics and starred in several major films. Of course, when he passed away on Saturday, 18 April 1992, the day before Frankie Howerd died, the celebrities couldn't wait to tell the press what a brilliant comedian Benny was. Even a certain Mr B. Elton, who vigorously denied ever saying a bad word about Benny.

Bullshit and bollocks! Who was it accused Benny of sexism then, another bespectacled comedian with the same name, jacket and smug expression?

Ben is a clever man, I realise that. His output as a writer is enviable – *Blackadder*, *The Thin Blue Line*, *Maybe Baby* – alright, two out of three ain't bad. And his musical collaboration with Andrew Lloyd Webber has been a success. But as a performer he lacks the charm and warmth (witness his appallingly misjudged performance hosting the 2000 Royal Variety Performance) that the great British comedians possessed. This is purely my opinion and my observation and I may well be proved wrong, but I don't think most of the university-educated comedians who have been pouring into television like soggy porridge since the early 1980s will be looked upon with fondness in twenty or thirty years' time, despite (or perhaps because of) their cleverness. They're all too cold and their comedy is the comedy of cruelty.

Alexei Sayle, remember him? Like a lot of them he ran out of material so he turned to writing books. He was being interviewed by Michael Parkinson quite recently, to plug his latest book I think, and he had the arrogance to say this: 'Before the alternative comedians came along, *there were no decent British comedians around, only a few naff Northern comics!*' I'm not kidding!

Now apart from the fact that Michael (a big fan of British comedians, who should know better) didn't challenge Mr Sayle's sweeping and obviously incorrect statement, it makes you wonder on what evidence he felt confident to open his ignorant gob on the subject. Because when the 'better educated' comedians came on the scene, we still had some brilliant British comedians around. Chic Murray. Eric Sykes. Max Wall. Jimmy Tarbuck. Tommy Cooper. Frankie Howerd. Benny Hill. Peter Cook. Dudley Moore. Tommy Trinder. Al Read. Michael Bentine. Spike Milligan. Dick Emery. Mike Yarwood. Arthur Askey. Bob Monkhouse . . .

Hey Alexei . . . ever heard of *The Two Ronnies*? No? OK, then Morecambe and Wise – do those two names mean anything to you?

For a man who has about as much warmth as an Arctic winter to speak so disdainfully of the hundreds of British comedians who had built up their careers in the 50s and 60s, some of whom are still working in TV and on stage, is nothing but a downright disgrace. Will there be a *Heroes of Comedy* documentary devoted to Mr Sayle in 2040, with his peers speaking of his genius with a lump in their throat? Let's wait and see . . .

I hear a lot about 'cutting edge' comedians. And 'pushing the envelope'. Young comedians are encouraged to 'push the envelope'. Which is very appropriate as many of them would be better off employed in a Royal Mail sorting office. They can't have a go at mainstream comedians for being sexist and then go on stage and television themselves and talk about what they like doing in bed or the back seat of a car, with their girlfriends or wives or both. But they get away with it because there's hardly anyone left in television who cares any more.

And can anyone tell me when performers stopped being introduced in this way – 'Will you please welcome . . .' and started being introduced in *this* way – 'Will you please *give it up for* . . .!'

'"Give it up"? What is it, Lent?'

Of course young people should have their own comedy icons, just like they have their own music that puzzles and irritates their parents. But it just seems to me that very subtly, the 'grown-up' comedians were gradually replaced by lesser talents who the TV bosses decided were younger and hipper – but were they any funnier? – to the extent now that alternative comedians who host and take part in 'comedy' panel games only ever invite the previous generation of comedians and impressionists on their shows just to take the piss out of them. Which is hardly creative comedy. But it seems young TV viewers love it, because these 'post-modern ironic' panel games seem to multiply every week.

But what about the viewers over forty? Don't they count? Over fifty-five? You can forget it mate! There are millions of mature people tired of the snide remarks and constant references to 1980s culture (the period the panellists grew up in and are still obsessed with) so why can't the older viewers be treated to just *one* well-made, star-packed variety show every week, preferably at eight o'clock on a Saturday evening? How would that possibly hurt the TV bosses? They give us countless detective shows, cookery shows, travel shows, soaps ... but they won't give us entertainment. I could sit down with the ITV Network Controller *tomorrow* (I can't today, I've got an appointment with the BBC Controller!), and plan out twelve variety shows featuring up and coming comedians, chart bands, rock 'n' roll legends, established comics, and a big star name to top the bill. But the brains behind television programming have lost the plot completely, totally ignoring the mainstream audience for years. Of course people still watch TV in their millions, but that doesn't mean they actually *enjoy* the stuff they're given. Television has got so bad now, I use the remote control to watch snatches of fifty or sixty digital programmes all night and never settle on any one for more than five minutes. Yes, admit it. You do too!

On terrestrial telly, five nights a week we have miserable people shouting at each other in soaps. We get docusoaps, garden and home make-overs and cookery. Bloody hell! No wonder the video shops are so busy. Then on Saturday night, which should be the big family entertainment night when the 18- to 25-year-olds are out enjoying themselves, what are we given? Ant and Dec, Dale Winton and *Casualty*. And who was the brain of Britain who decided that comedian Roy Walker, who had steered *Catchphrase* to continued ratings success over many years, should suddenly be removed and replaced by a grin on a stick?

And as for that amoeba with gelled hair, Steve 'I belong in local radio' Penk . . . don't get me started!

Harry Hill. Now I've carefully watched and analysed his TV shows and I'm convinced he's not an Earthling. No, he's a visitor from the furthest planet from ours, called 'Not-veryfuckingfunny', pronounced as you read it. He and several of his fellow visitors from Notveryfuckingfunny decided to invade Televisionland and thought the easiest route would be to take on the guise of a 'comedian'. They watched our Earth broadcasts for years until they thought they were ready to take over and morphed into their interpretation of 'comedians'. You can see them on your screens most nights. They *talk* like comedians. They *look* like comedians. They *even convinced TV bosses* they're comedians. But they're *not* comedians in my book.

Alright, I've told you what they're not, so it's only fair I tell you what they *are*.

They're well-educated, extremely articulate young men who have the ability to stand on stage or in front of a TV camera and talk with easy-going confidence. Which takes some doing. But it doesn't make them comedians.

Harry Hill's humour is often described by the TV trendies as 'surreal'. To them I say 'get real'. With his little catchphrases and furry animals and non sequiturs (I thought a non sequitur meant I'd lost my pruning shears) he is just plundering the comedy of his elders and betters like Milligan, Bentine and the Pythons without acknowledging his debt to them.

I love daft, wacky, off-the-wall humour that doesn't have to have any particular point and leaves everything unfinished before the next item appears. But when Harry Hill attempts it, he often slips back to his previous occupation as a doctor, because his approach to comedy is *very clinical*.

So where have all the *real* comedians gone?

Let's be honest, most of the 'greats' are dead. Those who are still around have been elbowed and forgotten by the new

TV bosses, whose average age is thirty these days. They must think Lenny Henry is an old-time music hall star!

There are a few younger mainstream comedians around, but you hardly ever see them on TV. Brian Conley is allowed one series most years. But what about Joe Pasquale, Bobby Davro, Shane Richie, Bradley Walsh? They're knockout comics, in no way old-fashioned in their approach to humour. They all learned their trade the hard way, in the working men's clubs and holiday camps and seaside resorts where you really had to be funny. Not for a five minute 'open mike' spot, but for forty-five minutes or longer. But it seems that just as they were establishing themselves as major stars, and getting their own TV series they were usurped (I looked it up and it's OK to use it) by the Oxbridge mob.

In America, the older generation of comedians are looked up to, put on pedestals, honoured for their contribution to showbusiness and usually, health permitting, keep working in TV, films and places like Vegas and Atlantic City. Jerry Lewis, Alan King, Joey Bishop, Don Rickles, George Carlin, Rodney Dangerfield. Do *we* do the same here for our elder statesmen of comedy like Eric Sykes or Norman Wisdom or Spike? Do we hell. And as upsetting as the thought is, these comedy geniuses won't be here in twenty years' time so let's give them all a telly series *now*!

By the way, just in case you think I'm obsessed with the success of the alternative comedians, relax. It's more of a detached, yet thoroughly researched observation. I'm not in competition with them. I've been there . . . done that . . . had the girl in the wet T-shirt. I was a headliner in 1970 after a twelve-year apprenticeship and when I feel like touring I can still pack out theatres. I have been honest with you and told you that I've been unhappy with some of my TV shows, but there have been some I thought were very good. Like my 1996 *An Audience with Freddie Starr* and the following year's *Another Audience With . . . Me*, both for London Weekend Television.

Why did I like them? Because they captured the essence of Freddie Starr's comedy. It wasn't just me who liked them – the audience figures for both were excellent. One of the main reasons the shows were so good *for me* was Nigel Lythgoe who was then Controller of Entertainment and Comedy at LWT – he's since become a household name thanks to *Popstars*.

He's a very creative person and having been a choreographer and producer of many TV entertainment series and Royal Variety shows, he's worked with hundreds of performers and writers, which gives him an advantage over many other television executives. He has a 'feel' for showbusiness and knows what the great big TV audience out there wants!

Nigel is a very approachable fellow (he's always being approached by young ladies in Old Compton Street) and will listen to my ideas, no matter how crazy. At the first production meeting for *An Audience With . . . Me* I was sat at the table with Nigel and the team of assistants and researchers and writers, who were all throwing ideas in which did nothing for me and after twenty minutes or so, I said, 'Nigel! Can I set fire to myself?'

'Yes,' he said, 'but not right this minute Freddie or your coffee will get cold!'

'No!' I said. 'Can I set fire to myself *on the show*?'

Everyone around the table dropped their pens or spilt coffee down their regulation black suits and T-shirts.

Except Nigel. Who was wearing his usual denim shorts, flippers and divers helmet. Well it *was* the second Tuesday after Pentecost. He looked at the team around the table and said, 'Look! If Freddie wants to set fire to himself, let him set fire to himself! It's your job to find out *how* he can set fire to himself!' Once Nigel had approved the idea they couldn't question it. So, when we taped the show, I set fire to my head. It was my quick impression of Robbie Burns. No, not really. Of course, I could only do it after stringent checks and tests by the Health and Safety people. The other proviso was I had to invite the entire cast of *London's Burning*!

It got a huge laugh. As I knew it would.

Thanks Nigel – you're not nasty at all!

CHAPTER SEVENTEEN

I'll never fprget the moment. I was sat in the same luxuriously over-the-top Las Vegas dressing room as my showbusiness idol. The icon of icons. I could see him talking to the boys in his band and some of his entourage, no more than ten feet away from me. For someone like me, the devoted fan who had grown up with his music, seen all his films at my local cinema and learned to copy his voice and his mannerisms so well that my impression of him was now one of the highlights of my act, just sitting there for half an hour, listening to him laughing and joking with his musicians would have been enough. Then I noticed him glancing over in my direction several times and that he seemed curious to find out who I was. My heart was in my mouth when I saw the tall, dark-haired man with the thick sideburns walking over to me. He put out his hand, smiled and said, 'Hi! My name's Elvis Presley!'

Let's go back a couple of days before that meeting. I was at the MGM Grand Hotel in Las Vegas to see Elvis 'live' and several of his shows were being filmed for inclusion in the film *Elvis – That's The Way It Is*, so the place was in chaos with cameras and lights and what seemed more like a small army than a film crew. But none of that spoiled the excitement of seeing 'The King' in concert. Even before the show started, the atmosphere was electric. Then the excitement went up several notches when the band, featuring legendary guitarist James Burton and pianist Glen D. Hardin started playing the intro to 'Blue Suede Shoes' and when Elvis walked out on that huge stage, I couldn't believe it was really him. To his fans in Britain, Elvis had always appeared to be a remote, almost mythical figure who only existed on film and records. The audience, evenly divided between men and women, went wild when they saw him. If he had just sung one song and left, that would have been worth the price of admission. But he gave us a fabulous, unforgettable selection of rock 'n' roll, ballads and gospel songs. 'Proud Mary', 'Sweet Caroline', 'Polk Salad Annie', 'The Wonder Of You' and more. I'd never seen a performer whip an audience into such a state of excitement. He gave every heartbeat and every fibre of his soul and mind to his devoted fans that night. Even if you were sat at the back of the auditorium, it felt like he was singing directly to you. I've never seen anyone sweat so much on stage. When he finally left the stage, the audience were almost as drained as he was.

On the way out I kept thinking, 'I just have to try and meet Elvis! I *have* to!' but the Americans are incredibly strict on allowing anybody backstage. Then and now.

I tried to think how I could get to see Elvis. I saw a guy named Jim standing at the back who was in charge of all of the entertainment venues in Vegas. I can't remember his exact job title, but I guessed he could open a few doors, possibly the one that said 'Elvis Presley – Strictly Private'. We'd spoken a few times and he knew I was an entertainer from Britain, so I walked up to him and he asked me if I'd enjoyed the show and I mentioned that I happened to know one of Elvis's entourage, a man named Charlie, who I hadn't seen for a few years. Jim said, 'Come with me Freddie', and took me through a door marked 'Keep Out!' A few minutes' walk down a neon-lit concrete corridor and we were in the backstage area.

'Would you please stay here?' Jim said and disappeared among the throng of musicians, singers, camera, sound and lighting crew and dozens of other people with vital roles to play.

Of course I didn't particularly want to meet Charlie, but wherever he was, Elvis might be nearby. Possibly. Maybe he'd already gone up to his suite. Or gone out on the town. It was worth taking a chance, anyway.

Jim was gone a long time, almost half an hour and while I was standing there pacing up and down with my stomach in knots with excitement and fear, a security man came over to me and asked me what I was doing there. I used excuse number one for getting backstage. 'I'm with the band.' Shit! Why couldn't I be more original!

He looked at me and rested his right hand on the gun that hung by his side.

'With the band, huh?' He didn't seem very convinced. He pointed with his thumb at yet another door, this one marked 'Strictly Private' and said, 'The band are on the inside and you, mister, are on the outside. How d'ya explain that?'

I was going to get close to Elvis whatever happened and no big security guard toting a gun was going to stop me! Didn't he know I was a personal friend of Karl Denver?

I lied through my teeth. 'Yes I know, but I've got a bad stomach. The shits. So I had to use the john in a hurry!' I clutched my stomach. It did hurt, but through nervous tension not the runs. He looked at me very suspiciously. As I was attempting to convince him of my digestive problems, I suddenly saw Jim approaching. What was he going to say? He ignored the security man and said, 'Come on, Freddie, follow me', and I smiled at the guard and followed Jim.

For all I knew he might have been taking me to a side exit so he could boot me out into the carpark, but he led me through the door marked 'Strictly Private'. I was actually at the back of the stage and he led me down a few steps to a large, well, not so much a dressing room as a dressing aircraft-hanger. Jim showed me into the room, nodded to me in the way Americans do to signify 'I've sorted it all out for you' and left. The room was huge with large comfortable sofas everywhere and a piano, drum kit and several guitars in one corner. I guessed it doubled as a rehearsal room. Dozens of well-dressed couples stood around, all Americans and all immaculately groomed. From the way they were talking to each other about what big deal they were just about to do or what contract they were just about to sign, I could tell that most of them had never met until that evening. So they were free to converse in the universal language of showbusiness – fluent bollocks.

Charlie came into the room and walked over to me, warmly shaking me by the hand. At last, someone I could talk to! We chatted about the show and the film that MGM were making which would give the rest of the world a taste of Elvis in concert. A short while later, Elvis walked in and he seemed larger than life to me. Like he'd stepped out of a cinema screen. I've met hundreds of big stars since, but I've never

ever got that feeling again. He was dressed in a red shirt and black trousers and I noticed his hands were long and slim. I studied every move he made. After all, that was as close to Elvis I would ever be, so I had to memorise everything so that when I got back to Britain and people asked me what he was like I could give them a full description. I could see Elvis's hair was a sort of bluish-black, possibly dyed and his skin colour was a mixture of orange and bronze, suntan and make-up. Which only added to his unreal appearance. Elvis looked around the room in my direction a couple of times and *I could not believe that Elvis was looking at little Freddie Fowell from Liverpool!*

Charlie left me and went over to talk to Elvis and the band and a bunch of other men who I took to be his entourage After ten, fifteen minutes, I saw Elvis nodding at something Charlie had said and then he started walking towards me, hand outstretched.

'Hi! My name's Elvis Presley.'

Bloody hell! I've never been a showbiz show-off, and I don't drop too many names, but ask yourself this.

Has anyone ever said, 'Hi! My name's Elvis Presley!' to you?

Anyone who hasn't been let out of the home for a couple of hours, I mean.

The King sat next to me and I introduced myself. We went through some trivial talk and then he wanted to know where I was from. When I told him 'Liverpool, England', it seemed to intrigue him. He was admiring the green jacket I was wearing which was cut high at the waist (ah, those 70s fashions!) and I told him I'd bought it in London. Anyway, this all led up to my telling him I was a performer and as I did, Charlie walked over and said, 'Elvis, over in the UK, Freddie is one of their top entertainers.'

Elvis said, 'Is that so? What is it you do?'

I said, 'I sing . . . tell gags . . . you know . . . oh and I do impressions.'

Charlie said, 'Do your Columbo for Elvis, Freddie!'

I couldn't say 'No! What if Elvis thinks I'm crap?' and by now several of the people in the room were staring at me. Well, it's more likely they were staring at Elvis talking to some guy they didn't know, so I went straight into a Columbo impression. Elvis laughed and I could see that he was wearing mascara and eye shadow. I thought he just hadn't had time to wash off his 'stage face' but I was told later that he wore make-up and mascara all the time. I'm *not* saying that's the gospel truth, I'm just telling you what I was told. But remember . . . I met the man and saw him wearing it, so don't send me hate mail!

Elvis wasn't gay, bi or the slightest bit effeminate, despite his make-up and mascara. Maybe he wanted to look permanently tanned. Or perhaps he thought his fans would be disappointed if they saw him looking pale and 'unstarry'. Whatever, he was 1000 per cent heterosexual. Next time you watch one of the *Naked Gun* films and the gorgeous Priscilla Presley sashays across the screen, just remember who was lucky enough to share a bed with her for a few years. What a woman! Phwoar! (Is that how you spell it?)

I went into several more impressions which made Elvis rock back and forth, tears of laughter streaming down his face. I thought, Please God, don't let his mascara run or I'll be thrown out! The rest of my time with him went by in a blur. I could have been there an hour. Or five. I just know he and I connected. Maybe it's because we're both Capricorns. He was born on 8 January 1935, I was born on 9 January 1943.

Elvis died on 16 August 1977. I was in summer season at Margate at the time and when I heard the news it upset me as much as if he'd been a member of my family.

I just couldn't take it in that my all-time idol was dead at the age of 42. When I went on stage that night, before I went into my Elvis impersonation, I announced I was doing it as a tribute to the man. I was crying, the audience were crying, even some of the orchestra were human enough to shed a tear. I couldn't get through the number because I was so choked. If that all sounds a bit too sentimental to you, all I can say is you should have been there that night. This was no false, American-style schmaltz.

I could tell the audience were genuinely moved. A lot of them were from my generation and when you love someone's music from the time you're a teenager, it stays with you for the rest of your life. You feel you know them through their lyrics and live appearances or just from interviews they do on TV When they die, it hits you hard that someone of your generation has gone. If you've been lucky enough to have met those people, like Elvis and John Lennon, it hurts ten times as much.

I've visited Vegas several time since that first, unforgettable time. In 1987 I supported Engelbert Humperdinck at the Las Vegas Hilton. He'd told me I should do well out there and asked me to open for him. So, after some massive reorganisation of my UK booking, I went out to Nevada. Engelbert was quite right. My impressions and my singing went down great. But the trouble was my spot was received too well. The audience reaction was fantastic and although I'm not going to say Eng found it hard to follow me, I will tell you that he refused to let me use his band after the first couple of nights. That's a sign of an insecure performer, wouldn't you say?

While I was out there I became friends with another comedy hero of mine, Jerry Lewis. His live act is like mine, mostly visual and he doesn't use gags as such. At the time of writing this book, Jerry is 74 and still touring the world in the musical *Damn Yankees*. He says of his ten-year partnership with Dean Martin, 'It was the perfect working relationship. I wrote all our material, rehearsed all day every day and got ulcers. And Dean played golf!'

I was very lucky during the times I went out there. In the early 1980s many of the legendary names in showbusiness were still around and appearing at the big hotels. One night Sammy Davis Junior walked up to me after a show and said, 'Hey, Freddie Starr! I've heard a lot about you. I'm told you're kind of a white Sammy Davis Junior!' and broke up laughing in the way you've seen him do in so many films.

I also had the privilege of meeting Dean Martin after watching his show at one of the hotels. When he first came on stage, I thought he was going to go straight into a song, but instead he stopped the band and started talking to the audience. I was dumbstruck when I heard him say, 'You folks don't want to throw your money away in the casino next door. That's all the guys in charge want, for you to lose your money here!' I don't know if someone had rubbed him up the wrong way before the show but for about ten minutes he did nothing but run down the casino bosses and even mentioned they were linked with the Mafia! He went into a 45-minute set, which was just superb, and before he left the stage he repeated his warning, 'Don't throw your money away in the casino, folks!'

I'd been told that Dean could be a right awkward bastard and having seen him deliver his anti-Mafia speech I didn't think he'd be in the mood to speak to a comedian he'd never heard of from Britain. But earlier in the evening, one of the entertainment bosses who had seen me open for Engelbert and thought that I was a 'funny guy' told Dean he should meet me. Once again I was taken through to a busy backstage area and eventually found Dean's room, where we found him relaxing in his chair.

He was a legendary boozer but from his healthy tan he looked more like a man who spent more time on the golf course than nursing a Jack Daniels in a gloomy bar. Jerry Lewis's summing-up of him must have been true. Dean shook my hand.

'How are ya, Freddie?' It was more a greeting than a question, but I answered, 'I'm fine! And I loved the show tonight.'

I was talking like Freddie Fowell, the film fan from Liverpool. But, why wouldn't I for crissake? This was *Dean Martin*! Dino Crocetti himself!

He went into another room for a couple of minutes and came out wearing a dressing gown. A man whom I took to be his dresser, poured him a drink. He then asked me if I'd like a drink.

'No thanks,' I said, 'I'm a teetotaller!'

Dean started laughing and said, 'A teetotaller! Get the fuck out of here!'

'Really,' I said. 'I don't drink. Never have.'

This really amused Dean. He couldn't have come across many people in showbusiness who didn't enjoy a drink. Apart from the Singing Nun and even she drank the Communion wine.

I asked him about the period he worked with Jerry Lewis and he just looked at me and smiled to himself.

'We had our times, but that's all in the past. I'd just do what I had to do, but Jerry never knew when to stop sometimes.'

I hated hearing him put Jerry down like that, but I knew they'd fallen out in the 1950s. They eventually made up 'live' on television in the 1980s, in the middle of one of Jerry's annual TV telethons for Muscular Dystrophy.

In 1979 I was booked to appear on BBC Television's *Parkinson, the* big Saturday night chat show of the 1970s (now dusted off, given a fresh coat of gloss paint and revived for the twenty-first century – and Parky looks all the better for it, don't you think?) and while I was rehearsing my Ray Charles impression, the director came down to the floor and told me he'd rather I dropped it from my act because Muhammed Ali was also guesting on the show and he might possibly be offended by the sight of a white man wearing a black stocking over his head, stumbling around the set, pretending to be a blind, coloured soul singer.

What he and the rest of the team, even Parky, didn't know was Muhammed Ali and I had been good friends for some years. He'd already seen and enjoyed my Ray Charles impression and I thought if one of the most powerful and influential black men in the world hadn't taken offence at my impression, I wasn't going to drop it for a nervous, white TV director. And I wasn't going to reveal my friendship with Ali.

'I don't care what Ali thinks,' I said. 'The impression stays in. And if he takes offence and gets the right hump with me, I'll knock him spark out!' I looked really pissed-off and capable of punching anyone's lights out!

They couldn't believe what I was saying. That I would dare take on a Heavyweight Champion of the World to defend an impersonation? Ali was in Britain to publicise his new film *Freedom Road* and Sandy and I had been guests at the London premiere a few nights before and even shared his limo to the cinema.

But I kept all that to myself. Every time they begged me during the afternoon, I told the director and the producer that I refused to take out the impression. Everyone around me got very sweaty and twitchy because they didn't want Ali upset again. He'd had a famously enormous row with Parky during his previous appearance on the show – you've probably see the clip more than once – and they didn't want a repeat performance. Ali and I had already discussed that classic confrontation and you might be interested in hearing his version, which may give you a different perspective next time the clip is reshown on 'Parky at the BBC – The First Eighty Years'!

There was an unauthorised biography of Ali out at the time, which he was very upset about because it was full of untruths. Parkinson had told him he would not mention it during the interview, but when Ali walked on to the set for the interview, he could see the book on a low table by Parky's feet. He asked Parky not to bring it out, but halfway through the show he did and started talking about it, which got Ali's back up. In fact I remember watching the show at home and being certain at one point that Ali was so angry he was going to hit Parky.

He let rip with a red-hot torrent of anger at Parkinson's behaviour and made it very clear that the book was full of lies about him and his religious beliefs. If I had been on the receiving end of Ali's wrath, I don't think I would have looked as cool as Parky seemed to be. He didn't even try to calm Ali down. In fact he managed to work him up into an even bigger lather. But, it was terrific television that people still talk about today. Well, you and me are talking about it right now!

Walking back to my dressing room after the rehearsal I bumped into Ali and we put our arms around each other and hugged. I don't know to this day why we got on so well, but he was another Capricorn, born on 17 January and always called me his soul brother, which was the biggest compliment he could have paid me. Maybe there was some sort of spiritual connection between us. We went into his dressing room and he mentioned what had happened when he'd been on the Parkinson show before, which he still felt a little upset about. I asked him if he would like to get his revenge on Parky and his eyes lit up. I said, 'Parky's producer and director have begged me not to include my Ray Charles impression in tonight, but I take it you wouldn't mind if I did it?'

'Not at all,' Ali said. 'It makes me laugh!'

'Great!' I said. 'Look, I've got an idea how we can have some fun with Parky tonight, but to make this work you have to keep a straight face because he doesn't know we're friends. This is what we'll do . . .'

A few hours later the show started and Michael introduced Ali who came on to fantastic applause. He was smiling and talkative and gave no sign that there was mayhem lined up for later. The interview lasted about 25 minutes and Michael said, 'For the moment, Mohammad Ali, thank you very much,' scratched his nose and rubbed it in his sideburns, something he did most weeks, and said, 'Please welcome Freddie Starr.' I came on with the orchestra playing and the audience went wild.

The director, producer, floor manager and the entire crew were pooping their pants that my Ray Charles impersonation would inflame Ali. After I did each impression I gave a sly glance to Ali who had a cheeky smile on his face, which nearly set me off laughing, and once I start laughing on stage I can't stop. I did my comedy Elvis with the black wig and everyone knew that Elvis was the last but one impression before Ray Charles, and were hoping I might 'see sense' and finish with The King and drop Ray. But they were disappointed.

'And now ladies and gentlemen,' I said, 'Mr Ray Charles!' On went the stocking and the dark glasses and I got straight into the impression. All the crew were looking at Ali for his outraged reaction but I could see he was hiding his smile behind his hand. I finished my set and walked over to where Parky and Ali were sitting and I pretended the Champion and I had never met before.

As he shook my hand he said, 'Freddie, that was the best Ray Charles impersonation I've ever seen!'

I said, 'Thank you, Mr Ali!'

Parky was just about to ask me a question when Ali said, 'Yes . . . what a great Ray Charles that was! You're so good! And Elvis too!'

I had my back turned slightly to Michael and didn't give him the chance to get a word in.

'I believe you have a film out at the moment, Mr Ali,' I said. 'What's it called?'

'*Freedom Road*,' he said, and went on talking about it for a few minutes.

I still kept my back to Michael and said, 'I know Kris Kristofferson's in it. How did you two get on?' And so we kept up this two-man conversation, totally ignoring Parky. The audience were with us, laughing hysterically at Michael's predicament. He wasn't likely to get stroppy with Ali after what had happened on the previous occasion. Then I steered the chat towards boxing, which I'm a big fan of, and I asked Ali what it took to be a champion.

'If you want to be a champion in the ring,' Ali said, 'you have to train so hard, so much, that when you get knocked down onto the canvas, no matter how bad you're hurting, you have the strength and the stamina to get right back up again, even if your legs are buckling under you and your lungs are on fire. Joe Frazier's jabbing at you and you just *know* the one thing he wants to do in life is to knock your head right off, so you have to keep punching and moving and every muscle in your body is aching and the sweat's stinging your eyes and the noise of the crowd is deafened by the blood pounding around your ears and you fight against the pain and the tiredness as much as you fight your opponent. Then "Bam!" you connect with one powerful punch, then "Bam! Bam!" two more and you watch your opponent fall to the floor. The fight's over, the bell rings and you're still the Heavyweight Champion of the World. That's all it takes!'

Is *that* all?

He said that the younger fighters who came along after him had it easy because they only had one fight a year, whereas he had to fight every three months. Four heavyweight fights a year! His body must have taken a hell of a pounding.

Parky had something to say then, but I jumped in again and started telling Ali about a film I'd just made about the Mafia (who, like the film I was talking about, don't really exist!) and I could see he was getting more and more enthralled by it.

I was making it up as I went along and the story got more and more suspenseful as my face got closer and closer to Ali's and when it was just six inches from Ali's, I let out a scream and he practically jumped out of his seat in fright.

'No one's ever scared me like that before!' he said. 'I'm going to tell everyone back home what you did to me.' We were having the time of our lives together so I took a chance and asked him if he'd like to sing a duet with me and he accepted. We'd hijacked the show from Parky but he knew it had been one of his most memorable evenings. When Ali and I finished our song it brought the house down. The sad thing is, because of the expensive cost of videotape back then, the BBC rarely kept complete editions of *Parkinson*. They had no idea that twenty years later, the satellite and digital channels would be buying up hundreds of old TV series which they'd repeat over and over again. So all that remains of the show I did with Ali is the section when I tell him the Mafia story. Unless . . . some BBC person has built up a private collection . . .?

Muhammed Ali has suffered from Parkinson's disease for many years but still visits Britain occasionally to attend fund-raising events. In fact his latest visit was at the beginning of 2001 when he proved once again that he is still as loved by the public as he was when he was the Heavyweight Champion of the World. The British seem to hold a special affection for boxing heroes, especially our own. Fighters from Freddie Mills to Henry Cooper to Frank Bruno crossed over into television, stage and radio after they hung up their gloves and were accepted warmly by the public and Muhammed Ali has joined that special brotherhood.

Ali, my courageous friend, I hope you still consider me to be your soul brother.

I've saved the best story till last. If I tell you it involves that giant of comedy, Tommy Cooper, you'll be smiling already.

I can't remember if I'd gone to see him working or if he'd come to see me working that night. But we'd had a drink (him whisky, me Coca Cola) and a chat afterwards and when I looked at my watch and saw it was well after midnight, I offered to give him a lift home.

We pulled into his road and he said, 'Would you mind stopping just by here?'

'I don't mind, no,' I said. 'But you live about six houses further down.'

'I know,' he said. 'But Dove's in bed' (he always called his wife, Gwen, 'Dove') 'and if she hears a car door slam, it'll wake her up and she'll be annoyed. Besides, this is a very refined neighbourhood and we rarely hear any noise after eleven o'clock.'

'I understand,' I said. 'Goodnight then, Tom.'

'Aren't you coming in for a cup of tea?' he said.

'Yeah, if you like!' I said.

'Come on then,' he said. 'But close your door quietly. Remember the neighbours.'

So we both got out of my car and very gingerly closed the doors. There was no one in the street and Tommy walked ve-ry slowly and ve-ry quietly, one foot after the other, as if he was walking across an expensive carpet and indicated that I should walk the same way. He opened his front gate and managed to close it without making a sound, which took some doing. I thought he might well have had some practice at it. Outside his front door he got his key out and just before he put it in the lock, he put a finger to his lips and went 'Ssshh!' The hall light was left on for him, so there was no clattering about in the dark. He closed the door and pointed to the front room. I went in and he followed me, switching on the light.

'Sit anywhere you like,' he said, so I parked my backside in an armchair and he sat opposite me.

'Shall I put the kettle on?' I said.

He looked puzzled and then said, 'Oh, yes. Tea!' but he didn't move.

'I'll put the kettle on if you like,' I said.

'Do you fancy some soup?' he said. 'I fancy some soup.'

'Yes, that'd be great,' I said. 'What sort have you got?'

'Hang on,' he said. 'I'll go and find out.'

I expected him to go into the kitchen to look at the cans of soup, but of course, this is Tommy Cooper I'm talking about. I heard him go upstairs, a door open and a light was switched on. I then heard a woman's voice, but because it was coming from upstairs and Tommy must have half-closed the bedroom door, it sounded very muffled. Then I heard Tommy's voice. Then a woman's, which I guessed belonged to Dove. All it sounded like to me was 'Rhubarb, rhubarb, rhubarb . . . *soup?*' 'Rhubarb, rhubarb, rhubarb, rhubarb . . . *yes . . . soup!*' for about five minutes.

Tommy came back into the room and said, 'It's alright. Dove'll make us some soup now!'

Sure enough, I heard Dove storming downstairs, but she didn't come in to say hello to me, she made straight for the kitchen. I heard her rattling cans and saucepans and soup bowls and ten minutes later she walked in with a face like thunder. She was wearing a dressing gown and slippers and carried two bowls of tomato soup on a tray which she banged down on the table, before turning around and going back upstairs without a word to either of us.

'If I were you I'd hurry up drinking your soup,' Tommy said, so we attacked it with our spoons and it had all gone in a couple of minutes.

'I think I'll go now,' I said. 'It's gone one o'clock.'

Tommy then walked me to the front door and he whispered, 'Remember, close the front gate quietly and when you walk back up the road to your car, I'd appreciate it if you'd walk very quietly. This time of night, even the smallest sound echoes up and down this road and it upsets the neighbours. It really is a *very* refined area. Goodnight, Freddie!'

In a voice just above a whisper, I told him to thank Dove for the soup and said, 'Goodnight, Tommy!'

I was very careful opening his front gate and as I closed it, equally as silently, I mouthed another 'Goodnight, Tommy!' before I walked silently up the road in the step-by-step manner he'd asked me to. There wasn't a soul about. It was true what Tommy had said about the area. Very refined. As I was opening my car door, being very careful not to drop the keys on the ground in case the noise woke up the entire road, I looked back at Tommy who was standing just inside his front gate watching me. I gave him the 'thumbs up' to signify I had accomplished my silent mission and he nodded. I was just about to climb into my car when he shouted out at the top of his very distinctive voice, 'Now fuck off! And don't fucking come back!'

With that he slammed his front door with an almighty crash and went inside.

Tommy's last television appearance was on one of LWT's weekly entertainment shows *Live from Her Majesty's* on Sunday, 15 April 1984. It was his first time on television for almost four years, but he had lost none of the Cooper comic genius. He'd had the theatre audience and the viewers in stitches with eight or nine minutes of wonderful nonsense and got to the section of his act where he put on a magic cape, out of which he would produce various items which were actually being passed to him through a gap in the curtains behind him. One of the girls from the Brian Rogers dancers brought the cape on for him and as she helped him to put it on, he said, 'Thanks love!'

Those was the last time we ever heard his voice, because a minute later he suffered a massive heart attack and died on stage, in front of 12 million television viewers.

It probably doesn't mean a lot to most people, but I've never forgotten that Tommy Cooper's last word was 'Love'.

'Goodnight, Tommy!'

CHAPTER EIGHTEEN

Writing your autobiography is very therapeutic work. I'd recommend it to anyone, whether you're a comedian or a copper-miner, an accountant or an acrobat. No. I take that back. If you're an accountant you can be excused writing your life story. *Please.*

Why therapeutic? Because if you harbour the feeling that life has dealt you a rotten hand of cards, when you start putting your past on paper from the vantage point of the present, you can see that the good and the bad times in your life are, on the whole, fairly evenly balanced. Just like *your* life has been (or will be, because none of us can escape them) touched by tragedies, so has mine.

I've told you that my father died when I was in my teens. My mother Hilda died in December 1992 at the age of 82, after nursing her second husband Jack for 14 years. He died of cancer aged 89 just a few weeks after Mum passed away.

The day my mother died I had to go on stage at Caesars Palace at Luton. I'll remember December '92 as a terrible month for me, personally, because that's also when Sandy and I split up for the first time.

I think it's a tragedy that my brother Richard no longer speaks to me.

My children Carl, Donna, Jody and Stacey want nothing to do with me, but I'm willing to talk to them or meet them any time, anywhere. I've missed out on so much as they grew up.

I have lost thousands and thousands of pounds because people who worked for me betrayed my trust.

I chose to make my career my top priority so my family could want for nothing and the irony is that my family life crumbled because I worked too hard, too much, too often.

All sorts of crap has been written about me in the papers which I chose to ignore at the time. I hope this book has helped to set the record straight about some of them at least. And so it goes on. You get the picture. Tragedy followed scandal followed court case. But, bear with me please. I don't intend to finish this book on a downer!

I now realise that those crazy days in Hamburg with the birds and The Beatles, the sell-out seasons in Bournemouth and Blackpool, those spine-tingling encounters with the greatest stars in the world and my history-making encore at the Royal Variety, all came at a price. And I have to be honest here. I think I've paid it several times over! So far, no one's thought to give me a receipt.

But I've still got more positives in my life than negatives and I found the biggest reason why my life is so positive, in 1997, in a furniture shop in the Midlands. It was a beautiful bow-legged Georgian dressing table with glass handles. I'm only kidding! I used to pop into Branson's Furniture in Redditch, Worcestershire when I was living in the area (yes, I know, I've lived all over the place ... but somehow the *Readers Digest still* manages to find my address) to buy bits and pieces from the owner Brian and got to know a young lady who worked for him, just to chat to over a cup of tea.

The lady's name was Donna and, from talking to her and Brian, I learnt that she was going through a divorce. I happened to be in the shop one morning talking to Brian, when she arrived late for work because her husband (soon to be her ex-husband) refused to let her borrow their car to drive to work. I had two cars at the time. A smart one which I only used on long journeys and a little run-around which was parked outside the shop.

'You can borrow my car today,' I said to Donna. 'Here's the keys. Will you give me a lift home, Brian?'

He said it was no problem so Donna borrowed my car for the day.

At first Donna and I would meet at the shop and just chat and joke around. I found her very attractive and great company but as the divorce was going through, out of respect for her, I didn't attempt to make any romantic advances towards her. Then after the divorce came through, I invited her around to my house a few times. Still nothing happened. I wasn't going to rush things. She was great company but I didn't want to push it. She had two small children to think about. This tentative relationship went on for about a year, and then our cautious romance was suddenly spoiled when her ex-husband came out of the woodwork and sold a rubbish story to the papers – 'Freddie Starr Stole My Wife'. How can an adult 'steal' another adult who was already divorced from her husband? But as usual, the papers wouldn't let the truth spoil a crap story. Donna had seen the press hanging around our house looking for more juicy details. Bastards!

So I called a press conference at the Oakley Court Hotel in Bray, and said to the various reporters gathered there, 'Will you stop creeping around my house? I'm divorced. Donna's divorced. That's it. She'll tell you her side of the story now.' And she did. The press took their notes with them and set the record straight. But if it hadn't been for them printing lies in the first place, they wouldn't have had to set the record straight!

Donna and I were married at Maidenhead Register Office in January 1999.

Yes, it's far too late to send us a bouquet.

We live in Spain for most of the year now and we both love the climate, the lifestyle and the people. We have a villa in the mountains and from our living room window we can look out at our outdoor swimming pool just below the balcony and beyond that we can see a wide expanse of the Mediterranean only a mile or two away. Sometimes at night we sit outside with a cold drink and watch the lights of the fishing boats and the yachts and tourist boats sailing by in the darkness, while a million stars look down on us from the night sky. And that's in January! The great thing is we're just over two hours from London by air, which is helpful when Donna has to fly there and back in a day to collect her two beautiful children Rhys and Paige, to bring them out for a visit during the school holidays.

When I refer to Donna as the backbone of my life, that is no exaggeration. I cannot imagine life without her love and patience and superb organisational skills.

But it's now the spring of 2001 and I started writing this book twelve months ago, so my fingers are very, very tired.

Will I tour again? Anything's possible.

Although I've been a household name since 1970, I'm still only in my fifties and as long as I still get a rush from the sound of a theatre packed with people crying with laughter at my on-stage antics and as long as the British public want to come out to see me 'live' on stage, I can always be tempted away from the warmth of the Spanish hills.

As for television projects I've got a suitcase full. Sitcoms. Game shows. A straight and serious interview show in which I would confront the most evil people in the country and try to get into their minds. I could do it. Remember I grew up with villains and hard men. I've got a degree in the art of intimidation. But no one can intimidate Freddie Starr. I've also got ideas for entertainment documentaries combining my love for music and a sprinkling of comedy. Sixty-minute comedy specials full of new characters and up-to-the-minute TV and film parodies which I'd love some of my comedy heroes to take part in. My mind is always working on ideas.

But it's time I brought this account of my life so far to a close. I hope you've enjoyed it and it's made you laugh (where it was supposed to!) and that you weren't too shocked by some of my exploits and those of my fellow entertainers.

While I would never claim that I've been an innocent victim all my life, I have been stitched up by friends, family and the press many times over the years. But that's water under the bridge. It was a raging torrent for a while, now it's trickled away.

I wish all of you health or happiness. That's right. It's not a misprint. I said health or happiness. You can't expect to have *both* you greedy bastards! Life's not like that.

And if you're still reading this in a bookshop during your lunch hour, I'm serious. Either take it and your wallet to the counter or put it back. Do you think I sweated a year over this book so you could read it for free? Now piss off out of the shop, you tightwad!

I'm off for my tea.

'Donna! What are we having with the roast hamster tonight? Salad or chips?'

INDEX